OECD
ECONOMIC
SURVEYS

2004

Korea

OECD

ORGANISATION FOR ECONOMIC CO-OPERATION AND DEVELOPMENT

ORGANISATION FOR ECONOMIC CO-OPERATION AND DEVELOPMENT

Pursuant to Article 1 of the Convention signed in Paris on 14th December 1960, and which came into force on 30th September 1961, the Organisation for Economic Co-operation and Development (OECD) shall promote policies designed:

- to achieve the highest sustainable economic growth and employment and a rising standard of living in member countries, while maintaining financial stability, and thus to contribute to the development of the world economy;
- to contribute to sound economic expansion in member as well as non-member countries in the process of economic development; and
- to contribute to the expansion of world trade on a multilateral, non-discriminatory basis in accordance with international obligations.

The original member countries of the OECD are Austria, Belgium, Canada, Denmark, France, Germany, Greece, Iceland, Ireland, Italy, Luxembourg, the Netherlands, Norway, Portugal, Spain, Sweden, Switzerland, Turkey, the United Kingdom and the United States. The following countries became members subsequently through accession at the dates indicated hereafter: Japan (28th April 1964), Finland (28th January 1969), Australia (7th June 1971), New Zealand (29th May 1973), Mexico (18th May 1994), the Czech Republic (21st December 1995), Hungary (7th May 1996), Poland (22nd November 1996), Korea (12th December 1996) and the Slovak Republic (14th December 2000). The Commission of the European Communities takes part in the work of the OECD (Article 13 of the OECD Convention).

Publié également en français.

Table of contents

AUG 2 1 2004

Figures

BASIC STATISTICS OF KOREA

THE LAND

Area (thousand sq. km)	100	Major cities, 2001 (million inhabitants):	
Agricultural area (thousand sq. km)	14	Seoul	10.3
Forests (thousand sq. km)	65	Pusan	3.8
		Taegu	2.6
		Incheon	2.5

THE PEOPLE

Population, 2003 (million)	47.9	Civilian labour force, 2003 (million)	22.9
Per sq. km, 2003	479	Civilian employment	22.1
Annual rate of change of population, 2003	0.5	Agriculture, forestry, fishing	1.9
		Industry	4.2
		Construction	1.8
		Services	14.2

PRODUCTION

GDP, 2003 (trillion won)	720.9	Origin of GDP, 2003 (per cent of total):	
GDP per head (US$)	12 630	Agriculture, forestry, fishing	3.9
Gross fixed investment, 2003 (trillion won)	183.2	Industry	32.7
Per cent of GDP	29.6	Construction	8.6
Per head (US$)	3 735	Services	54.8

THE GOVERNMENT

			Number of seats
Public consumption, 2003 (per cent of GDP)	13.3	Composition of the National Assembly: June 2004	
Central government revenue, 2003, consolidated basis (per cent of GDP)	23.9	The Uri Party	152
		The Grand National Party	121
Central government budget balance, 2003, consolidated basis (per cent of GDP)	1.1	Other	26
			299

FOREIGN TRADE

Commodity exports, 2003, f.o.b. (per cent of GDP)	32.0	Commodity imports, 2003, c.i.f. (per cent of GDP)	29.5
Main exports (per cent of total exports):		Main imports (per cent of total imports):	
Light industry products	14.1	Consumer goods	13.2
Heavy industry products	79.8	Industrial materials and fuels	48.3
Electronic products	30.6	Crude petroleum	12.8
Cars	9.0	Capital goods	38.5

THE CURRENCY

Monetary unit: won	Currency unit per US$, average of daily figures:	
	2002	1 251
	2003	1 191
	May 2004	1 169

Note: An international comparison of certain basic statistics is given in an annex table.

This Survey is published on the responsibility of the Economic and Development Review Committee of the OECD, which is charged with the examination of the economic situation of member countries.

•

The economic situation and policies of Korea were reviewed by the Committee on 3 May 2004. The draft report was then revised in the light of the discussions and given final approval as the agreed report of the whole Committee on 1 June 2004.

•

The Secretariat's draft report was prepared for the Committee by Randall Jones, Yongchun Baek and Michael Wise under the supervision of Willi Leibfritz.

•

The previous Survey of Korea was issued in March 2003.

Executive summary

Korea has been one of the fastest-growing economies in the OECD area over the past five years, with an annual growth rate of about 6 per cent. Such rapid growth, which has lifted per capita income to two-thirds of the OECD average, reflects Korea's underlying dynamism and its progress in implementing a wide-ranging reform programme in the wake of the 1997 crisis. However, the recession in 2003 – which was due in part to structural problems in the labour market and in the corporate and financial sectors – indicates that the reform agenda is unfinished. Sustaining rapid growth over the medium term as the contribution from inputs of labour and capital slows requires further progress in structural reform, particularly in the labour market and in the corporate and financial sectors, accompanied by appropriate macroeconomic policies.

Macroeconomic policies to promote stability and deal with rising spending pressures

Monetary policy should focus on the newly established medium-term inflation target. Putting a stop to foreign reserve accumulation would limit the need for higher interest rates over the business cycle and tend to promote a more balanced expansion over the medium term. Given the pressure for increased public expenditure due to population ageing and the development of the social safety net, as well as the potential costs of economic co-operation with North Korea, fiscal policy should aim at a balanced budget, excluding the social security surplus, over the business cycle. Anchoring spending decisions in a medium-term framework and increasing the efficiency of the public expenditure system would also help contain spending pressures. In addition, fundamental reform of the pension system is essential to ensure its sustainability in the context of exceptionally rapid population ageing. Reform should aim at expanding the effective coverage of the public pension system and developing private-sector saving for retirement.

The key long-term challenge is to raise productivity growth by:

Improving the functioning of the labour market

A comprehensive reform package is needed to increase employment flexibility, create more co-operative industrial relations and reduce the extent of dualism in the labour market, which creates equity concerns. Relaxing employment protection for regular workers and improving the coverage of the social safety net, especially for non-regular workers who account for about a quarter of all employees, would enhance flexibility and reduce labour market dualism. The government should promote an industrial relations framework in which workers and management settle their disputes autonomously. Active labour market policies should be improved while limiting deadweight costs. Over the longer term, boosting labour force participation rates, focusing on older workers and women, is essential to cope with rapid population ageing.

Reforms in the corporate and financial sectors

Further progress in implementing the new corporate governance framework, combined with improved financial supervision and strengthened competitive pressures, are important to effectively discipline chaebol behaviour and guide corporate restructuring. The 2003 accounting scandal demonstrates the need to improve auditing procedures to enhance transparency. In the financial sector, the privatisation of the commercial banks should continue. It is also necessary to promptly resolve the problems in the non-bank sector, notably in the credit card companies, which have impinged on private consumption, and in the investment trust companies. Shifting financial supervision to a more pre-emptive and risk-based approach would help avoid future problems in the financial sector.

Strengthening competition to enhance productivity growth

Competition policy should be strengthened by granting the Korea Fair Trade Commission compulsory investigative powers, making the threat of individual sanctions more credible and removing exemptions from the competition law. The benefits of increased competition are likely to be strongest in the service sector, where productivity levels are significantly lower than in the manufacturing sector. Competition should be strengthened by removing barriers to large retail outlets and eliminating unnecessary constraints on professional services. Simplifying land-use regulations, which are governed by 112 laws, may also reduce entry barriers. It is also important to accelerate efforts to expand the scope of competition in network industries through privatisation and the unbundling of their activities. Another key to competition is the establishment of sectoral regulators that are independent of the ministries responsible for promoting the development of network industries. Foreign competition should be increased by further reducing barriers to imports while addressing features, such as labour market problems, that tend to discourage inflows of direct investment.

Assessment and recommendations

Economic growth has been among the highest in the OECD area in recent years

Korea stands out as one of the fastest-growing OECD countries over the past five years, with an annual growth rate of around 6 per cent. This very good performance has sustained the convergence process, lifting per capita income to two-thirds of the OECD average. The return to high growth rates following the 1997 crisis was based in part on Korea's progress in reforming its economic framework to correct some of the weaknesses that had made it vulnerable to the Asian crisis. Rapid growth also reflects the country's underlying economic dynamism, particularly in the information and communications technology (ICT) sector. Korea has also benefited from strong demand from China, which has emerged as its biggest trading partner. Korea's outstanding performance is underpinned by large inputs of labour and capital, reflecting still-rapid population growth, rising labour force participation rates and a high level of investment.

Sustaining rapid growth requires appropriate macroeconomic policies and further progress in the post-crisis structural reform agenda...

The key long-term challenge is to continue the rapid convergence to the average income level in the OECD area by accelerating productivity growth as inputs of labour and capital slow. The government's emphasis on maintaining high growth is reflected in the recently established goal of doubling per capita income from $10 000 to $20 000, although the time frame is unspecified. With labour productivity (per hour worked) at around one-half of the OECD average, there is considerable scope for convergence to sustain high growth, all the more so given the positive effect stemming from the rising education level of the workforce. With some pick-up in total factor productivity gains, Korea may be able to sustain growth at around 5 per cent over the medium term. However, achieving such an outcome will require polices to:

- Maintain macroeconomic stability in the face of spending pressures stemming from exceptionally rapid population ageing, the development of a social safety net and the potential cost of economic co-operation with North Korea.

– Ensure that the labour market functions effectively by encouraging more co-operative and harmonious industrial relations, enhancing employment flexibility and limiting dualism in the labour market, which has negative implications for equity.

– Further improve the corporate governance framework and accounting transparency to boost efficiency in the corporate sector, while ensuring better supervision of the financial sector.

– Strengthen competitive pressure by overcoming the legacy of extensive government intervention in the economy, upgrading competition policy and continuing the opening to international trade and foreign direct investment.

In short, it is essential to continue the reform agenda launched after the 1997 crisis.

... to overcome weaknesses that played a role in the 2003 recession

Indeed, remaining weaknesses in the economic framework contributed to the economic recession in the first half of 2003, which slowed growth for the year to around 3 per cent. Private consumption was negatively affected by the liquidity and solvency problems of the credit card companies following the sharp rise in the delinquency rate in the wake of the credit boom to the household sector. Lending by the credit card companies to households has fallen by a quarter from its peak. The 1.4 per cent decline in private consumption in 2003 despite continuing household income growth also indicates that the household sector had become over-indebted. The instability in financial markets resulting from the problems of the credit card companies was aggravated by a serious accounting scandal that caused the failure of SK Global. The negative impact on business investment was magnified by the deterioration in already difficult industrial relations and labour strikes at major firms. In addition to these structural weaknesses, Korea was hit by a series of external shocks, notably SARS and the North Korean nuclear issue, which weakened confidence.

With an economic rebound underway...

The recession in 2003 continued the pattern of volatility experienced in recent years. The ICT-led expansion in 2000 and the credit card boom in 2002 were followed by marked slowdowns in 2001 and 2003. The rebound in exports, at 16 per cent in volume terms in 2003, led to an economic recovery beginning in the second half of the year. China continues to exert a strong positive effect, with its imports from Korea rising at a 50 per cent year-on-year rate. The conflicting signals given by buoyant export growth and sluggish domestic demand make it exceptionally difficult to project the path of the economy. Nevertheless, robust export growth should stimulate sluggish business investment and private consumption, resulting in growth in the 5 to 6 per cent range in 2004 and 2005 that would absorb the excess capacity in the economy. The unemployment rate, 3.4 per cent in the first quarter of 2004 (seasonally-adjusted), is about the same as the average of the past three years, while core inflation (which excludes petroleum-based fuels and non-grain farm products) has remained around the midpoint of the medium-term target range of 2.5 to 3.5 per cent, despite the economic downturn.

... monetary policy should focus on its medium-term inflation target

With the economy gaining momentum, *monetary policy should enhance macroeconomic stability by focusing on the medium-term inflation target introduced in* 2004. The increased independence that was granted to the central bank under the revised Bank of Korea Act that came into effect at the beginning of the year should facilitate the shift in emphasis to the medium term. In an effort to stimulate sluggish domestic demand, the central bank reduced the overnight call rate to a record low of 3¾ per cent in July 2003, a rate only slightly above the 3.6 per cent rate of headline inflation in 2003. *Maintaining stability over the business cycle will likely require some withdrawal of monetary stimulus*, leading to higher real short-term rates, as the economy accelerates. However, given the run-up in household debt from 56 per cent of GDP in 1998 to 74 per cent in 2003, higher interest rates may slow the recovery in private consumption.

There is no need for continued foreign exchange accumulation

The extent of the rise in interest rates needed to keep inflation in the medium-term target zone depends to some extent on exchange rate developments. By December 2003, the exchange rate of the won relative to Korea's 41 major trading partners had fallen 6 per cent below its year-earlier level. This may have contributed to the acceleration of exports, though possibly weakening domestic demand by reducing the purchasing power of Korean households and firms. The fall in the won took place in the context of continued large accumulation of foreign exchange reserves, which rose by $34 billion during 2003 to reach $155 billion, the second highest level in the OECD area, thus reducing Korea's vulnerability to crisis. However, there is some risk associated with intervention to limit the upward pressure on the currency, which generally has limited effectiveness except in the very short run. At the same time, the opportunity cost of holding such a large amount of reserves is significant. *Therefore, now that Korea's reserves are almost three times larger than its total short-term foreign debt, there is no need for continued foreign exchange accumulation.* Although this may allow more upward pressure on the exchange rate, with a moderating effect on exports, it would have some offsetting positive effects, including a real income gain for households and firms. In addition, it would reduce the burden of companies' foreign debt. In sum, these factors may promote a more balanced expansion over the medium term.

While fiscal policy's automatic stabilisers should be allowed to function...

A monetary policy focused on the medium term should be accompanied by a fiscal policy anchored in a medium-term framework to ensure fiscal sustainability. Such a framework would allow automatic stabilisers to function in order to limit volatility. However, such stabilisers are relatively weak in Korea, reflecting the small size of government and the early stage of development of the social safety net. In 2003, two supplementary budgets in the latter part of the year boosted total government spending, after adjusting for special factors, by 6½ per cent, slightly faster than nominal output growth. However, government revenue grew even faster, at 8 per cent, due in part to large tax receipts from corporations on their profits in 2002. Consequently, the consolidated central government balance (excluding the social security surplus, the cost of bringing part of the financial-sector restructuring programme into the budget and privatisation revenues) was in balance in 2003 for the first time since the crisis. The elimination of the small deficit, which was ¼ per cent of GDP in 2002, suggests that the stance of fiscal policy was slightly contractionary in 2003.

... it is essential to maintain a sound fiscal position...

The fiscal stance for 2004 is uncertain. While comparing the initial budget to the outcome in 2003 shows an 8 per cent rise in spending – in line with expected nominal income growth – the frequent use of supplementary budgets may lead to higher expenditures. Moreover, tax cuts have recently been introduced to encourage private consumption and job creation. The recovery projected during the course of the year, though, would negate the need for fiscal stimulus. *The authorities should aim to keep the consolidated central government budget (excluding the social security surplus) in balance over the business cycle once the process of bringing the costs of financial-sector restructuring into the budget is completed in 2006.*

... in part by improving the public expenditure system...

Maintaining a sound fiscal position in the face of the pressures for increased outlays would be facilitated by an effective medium-term expenditure framework that anchors annual spending decisions and provides discipline for policymakers. *The National Fiscal Management Plan, which is currently under discussion by the cabinet, has many positive features, and should be used to bind annual budgets as from 2005.* This should be accompanied by a comprehensive reform of the budget structure aimed at:

- *Strengthening aggregate spending control and enhancing transparency by making the budget less compartmentalised and fragmented;*

- *Increasing efficiency by strengthening accountability for results and relying more on market mechanisms in supplying publicly financed services;*

- *Improving inter-governmental fiscal relations.*

Similarly, on the revenue side, it is important to minimise the distortive effects of the tax system by reducing generous allowances and tax credits in the personal income tax system and broadening the base for corporate and value-added taxes. The negative features embedded in the tax system should be removed before boosting government revenues to accommodate growing expenditure resulting from the development of the social safety net, economic co-operation with North Korea and population ageing.

*... and reforming
the public
pension system to
cope with rapid
population ageing*

The fiscal impact of ageing will be large in Korea given the rapid pace of demographic change. Indeed, the share of the population over age 65, which is projected to double from 7 to 14 per cent between 2000 and 2019, is increasing substantially faster than in other OECD countries. Although the law requires changes in the pension system every five years to ensure its long-run sustainability, the proposal in 2003 to raise the contribution rate gradually and to cut the replacement rate from 60 to 50 per cent was not approved by the National Assembly. Maintaining the current benefit replacement rate would require a rise in the contribution rate, currently set at 9 per cent, to nearly 20 per cent, which would have a significant impact on the labour market. *An overhaul of the pension system is essential to ensure its sustainability, while providing adequate coverage.* At present, around a quarter of those who are supposed to participate in the National Pension Scheme, notably the self-employed, do not contribute. *There is thus a need for measures to include more of the self-employed and encourage them to report their income more accurately. Private sources of retirement income should be further developed, notably by creating a corporate pension system. In addition, it is important to raise the age of retirement of regular workers, which is typically around age 55, and ensure that the pension system does not discourage older persons from working. Given the small number of persons receiving public pensions at present, it is essential that the social safety net be adequate to limit poverty among the elderly.*

*Reforms to
improve the social
safety net and
upgrade active
labour market
policies...*

The effective coverage of the social safety net should also be expanded to ensure adequate support for unemployed persons. Although the legally-mandated coverage of the Employment Insurance System has been progressively increased since its establishment in 1995, less than one-fifth of the unemployed in 2003 received unemployment benefits, reflecting in part the low effective coverage of the System. The recent changes to expand the coverage, in particular by including more non-regular workers – who account for at least a quarter of employees and are paid about 20 per cent less on average than regular workers – are commendable but enforcement needs to be further improved. *There may be scope for greater use of active labour market policies, such as training for the unemployed and job placement services to overcome mismatch problems, provided they are subject to rigorous cost-benefit analysis.* However, as wage subsidies are generally associated with high deadweight costs, measures are needed to minimise such effects.

... should be combined with steps to improve industrial relations and to increase labour market flexibility...

Measures to expand the safety net and improve active labour market policies should be part of a comprehensive package addressing labour market problems. Such a package should also include steps to improve industrial relations, enhance employment flexibility and raise labour force participation rates of women. Unstable industrial relations appear to be one of the obstacles to a sustained economic recovery. *The government should develop an environment more conducive to harmonious industrial relations and avoid getting involved in individual disputes.* More co-operative industrial relations may facilitate more employment flexibility, while it is also necessary to reform the labour law. Although it was revised in 1998 to allow collective dismissals of regular workers for managerial reasons, this has not created enough flexibility in practice, given the constraints on management wishing to take such actions. *Reducing the employment protection provided to regular workers is important to reduce the incentives to hire non-regular workers, thus limiting the extent of dualism in the labour market, while enhancing labour market flexibility.*

... to facilitate structural change in the corporate sector, which also requires improved corporate governance and auditing frameworks

Greater flexibility in the labour market is essential to cope with rapid structural change in the corporate sector, which is driven by technological advances and Korea's increasing integration in the world economy. Another important element is effective corporate governance to guide investment decisions and prevent abuses by controlling shareholders and management. Significant improvements have been made in the corporate governance framework since the 1997 crisis. However, the failure of SK Global as a result of accounting fraud suggests that there is a lack of transparency and a need for better auditing practices. *The measures recently introduced to require the certification of financial reports by CEOs and CFOs, prohibit loans or collateral for major shareholders and executives, and strengthen protection for whistle-blowers should be effectively implemented to prevent such abuses. In addition, the steps introduced to ensure the independence of auditors should help enhance transparency. However, it is also necessary to increase the number of auditors significantly. The government should also encourage firms to adopt the recently introduced* OECD *Principles of Corporate Governance.* Finally, the decision to allow class action suits to protect shareholders of the largest firms – about 80 in number – from fraudulent practices related to securities is already influencing managerial behaviour. *Expanding the coverage of such suits to cover related party transactions should be considered to further reduce the scope for managerial abuses.*

Further restructuring in the financial sector, notably in the non-bank sector, is essential...

Such abuses have created financial-market instability. In particular, the investment trust companies (ITCs) were vulnerable to liquidity pressures in 2003 after the collapse of SK Global and were also affected by the problems in the credit card companies. Credit card use expanded by a factor of eleven between 1998 and 2002, preceding the development of adequate expertise in the credit card companies and in the supervisory authorities. The rise in the delinquency ratio from 5 to 14 per cent and in the amount of rescheduled loans from 7 to 29 per cent of total credits led to serious liquidity and capital problems in this sector. In response, the government has encouraged related companies to roll over the debt of the credit card companies, although such a strategy tends to weaken market discipline. The authorities co-ordinated a rescue of the largest credit card company, fearing that its collapse could lead to a systemic crisis. However, this may increase moral hazard by suggesting that the "too big to fail" approach is still valid. In addition to the need for better supervision to cope with the rapid expansion of the credit card sector, the pace of the expansion of bank lending to households, which increased more than 40 per cent in 2002, raises concerns about risk analysis capabilities in the financial sector. *These problems demonstrate the need to develop a pre-emptive and risk-based approach to the supervision of financial institutions. In the banking sector, the privatisation of the government's holdings should continue. Finally, improving the health of the ITCs, in part by privatising the two large institutions that were restructured using public funds, is a priority to promote the development of the corporate bond market and provide more secure saving instruments for households.*

... as well as reforms in the real estate market

The development of long-term saving vehicles would help households prepare for retirement and reduce the concentration of their savings in real estate. Concern about persistent upward pressure on real estate prices, which resulted in a one-third rise in housing prices over the past three years, has led to a wide range of policy initiatives. Following through on measures to raise holding taxes and enhance the supply of housing should help alleviate such pressures. The plan to move the capital from Seoul to the middle of the country could also alleviate the concentration of activity in the capital region, where price increases have been largest. Given that Korea's population density is one of the highest in the world, achieving an efficient use of land should be a priority. Complicated land regulation, which is governed by 112 laws, is one of the key factors hindering investment by foreign and domestic companies in Korea. *Simplifying regulations on land use should therefore be a top priority.*

Competition should be strengthened by giving more authority to the KFTC...

Enhancing competition is a key to improving productivity growth. Indeed, markets with high concentration ratios tend to have higher mark-up ratios, which reduce consumer welfare and distort the allocation of resources. *Given the large potential gains, promoting competition should take priority over government interventions aimed at accelerating growth in certain sectors. In particular, the authorities should avoid undue emphasis on the ten areas identified as future growth engines.To enhance competition, the power of the Korea Fair Trade Commission (KFTC) should be expanded by strengthening its investigative powers. Boosting the level of sanctions to the levels in other member countries and establishing a credible threat of individual sanctions would increase the deterrent effect of competition policy. The scope for private legal actions should be expanded, while the special treatment provided for particular sectors, such as small and medium-sized enterprises, should be scaled back.* The emphasis on "fair trade" and concern about the power of the chaebol has led the competition authority to devote substantial attention to an enforcement programme to limit shareholdings and debt guarantees and control aspects of ownership structure. This may compete with the attention given by the KFTC to enforcement against other fundamental competition problems. The combination of improved corporate governance, more independent financial institutions, upgraded financial supervision and the increased role of foreign investors – who now own more than 40 per cent of listed Korean companies – is reducing the scope for abuses by managers of chaebol companies by strengthening market mechanisms that impose discipline on the groups. *Supervisory functions related to transactions that amount to misuse of corporate assets should be concentrated in regulators responsible for financial and securities matters, while transactions that have an exclusionary or distorting effect on product market competition in particular cases should still be subject to competition-law control.*

... reducing barriers in the service sector...

The potential gains from enhanced competition appear to be largest in the service sector, given its lower level of productivity. Therefore, facilitating competition in the service sector through market opening and regulatory reform is one of the most urgent tasks for the Korean economy. One priority should be the *retail sector*, which is characterised by a large number of outlets and a high number of employees. It *is important to simplify the application process for opening large retail stores and make it more transparent, while removing obstacles to foreign direct investment. Deregulation of zoning laws would also facilitate the development of large stores with higher productivity. Restrictions on entry in some professional services should also be relaxed, while avoiding the delegation of powers by the government to professional associations. Regulations that limit foreign competition by restricting commercial presence should be relaxed, while recognising the qualification standards of other countries would be beneficial.* As for prices, the Omnibus Cartel Repeal Act of 1999 made collusion over fee-setting illegal in nine professional services. *Similar action should be taken in other areas where exemptions from the Monopoly Regulation and Fair Trade Act allow cartel activity.*

... expanding competition in network industries...

The authorities should also intensify efforts to expand the scope of competition in network industries, notably electricity, natural gas and telecommunications. *One key to competition is the creation of independent sectoral regulators, which is the norm in other OECD countries.* The ministries' role in promoting the development of these sectors conflicts with the objective of encouraging competition. *In electricity and natural gas, it is important to spell out detailed liberalisation plans in order to encourage new entry in these sectors and to accomplish the planned privatisation of the electricity-generating companies.* This would help ensure the independence of the generation companies from the transmission system, a prerequisite for competition. *In addition, price distortions that favour agriculture and industry should be corrected by ensuring that prices reflect costs. In some sectors, notably telecommunications, an appropriate framework for interconnection and* local loop unbundling is needed to promote competition. Other measures, including an easing of entry requirements and the extensive adoption of number portability, would also be beneficial in telecommunications.

... and boosting international competition by increasing openness to imports and inflows of foreign direct investment

Reducing barriers to imports is an important aspect of strengthening competition. The relatively high tariff rates in Korea should be reduced, while ensuring that standards do not hinder imports. Trade barriers in the highly protected agricultural sector should be cut by transforming support for farmers into direct payments. Protection for agriculture should be lowered; the total support provided to farmers by Korean consumers and taxpayers amounted to 3½ per cent of GDP in 2003, according to the OECD. The liberalisation of agricultural barriers will contribute to the success of multilateral trade negotiations, as well as facilitate Korea's participation in regional free trade agreements, which would allow it to benefit from the economic dynamism of Asia. Stepping up inflows of foreign direct investment (FDI) has been a major government objective since the crisis and large inflows were recorded at the end of the 1990s. While the declining trend in inflows since 2000 may be primarily due to external factors, it is important to remove remaining impediments to FDI. Perhaps most important for attracting inflows of FDI is improving aspects of the Korean economy that discourage foreign investors, particularly problems in the labour market.

In summary

Maintaining the high growth rate of recent years will require appropriate macroeconomic policies and further structural reforms to boost productivity gains and offset the deceleration of labour and capital inputs. An effective medium-term public expenditure framework is essential to deal with rising spending pressures, combined with a fundamental reform of the pension system to cope with rapid population ageing. Monetary policy should focus on its medium-term inflation target, while stopping the accumulation of foreign exchange reserves would tend to promote a balanced economic expansion. Labour market flexibility is a key to maintaining growth in the context of rapid structural change. Further development of the social safety net, a reduction in employment protection for regular workers and efforts to create more harmonious industrial relations would enhance flexibility while minimising the extent of dualism in the labour market. Flexibility in employment will in turn facilitate corporate restructuring, which should be guided by improved corporate governance based on the effective implementation of recent reforms to strengthen transparency and accountability. Remaining problems in the financial sector should be dealt with effectively while limiting the use of public funds and moral hazard problems. A more preemptive approach to limit emerging risks would help prevent problems such as those in the credit card sector. An important key to productivity gains is strengthening competition, in part by making competition policy more effective. The scope for greater competition, as well as productivity gains, is largest in the service sector and the network industries, where some of the reform programmes are lagging behind schedule. Increasing openness to imports and inflows of foreign direct investment are also important aspects to strengthening competition. In sum, ensuring macroeconomic stability, further improving the economic framework and boosting competition are all essential elements necessary to continue Korea's high rate of growth and speed the convergence process.

1. Becoming a high-income OECD country: key economic challenges

In July 2003, the government announced a medium to long-term target of doubling per capita income from around $10 000 to $20 000.[1] Thirty years of extraordinary growth had boosted per capita income from about $100 in 1965 to the $10 000 level by the mid-1990s (Figure 1.1). However, weaknesses in Korea's economic structure, which lacked many of the basic elements of a market economy, left the country vulnerable to the financial crisis that swept through Asia in 1997, reducing per capita income by a third in US dollar terms, primarily due to the sharp fall in the exchange rate. In particular, close government-business links had created moral hazard problems, resulting in excessive risk-taking and insufficient attention to credit and exchange-rate risks. The government responded to the crisis, as discussed in previous OECD *Economic Surveys of Korea*, by introducing a wide-ranging programme of reforms in the corporate and financial sectors and in the labour market to create a more market-oriented economy. The economy rebounded with an annual average growth rate of 6 per cent over the past five years. Adjusted for price differences, per capita income has risen to two-thirds of the OECD average (Panel B).

There are a number of challenges to maintaining a high rate of growth. *First*, growth has relied heavily on inputs of labour and capital, which are likely to slow in the future. If the contribution to growth from labour productivity were to maintain its level of the past decade, the pace of economic growth over the next five years would slow to about 4½ per cent. *Second*, structural weaknesses, reflected in the problems that pushed the economy into recession during the first half of 2003, illustrate the difficulty of sustaining rapid growth. While the economy was negatively affected by external factors, such as the SARS epidemic and the North Korean nuclear issue, a series of negative domestic shocks also undermined business and household confidence, more than offsetting the positive impact of 16 per cent growth of exports in volume terms (see Chapter 2). In particular, the SK Global scandal created renewed concern about the health of the corporate sector, while the financial sector was troubled by the problems of the credit card companies. Meanwhile, contentious worker-management relations resulted in labour strikes and unrest. These problems have been

Figure 1.1. **Per capita income in Korea**[1]

A. Gross national income per capita in US dollars

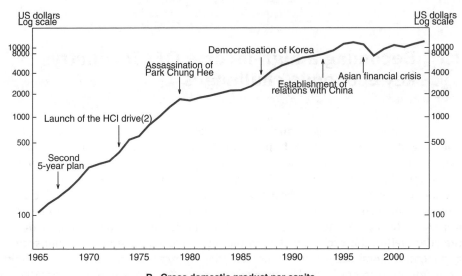

B. Gross domestic product per capita
2002 purchasing power parity exchange rates

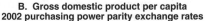

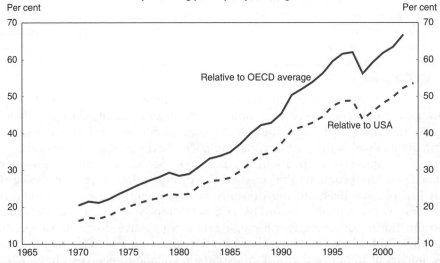

1. In March 2004, the Bank of Korea announced revised national accounts based on 1993 SNA for the period 1995 to 2003. This results in a sharp rise in per capita income in 1995.
2. Heavy and chemical industry.
Source: OECD.

compounded by unsettled political conditions. In short, this indicates that, despite recent progress, the reform agenda remains unfinished. This chapter begins by considering Korea's growth potential before discussing a number of obstacles to maintaining growth at a high level. These include the fiscal challenges associated with population ageing and eventual economic integration with the North, difficult labour market issues, problems in the corporate and financial sectors and weak competitive pressures in some parts of the economy. The chapter concludes with a brief assessment.

Korea's growth performance during the last decade

During the decade 1992 to 2002, Korea's output growth averaged 5.6 per cent a year, well above the 3 per cent rate recorded in the OECD area (Table 1.1). The most important factor was the increase of *labour productivity* at an average annual rate of 4¼ per cent, double the OECD average. Rapid productivity growth can be attributed, in part, to a high level of investment by the business sector. Although business investment as a share of GDP has fallen by a third since the 1997 crisis, it still remains the highest in the OECD area. Consequently, the level of fixed capital per worker has risen by more than two-thirds over the past decade, contributing to the strong labour productivity gains. Using a growth accounting framework, a recent study (Han *et. al*, 2002) estimated that capital inputs accounted for one-half of potential economic growth in the 1990s (Table 1.2).[2] A second factor has been the adoption of new technology, enabling Korea to continue its convergence to income levels in high-income countries. Korea's extensive use of foreign technology is illustrated by the fact that its deficit in the "technology balance of payments" is the second largest in the OECD area at 0.6 per cent of GDP.[3] High growth over the past decade is also explained by the expansion of *labour inputs*, which accounted for about 1¼ percentage points of growth. Increased labour inputs reflect the increase in the working-age population and the upward trend in the participation rate. These two factors have more than offset a modest decline in working hours and a small rise in the unemployment rate.

The OECD's study of economic growth (OECD, 2003e) identified a number of keys to growth, including boosting investment in physical capital, upgrading skills and human capital, encouraging innovation, removing barriers to trade and investment, stimulating firm creation, improving the regulatory environment, and strengthening the economic and social fundamentals. As noted above, fixed investment in Korea is exceptionally high. The following section discusses Korea's progress in upgrading skills and human capital and encouraging innovation, while becoming more open to foreign competition by reducing barriers to trade and investment.

Table 1.1. **Sources of growth over the decade 1992 to 2002**
Annual average

	GDP growth	Labour productivity growth (output per hour)	Labour input growth (hours worked)	Contribution to labour input growth (percentage points)							
				Working-age population		Participation rate		Unemployment rate		Hours worked per person	
				Contribution	Level[1]	Contribution	Level[2]	Contribution	Level[3]	Contribution	Level[3]
Korea[4]	**5.6**	**4.3**	**1.3**	**1.1**	**71.5**	**0.5**	**67.1**	**-0.1**	**3.1**	**-0.3**	**2 410**
Australia	3.9	1.9	2.0	1.2	67.1	0.3	75.8	0.4	6.3	0.0	1 837
Belgium	2.0	1.9	0.2	0.1	65.9	0.6	66.7	0.0	7.3	-0.6	1 528
Canada	3.6	1.5	2.0	1.2	67.6	0.3	78.6	0.4	7.6	0.1	1 783
Denmark	2.4	2.3	0.2	0.2	66.4	-0.2	80.4	0.4	4.5	-0.2	1 472
Finland	3.3	3.0	0.3	0.3	66.9	0.2	74.8	0.3	9.1	-0.4	1 685
France	2.0	1.9	0.1	0.3	65.0	0.5	70.1	0.1	9.0	-0.8	1 514
Germany	1.3	1.9	-0.6	0.0	67.3	0.4	76.1	-0.2	8.1	-0.8	1 459
Greece	2.7	2.2	0.5	0.3	63.5	0.5	63.7	-0.1	10.0	-0.1	1 922
Iceland	3.3	2.0	1.2	1.1	65.3	0.1	86.2	0.1	3.3	-0.1	1 838
Ireland	8.0	4.6	3.2	1.8	67.7	1.2	70.0	1.2	4.4	-1.0	1 674
Italy	1.6	1.6	0.1	0.0	67.5	0.3	61.3	0.0	9.1	-0.2	1 601
Japan	1.0	2.1	-1.0	-0.1	67.7	0.2	77.5	-0.3	5.4	-0.8	1 815
Netherlands	2.7	1.6	1.5	0.4	67.7	1.2	67.0	0.3	2.3	-0.4	1 333
New Zealand	3.6	1.1	2.5	1.4	75.4	0.5	76.4	0.6	5.2	0.0	1 818
Norway	3.3	2.6	0.7	0.6	65.1	0.5	80.4	0.2	4.0	-0.6	1 357
Spain	2.8	0.4	2.4	0.6	66.9	1.6	67.6	0.2	11.4	0.0	1 816
Sweden	2.6	2.3	0.2	0.4	64.7	-0.5	76.5	0.2	4.0	0.2	1 577
Switzerland	1.1	0.9	0.1	0.5	67.6	-0.1	87.3	0.0	3.1	-0.2	1 568
United Kingdom	2.9	2.2	0.7	0.3	65.2	-0.1	75.6	0.5	5.2	-0.1	1 707
United States	3.2	1.6	1.4	1.2	75.4	0.0	75.3	0.2	5.8	0.0	1 819
EU average	2.9	2.2	0.7	0.4	66.2	0.5	70.9	0.2	7.7	-0.4	1 607
OECD average	3.0	2.1	0.9	0.6	67.5	0.4	71.0	0.2	6.9	-0.3	1 693

1. As per cent of total population in 2002.
2. Persons in the labour force divided by the working-age population in 2002.
3. In 2002.
4. Based on SNA 68. In March 2003, the Korean authorities announced national accounts on an SNA 93 basis for 1995 to 2003. However, to maintain a consistent series, the SNA 68 national accounts are used.
Source: OECD.

Table 1.2. **Korea's potential growth rate**
Annual average contribution in percentage points

	Potential growth	Labour	Physical capital	Total factor productivity	of which: Human capital
1981-1990	7.8	1.7	3.6	2.5	0.8
1991-2000	6.3	1.2	3.2	1.9	0.9
2003-2012					
Scenario A[1]	4.6	0.6	1.9	2.1	0.6
Scenario B[2]	5.2	0.6	2.0	2.6	0.6

1. Assumes that Korea's economic system and international openness remain at the current level.
2. Assumes that Korea's economic system is improved through structural reform and increased international openness.
Source: Han et al. (2002).

Investing in knowledge

Korea has a high level of investment in knowledge, measured as expenditure on education and R&D outlays. Although public outlays on educational institutions are below the mean in the OECD area, private spending as a share of GDP is the highest. Consequently, total spending, at 7.1 per cent of GDP in 2000, is also the highest in the OECD area,[4] thus helping to finance the rapid development of the education system both in terms of quantity and quality (see the 2003 Survey). While the proportion of older people (aged 55 to 64) with at least an upper-secondary qualification is low, the share for young adults between the ages of 25 and 34 is the highest among OECD countries (Figure 1.2). The expansion of education has upgraded the skill level of the labour force; the proportion of workers with less than a secondary-school degree fell from 39 per cent a decade ago to under 29 per cent, while the share with a university degree has risen from 18 to 27 per cent (Table 1.3). The rising number of years of schooling is estimated to have added 0.7 percentage point to economic growth each year during the decade from 1993 (Panel B). The quantitative expansion of the educational system has been accomplished while maintaining outstanding levels of student achievement. In international tests of 15-year-old students in science, reading and math in 2000, Korea ranked among the top three countries in each subject. The education system emphasises science and engineering, which account for 40 per cent of new university degrees, the highest proportion in the OECD.

Korea also devotes a relatively large share of national income to R&D investment. By 2001, it had reached 2.9 per cent of GDP, the fifth highest in the OECD area (Figure 1.3), with an exceptionally large share funded and undertaken by the business sector (Panel B). The emphasis on R&D has resulted in a 25 per cent annual average increase in Korea's applications at the European Patent Office during the 1990s, the highest growth rate among OECD countries. The information

Figure 1.2. **Share of the population with at least an upper-secondary qualification**
Per cent in 2001

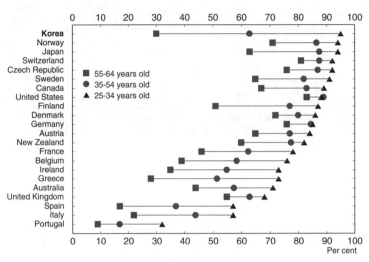

Source: OECD.

Table 1.3. **Educational attainment and economic growth**
A. Highest level of education classified by gender, per cent of employed persons

		1993[1]	2002[1]	2012[2]
Lower than secondary degree	Men	31.9	22.9	14.9
	Women	50.4	37.5	23.9
	Total	39.4	28.9	18.7
Secondary school degree	Men	45.8	47.0	49.5
	Women	37.9	40.8	48.6
	Total	42.6	44.4	49.1
University degree or higher	Men	22.2	30.2	35.5
	Women	11.6	21.7	27.5
	Total	18.0	26.6	32.1

B. Impact on growth

	1993-97	1998-02	2003-07	2008-12	1993-02	2003-12
Growth of human capital index (%)[3]	0.95	1.10	1.05	0.90	1.02	0.98
Contribution to economic growth[4]	0.62	0.72	0.68	0.59	0.67	0.64

1. Data from Korea National Statistical Office.
2. Projections by Han *et al.* (2002).
3. The human capital index is calculated based on the educational attainment of each age group and gender.
4. Percentage points.
Source: Han *et al.* (2002)

© OECD 2004

Figure 1.3. **R&D expenditure**

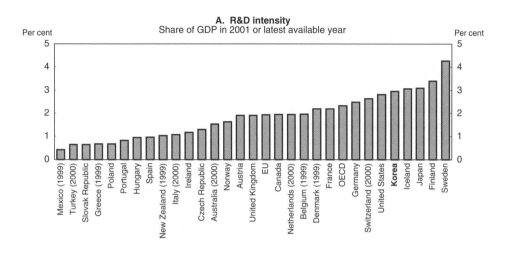

A. R&D intensity
Share of GDP in 2001 or latest available year

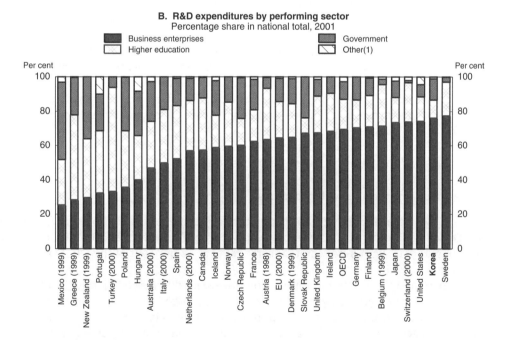

B. R&D expenditures by performing sector
Percentage share in national total, 2001

1. Private non-profit or not classifiable.
Source: OECD.

and communication technology (ICT) sector accounts for more than half of total R&D in the manufacturing sector.[5] Another aspect of investment in knowledge has been the rapid development of Internet connections. In 2002, the broadband penetration rate was the highest in the OECD area, while the price of Internet access was the lowest (Figure 1.4).

The priority attached to R&D and investment in human capital underpins the key role played by new industries in Korea. Industries classified as high and medium-high technology manufactures accounted for nearly 14 per cent of gross value added in 2000, the second highest share after Ireland (Figure 1.5). This reflects Korea's specialisation in ICT products, which account for nearly one-fifth of manufacturing output. Despite a significant contraction in 2001, ICT exports amount to nearly a third of total exports, the second highest proportion among OECD countries.

Increasing openness to international competition

Korea's strengths in technology-intensive products have boosted the importance of international trade in its economy. Indeed, world trade in high-technology products has nearly doubled during the past decade, outpacing the 50 per cent rise recorded for all manufactures. In addition, a reduction in Korea's import barriers has expanded trade. Perhaps most important was the phasing out by 1999 of the Import Diversification Programme, which had restricted imports of 924 items from Japan at its peak. All of this has helped to boost the share of international trade (the average of exports and imports) in the Korean economy from 25 per cent in 1993 to nearly 40 per cent at the start of the new century (Figure 1.6). An increase in inflows of foreign direct investment (FDI) following the 1997 crisis doubled the stock of FDI by 1999. Increased inflows reflected a change in the traditionally hostile attitude toward FDI inflows, the easing of restrictions and the urgency of corporate restructuring.

Korea's medium-term growth prospects

The large remaining gap in per capita income between Korea and the OECD average indicates considerable scope for rapid growth to narrow the difference (Figure 1.1). With a per capita income level at 67 per cent of the OECD average, Korea ranks in the bottom quartile of OECD countries by this criterion, along with Mexico and the Central European countries. The difference in labour productivity levels is even greater, given the exceptionally large input of labour in Korea. Indeed, labour input relative to total population in Korea is 21 per cent above the OECD average (Figure 1.7). The large labour input is primarily due to the fact that working time, at more than 2 400 hours per year, is the longest in the OECD area (Table 1.1). In addition, the unemployment rate is exceptionally low,[6] at around 3 per cent, while the proportion of the population that is of working age

Figure 1.4. **Internet access and its price**
September 2002

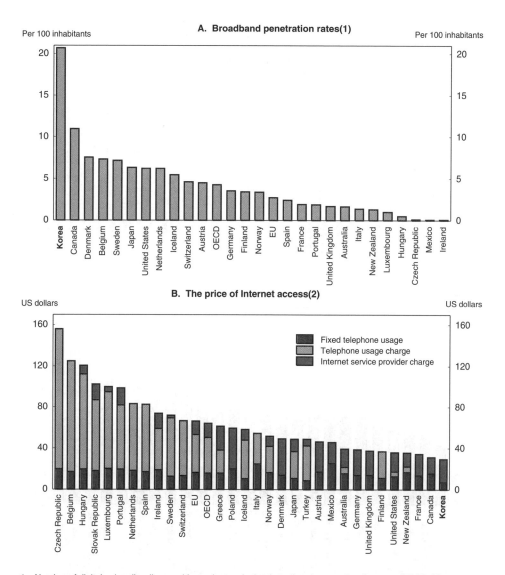

1. Number of digital subscriber lines, cable modem and other broadband connection lines per 100 inhabitants.
2. OECD Internet access basket for 40 hours of daytime discounted PSTN (Public Switch Telecommunications Network) rates, including VAT, in US dollars, converted using PPP exchange rates.
Source: OECD Science, Technology and Industry Scoreboard, 2003.

Figure 1.5. **Technology and knowledge-intensive industries**
Share of total gross value added in 2000

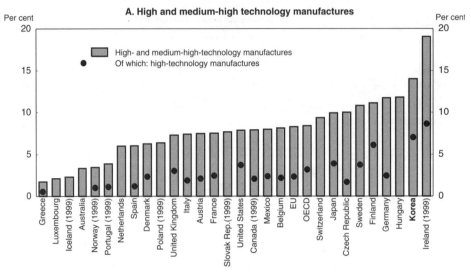

A. High and medium-high technology manufactures

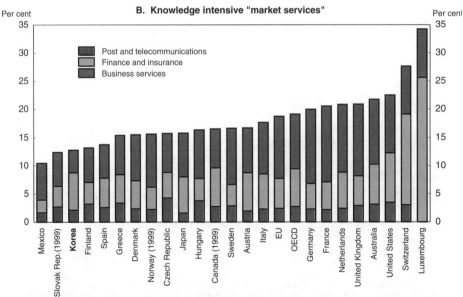

B. Knowledge intensive "market services"

Source: OECD Science, Technology and Industry Scoreboard, 2003.

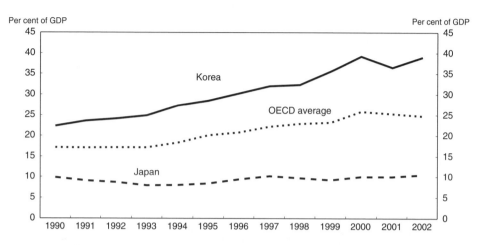

Figure 1.6. **Openness to international trade**
Trade in goods and services as a share of GDP[1]

1. Average of exports and imports on a national accounts basis. In March 2003, the Bank of Korea announced revised national accounts based on 1993 SNA for the period 1995 to 2003. This results in a substantial increase in the ratio in 1995.
Source: OECD.

is relatively high, reflecting the comparatively young population. The effect of these factors on labour input more than compensates for the low labour force participation rate that is mainly due to a smaller proportion of women who work. Taking account of the higher level of labour inputs, labour productivity per hour worked was about half of the OECD average in 2002.

In addition to abundant labour inputs, capital inputs have also been exceptionally high as noted above, accounting for about half of potential growth during the 1990s, according to Han *et al.* (2002). A high level of domestic saving has been available to fund this investment. In sum, economic development has been input-intensive, while total factor productivity growth, averaging around 2 per cent a year, has been responsible for less than one-third of economic growth (Table 1.2).

However, the contribution to growth from labour and capital inputs is projected to fall from 4½ per cent in the 1990s to around 2½ per cent during the coming decade (Table 1.2). The growth of labour inputs will be slowed by the gradual implementation of a five-day workweek under legislation passed in September 2003.[7] Assuming that overtime work stays near its 2002 level, this would cut working time by about 6 per cent by 2009. Declining working hours would largely offset employment growth, which is likely to remain robust, given

Figure 1.7. **Decomposition of the real income gap**
Percentage point differences in GDP per person relative to the OECD average,
PPP-adjusted, 2002

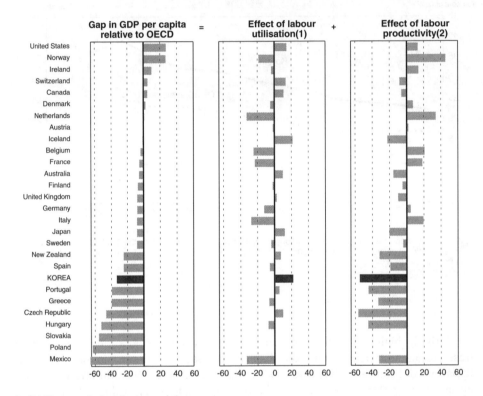

1. Total hours worked relative to population.
2. Productivity is measured on a per-hour basis.
Source: OECD.

the continued expansion of the working-age population, and assuming that the
upward trend in the labour force participation rate continues and that the unemployment rate remains near its current level. Consequently, the contribution to
growth from labour inputs would slow to about ¼ percentage point a year, well
below the 1¼ per cent contribution during the past decade. As for capital, the
downward trend in the large share of business investment in GDP is unlikely to be
reversed as firms become more sensitive to risks. Moreover, the domestic savings
pool has been reduced by the significant fall in the household saving rate.

The slower rise in labour and capital inputs means that economic growth
will become increasingly dependent on total factor productivity gains. If such gains

were to remain at the level of 2 per cent recorded in the 1990s, potential output growth would fall to 4½ per cent (Table 1.2, Scenario A). Achieving potential growth of 5¼ per cent would thus require that total factor productivity growth accelerate to more than 2½ per cent, an increase that may be harder to achieve as Korea moves closer to average productivity levels in the OECD area. In terms of labour productivity, there would have to be an acceleration from the 4¼ per cent recorded during the 1990s to around 5 per cent (Table 1.4). In summary, as labour and capital inputs are expanding at a slower rate, the challenge is to use these factors more efficiently.

Table 1.4. **Potential output growth over the medium term**

Annual average from 2003 to 2009 in percentage points

| | Potential GDP growth rate | Potential labour productivity growth (output per hour) | Potential labour input (total hours worked) | Components of potential employment | | | | Hours worked |
				Trend participation rate	Working-age population	Structural unemployment	Potential employment growth	
Korea								
Scenario A[1]	4.6	4.3	0.3	0.4	0.9	0.0	1.3	−1.0
Scenario B[2]	5.2	4.9	0.3	0.4	0.9	0.0	1.3	−1.0
Australia	3.6	2.2	1.4	0.0	1.4	0.0	1.6	0.1
Austria	2.0	1.6	0.4	0.1	0.1	0.0	0.3	0.0
Belgium	2.0	1.5	0.6	0.4	0.3	0.0	0.8	−0.3
Canada	3.0	1.9	1.0	0.1	1.0	0.0	1.1	0.0
Denmark	2.0	1.5	0.5	0.0	0.0	0.0	0.0	0.3
Finland	2.1	2.3	−0.2	−0.4	0.2	0.1	−0.3	−0.3
France	2.1.	1.6	0.5	−0.2	0.4	0.1	0.3	0.3
Germany	1.6	1.4	0.2	0.3	−0.2	0.0	0.2	−0.2
Greece	3.6	3.3	0.3	0.2	−0.1	0.1	0.3	0.2
Iceland	2.9	1.9	1.0	0.0	0.9	0.1	0.9	−0.1
Ireland	4.5	3.4	1.0	0.3	1.0	0.1	1.5	−0.2
Italy	1.4	1.0	0.5	0.6	−0.1	0.2	0.4	−0.1
Japan	1.3	1.1	0.2	0.2	−0.4	0.0	−0.2	0.0
Netherlands	1.8	1.1	0.7	0.5	0.4	0.0	0.9	−0.3
New Zealand	3.0	2.1	0.9	0.2	0.9	0.0	1.2	0.0
Norway	2.3	2.0	0.4	0.0	0.5	0.0	0.5	−0.2
Spain	2.6	1.0	1.6	1.4	0.3	0.3	1.5	−0.1
Sweden	2.3	1.5	0.8	−0.2	0.6	0.0	0.5	0.5
Switzerland	1.3	0.6	0.7	0.1	0.5	0.0	0.6	0.0
United Kingdom	2.4	1.9	0.4	0.0	0.4	0.0	0.4	0.0
United States	3.2	1.8	1.4	0.0	1.0	0.0	0.8	0.1
Total OECD[3]	2.4	1.7	0.7	0.2	0.4	0.0	0.6	0.0

1. Assumes that labour productivity growth remains close to the level recorded during the past decade with the economic system and the degree of international openness staying unchanged.
2. Assumes that productivity growth will accelerate enough to achieve the government's target of 5 per cent potential growth as a result of structural reform and increasing international openness.
3. Not including Korea.
Source: OECD.

Korea's success in upgrading human capital, promoting R&D and innovation and reducing its barriers to trade suggest that it is well positioned to achieve high total factor productivity growth. The impact of higher levels of education (Figure 1.2) will continue to make an important contribution. For example, the proportion of workers with a university degree is projected to rise further to 32 per cent in 2012 (Table 1.3). Consequently, the human capital index, which is based on the educational attainment of each age cohort by gender, is projected to continue rising at about a 1 per cent rate over the next decade, contributing 0.6 percentage point to the annual growth rate. Moreover, a successful reform of the labour market that allows Korea to more fully benefit from its human capital could lead to a larger contribution from the rising level of educational attainment.

Key challenges facing Korea

A major concern in Korea is that the traditional growth model, driven by high levels of investment in manufacturing industries to boost exports, is no longer capable of sustaining rapid growth. The government has established five strategies to lay the groundwork for achieving the income-doubling objective:

- *Labour-management relations*; establish socially cohesive labour-management relations.
- *Structural reform*; bring the Korean economic system in line with global standards.
- *Technological innovation*: develop science and technology and foster new growth engines.
- *Northeast Asian Economic Hub*; become an international business hub and strengthen economic ties in Northeast Asia.
- *Balanced national development*; promote local areas (*i.e.* outside of the Seoul metropolitan area) to lead innovation and development.

In August 2003, the government announced ten industrial sectors as new growth engines, in which it plans to invest 400 billion won in 2004.[8] The government is planning the development of technology for each sector and the necessary manpower and infrastructure, and acting as a promoter of these sectors.

A government policy of promoting certain industries to lead the economy, a policy that was tried in the past with mixed results,[9] contains considerable risks and may introduce important distortions in the economy, which may eventually dampen productivity growth. The evolution of the country's comparative advantage will depend primarily on the efforts and decisions of Korean firms and workers. While market forces, such as changes in demand patterns and advances in technology, should be the main drivers of growth, the government has an important role to play in upgrading the country's capabilities in education, infrastructure and the innovation framework in order to support an increasingly knowledge-based economy. Growth will be faster in an economy where resources are rapidly reallocated to high-productivity activities in response to market signals. It is thus important to reverse the legacy of government intervention, which is ill-suited to a complex, increasingly globalised economy. To accelerate the speed of adjustment, it is necessary to improve the functioning of the labour market in order to fully benefit from the increasing human capital available in Korea. At the same time, reforms in the corporate and financial sectors are essential to improve the allocation of capital, while limiting government intervention. In addition, strengthening competition is a key to boosting productivity. This section will briefly review the key problems faced in these areas after first discussing the medium-term macroeconomic challenges.

Macroeconomic challenges

Implementing the new monetary policy framework

Macroeconomic stability depends to some extent on monetary policy, which is conducted under a new framework introduced at the beginning of 2004. As recommended in the 2003 OECD *Economic Survey of Korea*, the independence of the central bank was enhanced and the inflation objective was changed from an annual target to a medium-term objective. The difficulty of achieving the desired targets has been heightened by the extensive restructuring of the financial sector since the crisis, which has increased uncertainty about the link between policy interest rates and market interest rates, as well as the impact of interest rate changes on economic activity. Moreover, the exchange rate and the persistent increases in real estate prices also influence the setting of monetary policy.

Spending pressures arising from population ageing and economic co-operation with the North

Korea has an exceptionally sound fiscal position. Gross public debt – at around 35 per cent of GDP, including guaranteed debt – is well below the OECD average and Korea is one of only three member countries in which the government is a net creditor. Government spending is the second lowest in the OECD area, at 24 per cent of GDP (Figure 1.8), reflecting the immaturity of the social welfare system and the relatively low level of public services. However, rapid population ageing will create considerable pressure for increased public expenditures. The old-age dependency ratio, the second lowest among member countries at present, is projected to surpass the OECD average before the middle of the century, reflecting the sharp fall in fertility and rising life expectancy (Figure 1.9). At the same time, increased urbanisation and the changing role of women have weakened the traditional support system for the elderly that was based on the extended family. The National Pension Scheme, created in 1988, promises to provide a pension set at 60 per cent of average earnings. However, it requires a major

Figure 1.8.   **Public spending in international comparison**[1]
Per cent of GDP

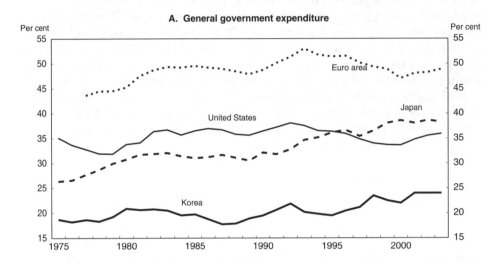

A. General government expenditure

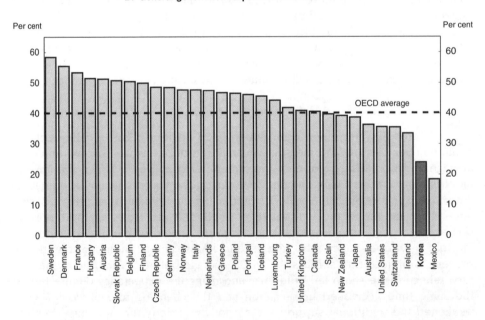

B. General government expenditure in 2002

1. Public spending is defined as the sum of current outlays and net capital outlays. Data are based on SNA93/ESA95.
Source: OECD.

Figure 1.9. **Old-age dependency ratios**

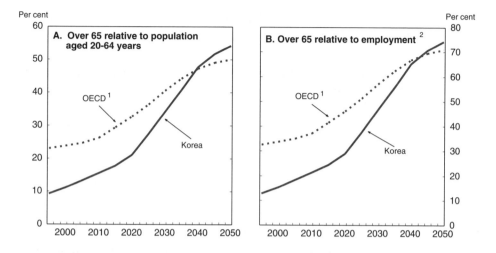

1. The average of the rates of individual countries (excluding Turkey and Mexico).
2. For the projections, the employment to population ratio is kept at its 1995 level.
Source: Eurostat for EU countries and United Nations for others.

overhaul to ensure its sustainability. Population ageing and the development of the social safety net is likely to boost publicly funded social expenditures, which were 6 per cent of GDP in 2001 compared to an OECD average of 21 per cent. Spending pressures will necessitate increased government revenue, which will result in signifi-cant deadweight losses resulting from such problems as overly generous allowances for individuals, large-scale and wide-ranging tax preferences for enterprises, an inappropriate taxation of property and a lack of strong and uniform tax enforcement.

The cost of economic integration with North Korea poses another poten-tially large fiscal burden. In the Berlin Declaration of 2000, the South promised to provide economic assistance to the North. While aid from the South and other countries may have helped stabilise conditions in North Korea, economic output remains well below the level of the early 1990s. Given the chronic food shortages and the deterioration in economic conditions in the North during the past decade, the cost of economic integration may be enormous. Compared to Germany, the burden of integration is likely to be heavier, given that the population of North Korea is one-half that of the South, while the per capita income gap may be more than 13 to one.[10] The challenges of rapid population ageing and North Korea underline the importance of establishing more effective budgeting frameworks and increasing efficiency in meeting the objectives of government spending programmes.

© OECD 2004

In sum, the key macroeconomic challenges, which are addressed in Chapter 2, are:

- Ensuring that monetary policy effectively promotes stability under the new framework in the context of pressure on the exchange rate and real estate prices.

- Coping with the fiscal pressures stemming from rapid population ageing, the development of the social safety net and economic co-operation with North Korea.

- Increasing the efficiency of the tax system, thereby reducing deadweight costs, as government revenue increases to match the rise in spending.

- Enhancing the efficiency and transparency of the public expenditure management system, while improving public service delivery and accountability for results.

The labour market: dualism and a lack of flexibility

Concerns about a "jobless recovery" have arisen as employment declined in 2003 despite the economic rebound in the second half of the year. This resulted in an unemployment rate of 7.7 per cent for young adults in the 15 to 29 age group in 2003, compared to an overall rate of 3.4 per cent. With the working-age population increasing about 1 per cent a year, achieving adequate job creation is a major challenge, heightened by the declining number of manufacturing jobs and the outflow of investment, particularly to China.

Korea's contentious labour-management relations did not improve significantly last year. In the Ministry of Labour's view, "Escalated industrial conflicts between monopolistic management and powerful trade unions are dragging down the nation's economy".[11] The uncooperative relationship between workers and management poses a stumbling block to labour market flexibility. Although the labour code was revised in 1998 to allow layoffs for managerial reasons, they are subject to a number of conditions, making it doubtful whether the reform enhanced flexibility in practice. Employment flexibility is also hindered by the strong opposition of workers to dismissals, which reflects to some extent the limited development of the social safety net, despite some progress. Indeed, less than one-fifth of the unemployed in 2003 received unemployment benefits. In addition, active labour market policies play a relatively minor role, accounting for less than 0.5 per cent of GDP, reflecting limited outlays on training for unemployed persons. Problematic industrial relations in some companies undermine business confidence and investment, as well as discouraging inflows of foreign direct investment, which have fallen by about half from the 1999-2000 level.

The higher level of employment protection granted to regular workers has encouraged firms to hire non-regular workers. Moreover, their wages are 20 to

27 per cent less on average than regular workers, after adjusting for employees' characteristics (Jeong, 2003), and they are excluded from some aspects of the social safety net. Non-regular workers are estimated to account for a quarter of total employees in 2003.[12] The emergence of a dualistic labour market in which one segment is subject to lower wages, less protection from the social safety net and greater job precariousness, creates equity concerns. Another labour market issue is the practice of seniority-based wages, which makes older workers relatively expensive. Consequently, firms tend to let workers go at around the age of 55, forcing them to seek self-employment or to exit from the labour force. Such a system is ill-suited for a rapidly ageing labour force as it tends to reduce participation in the labour force. The participation rate is also held down by the relatively low rate for women.

In sum, the key labour market challenges, which are addressed in Chapter 3, are:

- Reversing the decline in employment in 2003.

- Reducing the dualism in the labour market resulting from the increased use of non-regular workers.

- Increasing labour market flexibility.

- Expanding the effective coverage of the social safety net.

- Ensuring that active labour market policies are effective.

- Establishing more co-operative and harmonious industrial relations.

- Raising the labour force participation rate over the medium term in order to cope with population ageing.

Restructuring the corporate and financial sectors

Korea's corporate sector is still in the process of restructuring in the wake of the 1997 financial crisis, which led to significant changes, such as stronger competitive pressures, more independent financial institutions and a new corporate governance framework. The decline in the manufacturing sector's share of employment, which peaked at 28 per cent in the late 1980s, has resumed after being briefly reversed following the crisis in response to the one-third decline in the effective exchange rate between 1996 and 1998 (Figure 1.10). Indeed, there appears to be an accelerated shift of manufacturing abroad. A 2002 survey by the Korea Chamber of Commerce and Industry reported that 44 per cent of major companies had already moved some production sites outside of Korea and 34 per cent were planning such transfers. The major objective cited was to lower production costs. According to the Ministry of Commerce, Industry and Energy, labour-intensive manufacturing, which accounts for about a quarter of manufactured output, accounted for 46 per cent of that sector's overseas investment in 2003.

Figure 1.10. **De-industrialisation in the OECD area**

Source: Rowthorn and Coutts (2004).

Much of the concern about de-industrialisation is connected to competition from China. For example, in the survey cited above, four-fifths of the companies planning to move production abroad had chosen China as the destination. Korea is sandwiched both geographically and economically between a rapidly growing China, which is quickly moving up the product ladder, and Japan, which retains a comparative advantage in a number of advanced industries. The composition of exports illustrates Korea's position between its larger neighbours (Figure 1.11). In China, where wages are less than one-fifth of Korean levels, low and medium-low technology products, notably textiles, account for more than half of exports. However, Chinese exports of high and medium-high technology products, such as office, accounting and computing machinery, electrical products, radio, television and communication goods, are increasing rapidly. On the other hand, the strength of Japanese exports lies in more advanced products, while low and medium-low technology products account for only a quarter. Korea lies in between its two neighbours in terms of the proportion of high-tech goods in its exports. The evolution of Korea's comparative advantage will depend on the effectiveness of its large investment in knowledge.

However, the concern about de-industrialisation and the shift of jobs overseas appears to be exaggerated. The shift to fewer, but higher-paying, jobs in manufacturing is part of the process that allows income to increase at such a rapid

Figure 1.11. **The composition of exports of China, Korea and Japan**
By main sector and degree of technology intensity, 2001

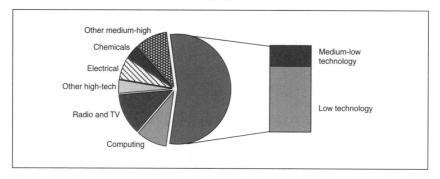

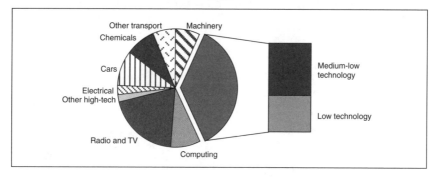

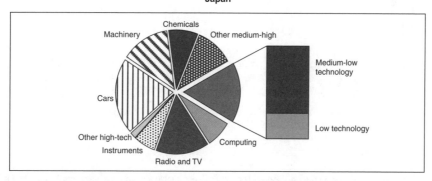

Source: OECD, Bilateral Trade Database, 2003.

rate in Korea. Part of this process in OECD countries has been a growing role for the service sector, an area where productivity in Korea is relatively low. The share of knowledge-intensive services – post and telecommunications, finance and insurance and business services – in GDP is the third lowest in the OECD area (Figure 1.5). As for business-sector R&D, only 12 per cent takes place in the service sector, about half of the OECD average. Moreover, in Korea, service sector productivity is around 60 per cent of that in manufacturing, the largest gap in the OECD area. The gap did not narrow during the latter part of the 1990s, as annual productivity growth was more than 7 percentage points higher in manufacturing than in the service sector (Figure 1.12).

Figure 1.12. **Productivity in the service sector**[1]
1995-2000

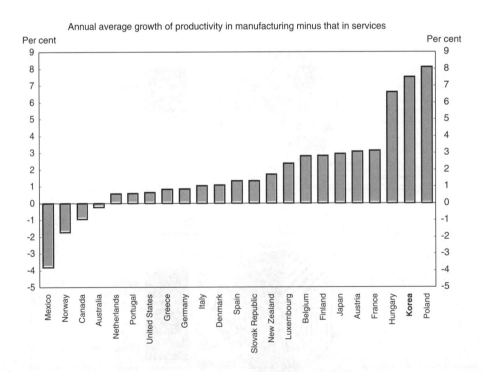

1. Productivity is defined as output per worker. The service sector includes wholesale and retail trade, hotels and restaurants, transport, storage and communication, financial intermediation, real estate and other business activities. Electricity, gas and water have been included in the manufacturing sector.
Source: OECD.

The corporate sector has evolved significantly since the crisis. In particular, the high leverage that was typical prior to the crisis has been sharply reduced. For the manufacturing sector, the debt to equity ratio fell from nearly 400 per cent in 1997 to 123 per cent in 2003. Increased competition, more independent financial institutions subject to improved supervision, a new corporate governance framework and measures to improve the auditing framework have been catalysts in changing behaviour in the corporate sector. However, the accounting scandal at SK Global demonstrated that there are remaining weaknesses in the auditing framework, leading to a lack of transparency. In corporate governance, current practices lag significantly behind the institutional changes. For example, while independent directors have been granted a larger role, their influence on corporate management appears to have been limited.

The restructuring of the corporate sector has had major repercussions on the financial sector. While considerable progress has been achieved in the banking sector, which has regained profitability, cut non-performing loans to record low levels and boosted capital adequacy ratios, the restructuring of the non-bank sector is less advanced. Despite the injection of nearly $7 billion in public funds for restructuring, the investment trust companies (ITCs) have not recovered from past shocks, such as the collapse of Daewoo in 1999, thus leading to problems in the corporate bond market. The ITCs were also negatively affected by the failure of SK Global in 2003 and the problems in the credit card companies. The sharp rise in the delinquency ratio and in the amount of rescheduled loans resulted in serious liquidity and solvency problems in the credit card companies, with adverse effects on private consumption. The government co-ordinated a rescue for the largest company, LG Card, by 14 financial institutions, including a state-owned bank, on the grounds that its failure could pose systemic risks, although this may increase moral hazard problems. More generally, the credit card bubble suggests that risk-management practices in the financial sector are still underdeveloped.

In sum, the key challenges in the financial and corporate sectors, which are addressed in Chapter 4, are:

- Upgrading the innovation framework in order to get the most benefit possible out of Korea's large investment in knowledge.

- Improving the corporate governance and auditing frameworks and practices in order to achieve a better allocation of capital, enhance transparency and reduce the scope for managerial abuse.

- Resolving the problems in the non-bank financial sector, notably in the credit card companies and the investment trust companies.

- Improving supervision to avoid future liquidity and solvency problems in the financial sector.

Enhancing competition to boost growth

The Anti-Monopoly and Fair Trade Act is enforced by the Korea Fair Trade Commission (KFTC), an independent and powerful agency. However, there are weaknesses in competition policy. In particular, the KFTC's power to obtain evidence is not backed up by effective judicial sanctions, while private actions and criminal enforcement are rare. Moreover, the law includes major exemptions and special treatment for some sectors, such as small and medium-sized enterprises. In some areas, the commitment to competition principles has been tempered by various forms of government intervention aimed at accelerating growth.

In addition, the emphasis on "fair trade" has led the competition authority to focus on financial oversight of the chaebol, which may limit its capacity to enforce more conventional aspects of competition law. The chaebol, which played a key role in both the rapid industrialisation of Korea and in the 1997 crisis, remain a difficult dilemma for policymakers. Chaebol are multi-company business groups operating in a wide range of markets under common entrepreneurial and financial control. A number of regulations have been introduced since 1987 to limit their growth,[13] although their effectiveness is questionable. However, the transformation of the economic environment following the crisis has led to significant changes in the corporate sector. Of the top 30 chaebol in 1997, seventeen have entered legal bankruptcy procedures or been forced into workout programmes, including Daewoo, which was the second largest group. Meanwhile, a number of others lost control of large affiliated firms. In addition, the average debt-to-equity ratio fell to 116 per cent from more than 500 per cent at the time of the crisis. Nevertheless, there remains concern about possible negative effects stemming from the concentration of power in the business groups, adverse impacts on competition in product markets and the possibilities of managerial abuse. The founding families have been able to exercise *de facto* control over legally-independent firms, although their ownership shares have fallen to an average of 4 per cent. This has created opportunities for the owner families to expropriate outside shareholders through transfers between affiliated firms.

Policymakers face the difficult questions of how serious these problems are in reality and what policies are necessary to address them. Moreover, policies to deal with chaebol issues are constrained by a number of considerations. First, the development of the business groups was linked to past authoritarian governments, raising questions about their legitimacy and making them politically unpopular. Second, the chaebol, which include key exporters such as Samsung and Hyundai, have a major impact on economic growth. Efforts to reform or change the behaviour of the business groups can therefore have a significant influence on growth and employment prospects in the short run. Third, the increasing integration of Korea in the world economy has weakened the rationale for the restrictions on the business groups. For example, allowing the chaebol's foreign competitors to purchase Korean firms while the chaebol themselves remain subject to invest-ment ceilings raises questions of fairness.

As noted above, the gap between labour productivity in the manufactur-ing and service sectors is exceptionally large in Korea. Consequently, continuing the process of convergence to the income levels in the advanced countries will depend to a considerable extent on raising productivity in the service sector, whose share of the economy is likely to continue expanding. Such gains depend in part on strengthening competition, particularly in the network industries. In the retail sector, the application process for opening large-scale retail stores limits competition. The important role of professional associations may also have harm-ful effects, such as creating entry barriers or price-fixing agreements. In the tele-communication sector, the market power of the dominant firms in both the fixed line and mobile telephony markets raises difficult challenges for competition. The government's ten-year plan to introduce competition in the electricity sector has fallen behind schedule, in part due to opposition from labour, while the initial efforts to privatise the generating companies have been unsuccessful. In both electricity and telecommunications, a key missing element is an independent and pro-active regulatory body, which has been found to be necessary for competition in other OECD countries.

International competition is hindered by an average tariff level that is more than double that in the major OECD countries. In particular, the level of pro-tection provided for the agricultural sector is exceptionally high. Strong opposition from farmers delayed the approval of Korea's first free trade agreement, with Chile, and limits the scope for Korea's participation in regional trade agreements that would allow it to benefit more fully from Asia's economic dynamism. As noted above, FDI inflows have declined during the past three years, in part due to labour market problems, following a surge in the late 1990s.

In sum, the key challenges to strengthening competition, which are addressed in Chapter 5, are:

- Upgrading the enforcement and coverage of competition policy.
- Reducing entry barriers in the service sector.
- Ensuring the necessary conditions for competition in the network indus-tries.
- Dealing effectively with the chaebol.
- Opening further to imports and inflows of foreign direct investment.

Conclusion

Korea's accelerated economic development has transformed it from one of the poorest countries in the world 40 years ago to a leading industrial nation. The economic growth rate during the past decade, at an annual pace of 5.6 per cent, has been one of the fastest in the OECD area. However, the contribution to growth from factor inputs is expected to slow over the medium term. Consequently, maintaining growth at an annual average rate of 5 per cent or higher would require that labour productivity growth accelerate from its 4¼ per cent pace during the past decade to at least 4¾ per cent, implying an acceleration of total factor productivity growth.

A number of factors, such as investment in physical capital, education and R&D, explain the country's success in moving into technologically-advanced sectors and suggest that it has the potential to maintain growth at high rates that would rapidly achieve the government's income-doubling objective. Moreover, the large gap between productivity levels in Korea and the OECD average indicates that there is considerable scope to continue the convergence process towards the income levels in the most advanced nations. However, effectively exploiting Korea's growth potential will depend on reforms in a number of areas. Although the wide-ranging programme implemented in the wake of the 1997 crisis made major improvements in key areas, the reform agenda remains unfinished. One challenge, discussed in Chapter 2, will be to maintain macroeconomic stability and ensure fiscal sustainability in the context of rapid population ageing and other spending pressures. Chapter 3 discusses measures to improve the functioning of the labour market, while Chapter 4 examines policies related to the corporate and financial sector. The final chapter examines the challenge of strengthening competition in the Korean economy. Action in all of the areas would allow Korea to continue its progress in becoming a high-income OECD country.

Notes

1. Ministry of Finance and Economy (2003), *Economic Policy Directions*. In 2002, per capita gross national income was around $10 000. The revision of national accounts in March 2004 boosted that figure by 15 per cent to about $11.500.

2. This study divided potential output gains into factor inputs and total factor productivity growth. This approach requires measuring the quality of inputs of labour and capital, although the latter is difficult to quantify. The output gain not explained by the quality-adjusted inputs is often used as an indicator of technological progress (see *The Sources of Economic Growth in OECD Countries* [OECD, 2003e]). In the growth de-composition shown in Table 1.1, growth is divided into labour inputs and labour productivity. The latter term shows the impact of changes in the quality of labour, changes in the quantity and quality of capital inputs and technological progress, as well as other factors.

3. The "technology balance of payments" is defined as the balance of international payments resulting from the transfer of techniques (through patents and licenses), the transfer of designs, trademarks and patterns, services with a technical content (such as engineering studies) and industrial R&D (OECD *Science, Technology and Industry Scoreboard*, 2003, Table C.5.4).

4. This does not include outlays on private educational institutes, known as *hakwon*, which account for 5 per cent of total household spending.

5. Business R&D in this sector amounts to nearly 1 per cent of GDP, a level second only to Finland.

6. As in other OECD countries, the rate would be higher if discouraged workers were included. Such workers may be relatively high in Korea, as reflected in fluctuations in the labour force participation rate. This may be one reason for the relatively low participation rate as noted below.

7. The amended Labour Standards Act reduces the maximum standard workweek from 44 to 40 hours. Implementation will begin at workplaces with more than 1 000 employees in July 2004 and will be extended gradually to those with more than 20 employees in 2008. For workplaces below this threshold, the five-day workweek will be introduced sometime before 2011.

8. The ten industries are: intelligent robots; future automobiles; next-generation semiconductors; digital television and broadcasting; next-generation mobile communications; next-generation computer displays; intelligent home networks; digital content and software solutions; next-generation batteries; and biomedical products and artificial organs.

9. In particular, the Heavy and Chemical Industry (HCI) drive of the 1970s targeted certain industries and provided a number of special incentives, notably the allocation of credit to favoured industries and selective trade and tax policies. This policy ended when

Korea faced serious economic problems in 1980 stemming from over-investment and low profitability in some of the sectors targeted by the HCI drive, which were compounded by the second oil shock and political instability.

10. In comparison, East Germany's population was less than a third of West Germany's at the time of German re-unification, while the income gap was smaller, with per capita income in East Germany around half of that in the West. Moreover, South Korea would face this challenge at a lower level of income than in the case of West Germany.

11. Ministry of Labour (2003), *Reform Proposal for Sound Industrial Relations*, Seoul.

12. Regular workers are defined as those that work more than one year at a firm and are paid standard wages, plus bonuses and overtime. Officially, the proportion of non-regular workers rose from 46 per cent of wage and salary employees in 1997 to 49 per cent in 2003. However, a significant proportion of employees classified as non-regular remain with their employer on a longer-term basis. Nonetheless, even the revised estimate of 24 per cent (see Chapter 3) is high by OECD standards and, in any case, has been increasing in recent years.

13. In particular, the Monopoly Regulation and Fair Trade Act prohibits cross-shareholding between affiliates of chaebol, limits loan guarantees and monitors commercial exchanges between them. In addition, shareholding in other domestic companies by chaebol-affiliated firms is restricted in order to limit the expansion and diversification of the business groups.

2. Economic prospects and macroeconomic policies

Korea is rebounding gradually from the downturn in the first half of 2003. Output growth at an 11 per cent seasonally-adjusted annual rate in the fourth quarter of 2003 suggests a strong recovery. However, the large gap between buoyant exports and still sluggish domestic demand, with private consumption still declining, indicates that a full-fledged recovery is not yet underway. On the other hand, there is not much slack in the labour market, where unemployment is at a low level and wage growth has been high. These conflicting signals make it exceptionally difficult to project the path of the recovery and the appropriate macroeconomic policies. This chapter begins by providing short-term projections before turning to the macroeconomic policy issues. The second section considers monetary policy and the related issues of exchange rate policy and the real estate market. Fiscal policy issues, including the pension system, are discussed in the third section, while the fourth section considers how to improve the efficiency of public expenditure, by providing a follow-up to the special chapter in the 2003 OECD *Economic Survey of Korea*. The chapter concludes with an assessment.

Economic prospects

Korea is gradually emerging from an economic downturn caused by sluggish domestic demand, despite buoyant export growth. Exports increased 16 per cent in volume terms in 2003 (Table 2.1), thanks in large part to China, which has become Korea's largest trading partner. Korean exports to China are increasing at nearly a 50 per cent year-on-year rate in dollar terms. The decline in the effective exchange rate during the course of 2003 also had a positive effect. However, robust export growth could not prevent a decline in both private consumption and investment in machinery and equipment in 2003. The dualistic nature of growth is reflected in the gap between the 5 per cent rise in manufacturing output and the 2 per cent increase in the service sector, an outcome that had negative implications for employment, which declined for the first time since 1998. With a recession in the first half of 2003, output growth for the year as a whole slowed to 3.1 per cent, the slowest since the crisis.

Table 2.1. **Economic outlook**[1]

Percentage change in constant 1995 prices

	Share of GDP in 2000[3]	2000	2001	2002	2003	2004	2005
Demand and output							
Private consumption	53.9	8.4	4.9	7.9	−1.4	2.5	5.0
Government consumption	12.1	1.6	4.9	6.0	3.7	3.0	3.0
Gross fixed capital formation	31.1	12.2	−0.2	6.6	3.6	4.7	5.7
Final domestic demand	97.1	8.7	3.1	7.3	0.8	3.2	5.0
Stockbuilding[2]	0.0	−0.2	0.1	−0.2	−0.7	0.0	0.0
Total domestic demand	97.0	8.5	3.2	7.1	0.0	3.3	5.0
Exports of goods and services	40.9	19.1	−2.7	13.3	15.7	18.0	14.0
Imports of goods and services	37.7	20.1	−4.2	15.2	9.7	14.0	13.5
Foreign balance[2]	3.2	0.2	0.5	−0.3	2.8	2.6	1.3
GDP	100.0	8.5	3.8	7.0	3.1	5.6	5.9
Prices							
GDP deflator		0.7	3.5	2.9	2.3	2.0	2.3
Private consumption deflator		4.7	4.8	2.8	3.4	3.2	3.2
Consumer price index		2.3	4.1	2.7	3.6	3.2	3.2
Labour market							
Employment growth		4.3	2.0	2.8	−0.1	1.7	1.2
Participation rate[4]		61.0	61.3	61.9	61.4	61.7	61.7
Average wage		8.0	5.1	11.2	9.2	6.0	7.0
Unemployment rate		4.1	3.8	3.1	3.4	3.3	3.0
Balance of payments							
Current account (US$ billions)		12.2	8.0	5.4	12.3	14.7	16.5
As a percentage of GDP		2.4	1.7	1.0	2.0	2.2	2.3

1. These projections are identical to those published in the OECD *Economic Outlook* No. 75 (June 2004).
2. Contribution to GDP growth.
3. The components shown below do not sum to 100 per cent due to a statistical discrepancy equivalent to −0.2 per cent of GDP.
4. Labour force as a share of population age 15 and over.
Source: OECD.

The failure of strong export growth to translate into a sustained recovery in domestic demand thus far is partly due to external shocks, such as the North Korean nuclear issue, that have undermined confidence. However, the main reason was the end of the private consumption boom due to several factors. *First*, the sharp run-up in household debt, from 56 per cent of GDP in 1998 to 74 per cent in 2002, was followed by a period of retrenchment for households (Figure 2.1). *Second*, the problems in the credit card companies, in the wake of the three-fold rise in the delinquency rate to 14 per cent by the end of 2003, caused them to reduce lending to the household sector (see Chapter 4). Domestic demand was also negatively affected by domestic shocks, notably labour unrest and the SK Global accounting scandal in 2003, which exacerbated the fall in both household and business confidence.

Figure 2.1. **Household financial assets and liabilities**
Per cent of GDP[1]

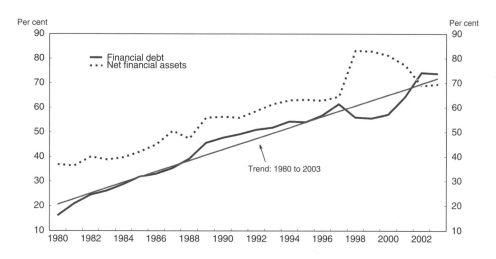

1. For the "Individual Sector" in the Bank of Korea's flow of funds data.
Source: Bank of Korea.

The further acceleration of export growth – to 38 per cent year-on-year in US dollar terms in the first quarter of 2004 – is expected to spark stronger growth in domestic demand during the course of 2004. Investment in machinery and equipment already turned positive in the final quarter of 2003 and should gain momentum during 2004. However, the rebound in consumption may be modest for a number of reasons. *First*, despite the decline in private consumption in 2003, the level of household debt is still somewhat above its long-term trend (Figure 2.1). *Second*, the on-going problems in the credit card sector may lead to a further reduction in lending to households. *Third*, consumer confidence has weakened in the most recent months. *Fourth*, in the Social Pact for Job Creation in February 2004, the major union confederation agreed that high-paid workers will accept wage stability over the next two years (see Chapter 3).

In summary, continued strong export growth in the context of rising world trade and a moderate pick-up in domestic demand is expected to lift output growth to the 5 to 6 per cent range in 2004 and 2005. The export-led nature of the recovery may keep the current account surplus at around 2 per cent of GDP in 2004 and 2005. The recovery is likely to quickly absorb the remaining slack in the labour market, where the unemployment rate is already low at 3.4 per cent (seasonally-adjusted) in the first quarter of 2004. The relatively low level of unemployment may also help explain the still-high increase in wages – 9 per cent

in 2003 compared to 11 per cent in 2002 – although this also reflects the importance of bonus payments, which are linked to the previous year's profits, in
employee compensation.[1] This contributed to unit labour cost increases of 6.8 and
5.8 per cent in 2002 and 2003, respectively. Thus far, the core measure of consumer
price inflation, which excludes petroleum-based fuels and non-grain farm products, has remained at around 2¾ per cent, near the mid-point of the Bank of
Korea's medium-term inflation target.

There are risks, though, attached to the projection of an expansion
through 2004 and 2005. In particular, there is uncertainty about private consumption, given the still weak level of household confidence. With their debt still at a
high level, there is a risk that households will raise their saving rate in order to
improve their financial position. A second risk is a slowdown in export demand,
particularly in China, which has been the major factor driving the growth of
exports.

Monetary and exchange rate policy

Monetary policy under the new framework

The revision of the Bank of Korea Act that took effect in 2004 has significantly changed the framework for monetary policy, as recommended in previous
OECD Economic Surveys of Korea. First, the inflation objective has been changed from
an annual to a medium-term target, which is the norm in OECD countries that target inflation. The medium term is defined as three years. This reform reflects the
fact that monetary policy changes only have an impact on the real economy with a
significant lag and on inflation with an even longer lag.[2] Consequently, attempting
to achieve an annual inflation target requires a more aggressive monetary policy,
which may increase the volatility of the real economy and financial markets. Second,
the independence of the central bank has been strengthened by replacing one of
the outside members on the Monetary Policy Committee by the deputy governor
of the Bank of Korea. In addition, the central bank's budget no longer needs the
prior consent of the government, although changes in wages and benefits still
require the approval of the Ministry of Finance and Economy.

Monetary conditions remain relaxed, as the central bank has left the
short-term policy interest rate at a record low of 3.75 per cent since July 2003
(Figure 2.2). Adjusted for inflation, the short-term rate fell close to zero in the final
quarter of 2003. The impact of interest rate declines is reinforced by the fall in the
exchange rate (Figure 2.3). In contrast to many major currencies, the rate of the
won relative to the dollar was relatively stable during 2003. Consequently, the won
had depreciated by 10 and 16 per cent against the yen and the euro, respectively,
at the end of 2003 compared to the year-earlier levels. In effective terms (relative
to Korea's 41 major trading partners), the won declined 6 per cent over the same

Figure 2.2. **Interest rates**

Nominal rates

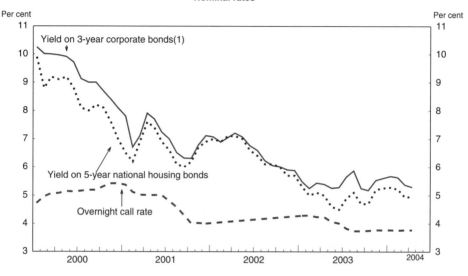

Real interest rates(2)

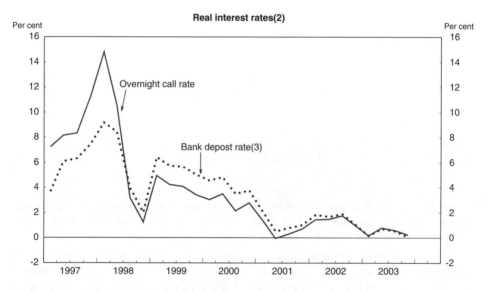

1. With a credit rating of A+ until September 2000 and a rating of AA- since October 2000.
2. Deflated by the year-on-year change in the consumer price index.
3. Rate on time deposits of less than six months.
Source: Bank of Korea.

Figure 2.3. **The exchange rate**[1]

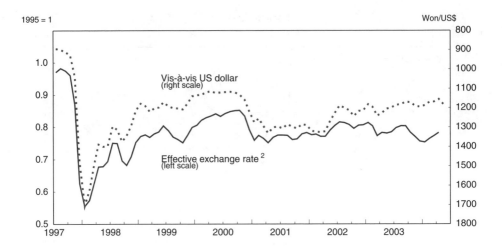

1. A rise indicates an appreciation of the won.
2. Calculated *vis-à-vis* forty-one trading partners.
Source: OECD.

period. Part of this decline was offset by some appreciation of the won in the first quarter of 2004.

The Bank of Korea has been successful in keeping core inflation within its annual target zone since 2000 (Figure 2.4). Under the new framework, monetary policy is supposed to achieve a core inflation rate of 2.5 to 3.5 per cent over the medium term. There is concern that rising prices of oil and raw materials will have a significant impact on inflation. Indeed, producer prices in early 2004 were rising at a 4½ per cent rate, the highest in five years, which may boost the headline CPI figure above the central bank's forecast of 2.9 per cent in 2004. In response, the government recently decided to freeze public service prices – notably the tariffs for telephone, electricity and other public utilities – in the first half of 2004 and asked local governments to take similar measures. Moreover, it plans to lower mobile telecommunications fees and pharmaceutical prices in June. However, a more serious threat to inflation may come from demand pressure as the recovery accelerates, since the slack in the economy will be absorbed. During the course of the recovery, therefore, real interest rates may have to rise from their current level of close to zero in order to achieve the central bank's medium-term inflation target, although this would have a negative effect on the heavily-indebted household sector. The extent of the interest rate rise that is appropriate, though, will be affected by exchange rate developments.

Figure 2.4. **Inflation targets and outcomes**

Year-on-year percentage changes

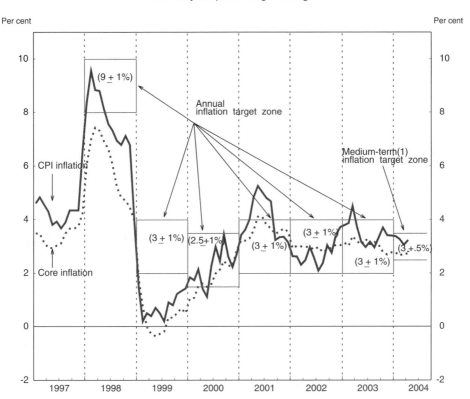

1. In 2004, the Bank of Korea changed the target to a medium-term objective.
Source: Bank of Korea.

Exchange rate policy

With an increase of $34 billion during 2003, Korea's foreign exchange reserves reached $155 billion (Figure 2.5), the second highest level in the OECD area. Consequently, reserves are now almost three times higher than short-term foreign debt, in contrast to 1997, when they were substantially less. While holding higher reserves tends to reduce vulnerability to crisis, there is little rationale from that perspective for further accumulation. The marked rise in reserves in 2003, which was significantly larger than Korea's combined surplus on the current and capital accounts, partially reflects intervention in exchange markets aimed at enhancing the

Figure 2.5. **Foreign exchange reserves and short-term foreign debt**

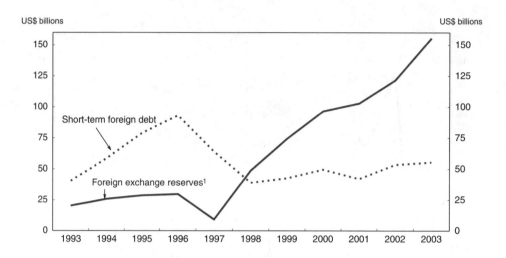

1. Useable reserves only, *i.e.* excludes illiquid deposits at offshore Korean banks.
Source: Bank of Korea.

stability of the exchange rate. However, there are substantial risks to a policy of intervention, which generally has limited effectiveness except in the very short run. Moreover, sterilised intervention requires the issuance of Foreign Exchange Equalisation Bonds and Monetary Stabilisation Bonds. The interest rate paid on such bonds is generally more than on the instruments in major reserve currencies.

Although slowing the pace of foreign exchange accumulation may increase the upward pressure on the won and eventually moderate export growth, there would be some offsetting positive effects. *First*, a stronger currency would provide income gains for households and firms. *Second*, it would reduce the burden of the corporate sector's foreign debt, which at $70 billion in 2003 (12 per cent of GDP), is still significant. *Third*, a stronger currency might help revive stagnant investment by lowering the price of foreign capital goods. *Fourth*, a gradual currency appreciation may impose less adjustment costs than if intervention aimed at stabilisation is followed by a significant appreciation. In sum, slowing the pace of reserve accumulation may promote a more balanced expansion over the medium term.

Real estate market considerations

The policy of keeping interest rates at low levels has also contributed to the rise in real estate prices in recent years. High land prices have a number of adverse impacts, including distortions in the distribution of wealth, high housing prices relative to income, a lack of social infrastructure, and weakened international competitiveness of corporations. Moreover, rising real estate prices may have contributed to the private consumption boom by raising households' collateral and hence their ability to borrow. Given the consequences for price stability, real estate price trends have become a factor influencing monetary policy decisions, not only in Korea but in other OECD countries that have experienced marked increases in housing prices. Preventing higher real estate prices has been used in the past as a rationale for tighter monetary policy in Korea.

However, rising real estate prices in Korea can be attributed to a number of other factors, such as government policies that limit the use of land, thereby restricting its effective supply, and the low rate of holding taxes on real estate. Moreover, the surge in housing prices during the past few years reflects, in part, a correction from the post-crisis decline (Figure 2.6). From a longer-term perspective, the nation-wide level of house prices has kept pace with the consumer price index. Perhaps most importantly, the recent increasing trend differs from previous episodes because it is highly concentrated in the capital region, in particular, Kangnam, an area in the southern part of Seoul.

The surge in house prices appears to have been at least temporarily subdued, as the recent moderation in price movements is larger than expected based

Figure 2.6. **Housing price trends**
1997 = 100

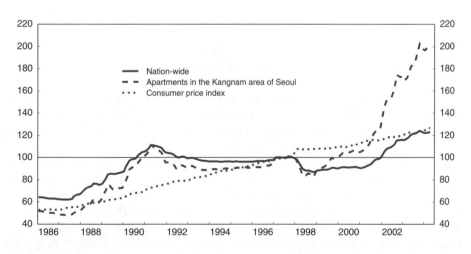

Source: Kookmin Bank.

on seasonal factors alone. The sluggish domestic economy and the slowdown in the growth of household credits have probably had an impact. In addition, government measures to expand the housing supply and discourage speculation have helped restore stability. Following a number of *ad hoc* measures over the past few years, the government announced in October 2003 a comprehensive policy package.[3] However, maintaining stability in real estate markets will be difficult in the face of population concentration in the capital region, resulting in a shortage of housing.[4] The plan to move the capital from Seoul to the middle of the country could alleviate the concentration of activity in the capital region (see Chapter 5). However, government policy should go beyond trying to maintain stability and aim at encouraging the efficient use of land and removing regulations that tend to restrict economic activity. In sum, the localised nature of the rise in real estate prices does not suggest that a monetary policy response is needed at the present time.

Fiscal policy directions

This section briefly considers the stance of fiscal policy in 2003 and the impact on public debt. After looking at indicators of the fiscal stance for 2004, this section will discuss longer-term spending pressures stemming from the impact of population ageing on pension outlays.

Did fiscal policy help to stabilise the economy in 2003?

The impact of fiscal policy on economic activity in Korea is relatively weak, reflecting the small size of the government and the early stage of development of the social safety net. Consequently, automatic stabilisers appear to play a minor role. In 2003, two supplementary budgets in the latter part of the year boosted total government spending by 6½ per cent,[5] somewhat faster than the 5½ per cent rise in nominal GDP. However, government revenue increased even faster, at 8 per cent, due in part to a rise in corporate income tax payments.

The overall measure of the consolidated budget balance, which shows a decline in the surplus from 3.3 per cent of GDP in 2002 to 1.1 per cent in 2003, would suggest an expansionary stance (Table 2.2). However, the reported deterioration was due to special factors. Most important was the decision to replace government-guaranteed borrowing used to finance restructuring of the financial sector with public bonds (see Chapter 4). Between 2003 and 2006, 49 trillion won (6.8 per cent of GDP) of such debt is being brought into the budget. The first tranche of 13 trillion won in 2003 reduced the budget balance by 1.8 percentage points of GDP. A second special factor was privatisation revenue. The sale of Korea Telecom in 2002 had generated revenue of about 1 per cent of GDP. The decline in privatisation revenue in 2003 accounted for 0.8 percentage point of the decline in the budget surplus. In sum, two special factors – financial-sector restructuring costs and the privatisation of Korea Telecom – more than accounted for the

Table 2.2. **Consolidated government budget**

Trillion won[1]

	1998	1999	2000	2001 Initial budget[2]	2001 Outcome[3]	2002 Initial budget[2]	2002 Outcome[3]	2003 Initial budget[2]	2003 Outcome[3]	2004 Initial budget[2]
	Outcomes									
A. Total										
Revenue	96.7	107.9	135.8	142.1	144.0	154.4	158.7	172.0	172.2	185.3
Growth (per cent)	-2.6	11.6	25.9	4.6	6.1	8.7	10.2	11.3	8.5	7.8
Per cent of GDP	20.0	20.4	23.5	22.8	23.1	22.6	23.2	23.8	23.9	23.8
Expenditures	115.4	121.0	129.3	142.5	136.8	148.4	136.0	165.3	164.1	178.2
Growth (per cent)	15.1	4.9	6.9	5.4	5.8	4.1	1.3	11.4	20.7	7.8
Per cent of GDP	23.8	22.9	22.3	22.9	22.0	21.7	19.9	22.9	22.8	22.9
Balance	**-18.7**	**-13.1**	**6.5**	**-0.4**	**7.2**	**6.0**	**22.7**	**6.6**	**8.1**	**7.1**
Per cent of GDP	**-3.9**	**-2.5**	**1.1**	**-0.1**	**1.2**	**0.9**	**3.3**	**0.9**	**1.1**	**0.9**
Of which:										
Social security balance	6.0	7.3	12.5	13.2	15.4	14.4	17.6	19.4	19.6	22.5
Per cent of GDP	1.2	1.4	2.2	2.1	2.5	2.1	2.6	2.7	2.7	2.9
Privatisation revenues	0.3	3.3	0.0	3.0	3.7	5.4	6.7	1.6	1.3	–
Per cent of GDP	0.1	0.6	0.0	0.5	0.6	0.8	1.0	0.2	0.2	–
Financial-sector restructuring costs	0.0	0.0	0.0	0.0	0.0	0.0	0.0	13.0	13.0	12.0
Per cent of GDP	0.0	0.0	0.0	0.0	0.0	0.0	0.0	1.8	1.8	1.5
B. Alternative measures of the balance										
Excluding social security	-24.8	-20.4	-6.0	-13.0	-8.2	-8.4	5.1	-12.8	-11.5	-15.5
Per cent of GDP	-5.1	-3.9	-1.0	-2.1	-1.3	-1.2	0.7	-1.8	-1.6	-2.0
Excluding financial-sector restructuring costs and privatisation revenues	-19.5	-16.4	6.5	-3.4	3.5	0.6	16.0	18.3	20.8	19.1
Per cent of GDP	-4.1	-3.1	1.1	-0.6	0.6	0.1	2.3	2.5	2.7	2.4
Excluding social security, privatisation and financial sector restructuring costs	-25.1	-23.8	-6.0	-16.1	-11.9	-13.8	-1.6	-1.4	0.2	-3.5
Per cent of GDP	-5.2	-4.5	-1.0	-2.6	-1.9	-2.0	-0.2	-0.2	0.0	-0.4
Memorandum item										
Adjusted expenditures[4]	116.2	124.3	129.3	145.5	140.5	153.8	142.7	153.9	151.9	166.2
Growth (per cent)	15.9	7.0	4.0	4.2	8.7	5.7	1.6	0.1	6.4	8.0

1. On a GFS basis. Includes public enterprises, but excludes local government.
2. Growth rate relative to previous year's initial budget.
3. Growth rate relative to previous year's outcome.
4. Excludes financial sector restructuring costs and privatisation revenues, which are treated as negative net lending under the Government Financial Statistics (GFS) methodology.
Source: Ministry of Planning and Budget.

2¼ percentage-point fall in the surplus. Excluding the financial-sector restructuring costs and privatisation receipts, the budget surplus increased from 2.3 to 2.7 per cent of GDP in 2003, implying a small contractionary effect from the government sector.

The government's preferred fiscal measure excludes the social security surplus, since this is intended to cover the future liability of pension spending. According to this measure, and adjusted for the two special factors discussed above, the consolidated budget (shown in the bottom line of Panel B in Table 2.2) was in balance in 2003 for the first time since the 1997 crisis. The elimination of the small deficit of ¼ per cent of GDP in 2002 in the context of the sharp slowdown in economic growth also suggests that the stance of fiscal policy in 2003 was contractionary.

This fiscal stance kept the total of general government gross debt, which includes local government, and government-guaranteed debt at about 34 per cent of GDP in 2003 (Figure 2.7). Even this combined amount is less than half of the 74 per cent average for gross government debt in the OECD area. Korea's gross debt did increase somewhat – from 19.5 per cent of GDP in 2002 to 23.0 per cent in 2003 (Table 2.3) – but this was offset by the fall in government-guaranteed debt related to financial-sector restructuring, as noted above. Meanwhile, the

Figure 2.7. **Government gross debt and guaranteed liabilities**
Per cent of GDP[1]

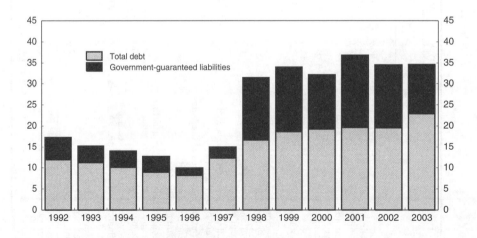

1. Intra-government debt is netted out beginning in 1997.
Source: Ministry of Finance and Economy.

Table 2.3.   **Gross government debt and guarantees**

Trillion won at the end of the year

	1997	Per cent of GDP	2000	2001	2002	2003	Per cent of GDP
Total debt (A + B – C)	**60.3**	**12.3**	**111.4**	**122.1**	**133.6**	**165.7**	**23.0**
A. Central government	50.5	10.3	100.9	113.1	126.6	158.8	22.0
Borrowing	18.5	3.8	21.9	22.5	20.7	15.8	2.2
Domestic	3.2	0.7	1.9	2.1	2.3	3.2	0.3
Foreign	15.3	3.1	20.0	20.4	18.4	12.6	1.7
Bonds	28.6	5.8	76.3	87.8	103.1	140.6	19.5
Treasury	6.3	1.3	42.6	50.9	55.6	81.5	11.3
Foreign exchange	4.2	0.9	13.5	14.1	20.7	28.5	4.0
Grain security	5.1	1.0	2.5	2.1	1.1	0.6	0.1
National housing	13.0	2.6	17.8	20.6	25.7	30.1	4.2
Contract authorisation	3.4	0.7	2.7	2.8	2.8	2.4	0.3
B. Local government	15.1	3.1	22.3	21.3	19.5	18.4	2.6
C. Inter-government debt	5.3	1.1	11.9	12.3	12.5	11.6	1.6
Government guarantees[1]	**13.0**	**2.6**	**74.6**	**106.8**	**102.5**	**80.6**	**11.2**
Guarantees on loans	2.2	0.4	6.2	9.2	7.0	3.2	0.4
Domestic	0.7	0.1	2.4	5.8	5.3	1.7	0.2
Foreign	1.5	0.3	3.8	3.4	1.7	1.5	0.2
Guarantees on bonds	10.9	2.2	68.4	97.5	95.4	77.4	10.7
Of which for financial sector restructuring	7.0	1.4	68.2	97.4	95.3	77.4	10.7
Total debt plus government guarantees	**73.3**	**14.9**	**186.0**	**228.9**	**236.1**	**246.3**	**34.1**

1. Includes only central government.
Source: Ministry of Finance and Economy.

government has accumulated a substantial stock of assets, making Korea one of only three OECD countries, along with Norway and Finland, in which the government is a net creditor.

The fiscal stance in 2004

For 2004, the stance of the initial budget appears to be neutral. The increase in consolidated central government expenditures, excluding financial-sector restructuring costs and privatisation, is set at 8 per cent, roughly in line with the expected increase in nominal GDP (Table 2.2). The largest spending increases are planned for R&D investment, as part of the objective of boosting such outlays to 5 per cent of total government outlays, and social welfare expenditures as part of the development of the social safety net (Table 2.4). Total outlays are held down by significant declines planned for foreign affairs and reunification, promotion of exports and small and medium-sized enterprises, the environment and social infrastructure and housing. The increase in spending is to be matched by an 8 per

Table 2.4.   **Central government expenditures**

Trillion won[1]

	2002	Percentage increase	2003[3]	Percentage increase	2004	Percentage increase
Education	22.5	12.5	24.9	9.6	26.4	5.9
Civil service salaries	20.8	9.9	22.6	8.6	24.3	7.1
National defence	16.4	6.5	17.5	6.7	18.9	8.1
Social infrastructure and housing	16.0	7.5	18.3	14.3	17.3	−5.4
Agriculture and fisheries	10.0	1.0	10.4	4.0	10.6	1.5
Social welfare	10.0	22.7	11.1	11.0	12.1	8.4
Interest payments[2]	1.8	−11.6	1.8	−1.3	1.8	3.3
R&D investment in science and technology	5.0	16.1	5.6	12	6.1	8.5
Promotion of exports and SMEs	3.6	10.1	3.9	8.3	3.6	−7.6
Environment	2.9	8.5	3.3	13.8	3.1	−6.3
Information technology	1.6	9.7	1.7	4.4	1.7	1.0
Culture, tourism and sports	1.4	12.5	1.4	2.0	1.5	3.2
Foreign affairs and reunification	0.8	4.6	0.7	−16.8	0.6	−13.2

1.   Includes the initial budgets for the general and special accounts.
2.   Does not include the interest payments on government-guaranteed bonds issued to pay for financial-sector restructuring.
3.   Includes supplementary budgets.
Source: Ministry of Planning and Budget.

cent rise in government revenue, led by a large expected hike in social security contributions (Table 2.5). However, this does not take into account the plans announced in March 2004 to promote consumption by temporarily cutting excise taxes to encourage purchases of cars and household appliances and reducing taxes on new enterprises to promote job creation.

The impact of population ageing on public expenditures

Families remain the main source of support for the elderly in Korea. However, increased urbanisation, smaller families, a changing role for women and a marked increase in life expectancy have had a significant impact on the traditional support system. Another form of support for the elderly is the lump-sum "retirement allowance" that firms pay regular employees when they leave. However, only a third of the labour force is covered by this allowance, which moreover is often used for purposes other than retirement saving. To provide a more secure source of retirement income, the partially-funded National Pension Scheme (NPS) was established in 1988 and will begin paying regular pensions in 2008. The NPS promises to pay a replacement rate of 60 per cent for workers with 40 years of contributions who earned the average wage. However, with the current contribution rate set at 9 per cent, the NPS would have large deficits beginning in 2030 that would exhaust the National Pension Fund by 2047.

Table 2.5. **Consolidated government revenue**

Trillion won

	2002 initial budget	2002 outcome	Percentage change[1]	2003 initial budget	2003 Outcome	Percentage change[2]	2004 Initial budget	Percentage change[3]
Total tax revenue	103.7	104.0	7.9	113.8	114.7	10.3	122.1	6.8
Income, profits and capital gains	36.3	38.4	7.3	41.8	46.4	20.8	45.6	8.3
Income tax	20.1	19.2	2.6	20.2	20.8	8.3	22.0	8.2
Corporation tax	16.1	19.2	11.5	21.6	25.6	33.3	23.6	8.5
Taxes on property	3.2	2.9	0.0	3.3	2.9	0.0	3.0	-10.0
Taxes on goods and services[4]	49.2	48.0	8.8	52.8	50.9	6.0	57.3	7.9
Custom duties	7.3	6.6	10.6	7.2	6.8	3.0	7.5	4.0
Others	7.7	8.0	6.3	8.7	7.7	-3.8	8.8	1.1
Social security contributions	18.2	19.7	11.2	20.9	20.7	5.1	24.8	15.7
Non-tax revenue	30.9	33.5	12.2	35.8	35.4	5.7	37.0	3.2
Capital revenue	1.7	1.5	13.3	1.5	1.4	-6.7	1.4	-7.1
Total revenue	**154.4**	**158.7**	**9.3**	**172.0**	**172.2**	**8.5**	**185.3**	**7.8**
Per cent of GDP	22.6	23.2		23.8	23.9		23.8	

1. Relative to the 2001 budget outcome.
2. Relative to the 2002 budget outcome.
3. Relative to the 2003 initial budget.
4. Includes value added tax, liquor tax, special consumption tax and transportation tax.
Source: Ministry of Planning and Budget.

With the population ageing more rapidly than in other countries, the projected rise in pension outlays over the coming decades will be one of the largest in the OECD area. Nonetheless, the resulting level of outlays would still be below the current level of pension spending in some other OECD countries. Ensuring the long-term sustainability of the NPS requires a doubling of contributions, a halving of benefits or some combination of the two. The government is legally required to review the sustainability of the NPS every five years. Following the review in 2003, the government proposed cutting the replacement rate from 60 to 50 per cent in 2008, while ensuring the vested rights earned prior to the reform. The contribution rate would be raised by 1.38 percentage points every five years beginning in 2010, boosting it to 15.9 per cent by 2030. Such a contribution would ensure the financial sustainability – defined as a reserve fund large enough to pay two years' of benefits – through 2070. However, the National Assembly has not approved the proposed reform.

The government also introduced a bill to create a corporate pension system following two years of discussion in the Tripartite Commission. The main elements of the proposed system are:

- It will provide benefits equivalent to those paid by the retirement allowance, which mandates one month of pay for each year of employment.

- The decision of whether to maintain the allowance or move to the corporate pension system will be left to workers and management at individual firms, although tax incentives will encourage the adoption of the corporate pension system.

- The decision of whether it should be a defined benefit or a defined contribution scheme will be left to individual workplaces.

- The pension will be based on individual accounts, thus allowing portability for workers who change firms.

- The coverage of the retirement allowance, which is currently limited to regular workers in firms with at least five workers, will be gradually extended to all firms and to temporary workers. The corporate pension system would thus become potentially available to all employees.

- Employers and retirement pension providers will be required to take responsibility for the sound operation of pension reserve funds, with supervision entrusted to a special organisation such as the Financial Supervisory Service.

However, the lack of consensus has delayed the introduction of the new system. Management opposes the extension of the system to small firms and favours a defined contribution system, while labour favours a defined benefit system.

Reform of the budgetary and tax systems

Although Korea has a tradition of fiscal prudence, generally avoiding budget deficits and keeping public debt at one of the lowest levels relative to GDP among OECD countries, the expected increase in demand for spending due to population ageing and the cost of co-operation with the North calls for further improvement in the efficiency of public spending. The extensive discussion of this issue in the 2003 OECD *Economic Survey of Korea* concluded with a comprehensive set of policy recommendations aimed at improving the management of public expenditures. This section follows up the recent progress in public expenditure reform, mainly focusing on the budgetary system. Even with an improved public expenditure system, increased government revenues will be needed to cover higher outlays. It is thus important to remove the distortions in the tax system before higher government revenues substantially boost deadweight costs. The status of tax reform, the special topic of the 2000 OECD *Economic Survey of Korea*, is briefly reviewed at the end of this section.

Improving the public expenditure system

One of the major deficiencies in the current system has been the lack of strategic prioritisation in allocating budgetary resources. Given the absence of a strong linkage between the medium-term fiscal plan and the annual budgeting process, as well as the bottom-up approach based on requests of line ministries, the budget formulation process tends to be geared to a single fiscal year, resulting in weak prioritisation of resources. However, some progress has been made in strengthening the medium-term framework by building on the first medium-term fiscal plan, which covered 1999 to 2003. A new medium-term plan for the years 2004 to 2008 will be finalised after discussions at the Cabinet Council in June and July 2004 (Table 2.6). It will differ from the earlier plan by including forecasts of fiscal objectives and will be linked to a top-down budgeting process, an approach that was already introduced in four government organisations in 2004. The new plan is expected to be used as a guideline for budget requests in 2005. However, the key to an effective medium-term plan is its power to bind the annual budgeting process, which remains uncertain in the new plan. Beginning in June, the plan will be updated to 2005 to 2009 and will be used in the formulation of the 2006 budget.

Performance-based management and accountability for results

In addition to greater reliance on a medium-term budget plan, the managerial flexibility of ministries in budgeting is also being enhanced by the introduction of a performance-based management system and the establishment of executive agencies. By 2003, 22 of 54 government organisations had been selected to conduct pilot projects for performance-based budgeting. These organisations

Table 2.6. **Changes in the medium-term fiscal framework**

	Medium-Term Fiscal Plan 1999-2003	National Fiscal Management Plan 2004-2008
Scope:	Budget, focusing on the general account	Consolidated budget, including public funds
Objective:	Setting broad directions	Presenting medium-term quantitative goals, overall directions, detailed resource allocation plans
Effectiveness:	Only a reference	Reflected in actual budget formulation and Public Fund Management Plans
Method:	Centred on the MPB	Broad participation of interested parties, including related ministries
Public announcement:	Used as internal information	Publicly announced to the press after reporting to the Cabinet Council
Revisions:	Revised only when necessary	Updated every year

Source: Ministry of Planning and Budget.

are required to apply this approach to all of their fiscal projects by the end of 2004. The evaluation results based on performance indexes are to be effectively linked to fiscal management beginning in 2005. Other government organisations are also required to introduce performance-based management systems by 2005. To increase managerial flexibility in providing public services, the government established 23 executive agencies by 2001 in fields where the introduction of competition was expected to boost efficiency. In exchange for operational independence, executive agencies bear responsibility for their performance. According to evaluations by outside experts, the implementation of the executive agency system has led to an improved operational performance by those agencies, in particular by increasing self-generated revenue, producing budget savings and providing higher quality public services and greater customer satisfaction.[6]

The introduction of greater autonomy in implementing the budget should be accompanied by stronger accountability for results through systematic *ex ante*, intermediate and *ex post* spending reviews and effective value-for-money audits. As for *ex ante* project evaluation, the establishment of an independent organisation in 1999 to conduct preliminary feasibility studies for large-scale public investment projects is a major step forward. Assigning this role to the Public Investment Management Centre (PIMA), which is located in the Korea Development Institute, ensures the objectivity of the feasibility studies, in contrast to the past, when the studies were conducted by the ministries responsible for the projects. Of the 153 projects examined by 2003, 78 were suspended (Table 2.7), resulting in budget savings estimated at around 55 trillion won (8 per cent of GDP). Given the

Table 2.7. **Preliminary feasibility studies on public investment projects**
Trillion won

	Total public investment projects		Selected for screening by PIMA[1]		Investment projects rejected	
	Number of cases	Estimated expenses	Number of cases	Estimated expenses	Number of cases	Estimated expenses
1999	19	26.7	12	6.9	7	19.8
2000	30	13.9	15	6.0	15	7.9
2001	41	19.8	14	6.4	27	13.3
2002	30	16.6	13	6.2	17	10.4
2003	33	21.5	21	17.5	12	4.0
Total	**153**	**98.4**	**75**	**43.0**	**78**	**55.4**

1. The Public Investment Management Centre, which is located in the Korea Development Institute.
Source: Ministry of Planning and Budget (2002).

success of this approach in eliminating wasteful investment projects, it should be expanded to other areas such as R&D and large-scale procurement. As for intermediate spending reviews of on-going projects, the "project ceiling budget management system" for multi-year projects adopted in 1994 did not immediately help to limit mid-project increases in costs. To bind costs to the project ceiling more effectively, a number of steps were taken in 1999, including establishing a government body exclusively responsible for the ceiling (the Budget Management Bureau), requiring the signatures of individuals involved in projects, and introducing inspections to check wages and unit prices. These steps significantly reduced the gap between *ex ante* budget allocation and *ex post* costs (Table 2.8).

In contrast, the adoption of systematic *ex post* review of projects and value-for-money auditing remains at an early stage. The government has just begun to develop *ex post* evaluation techniques for special areas such as R&D, job training and state-owned enterprises. Although the Board of Audit and Inspection (BAI) is

Table 2.8. **Intermediate spending reviews**
Trillion won

	1997	1998	1999	2000	2001	2002	2003
Number of projects	70	104	194	196	169	236	306
Requested increase in cost							
relative to initial plan	5.2	19.1	15.4	5.5	1.7	2.7	2.0
As a per cent of total cost	20.2	28.0	19.3	7.4	3.8	3.7	2.8
Approved adjustment in cost	2.6	8.5	6.9	2.6	0.1	0.2	0.1
As a per cent of total cost	10.0	12.5	8.6	3.4	0.3	0.2	0.1

Source: Ministry of Planning and Budget.

also trying to expand its scope by focusing more on *ex post* performance audits, human resource constraints have hampered this shift. However, the BAI has recently stepped up its efforts to increase its human resources.

Increasing transparency

Further progress has been made in increasing the transparency of the budget system. As noted in previous *Surveys*, Korea's budget structure is highly fragmented and compartmentalised due to numerous special accounts and public funds that are outside of the general account. This significantly reduces the transparency of the budget system and weakens control over public spending. The special accounts and the public funds are independently managed and their funding, which involves complicated financial transfers between them, are linked to earmarked taxes and so-called "quasi-taxes" (charges and contributions not imposed by the tax laws). Moreover, the extra-budgetary funds, many of which are excluded from the national budget, are involved in quasi-fiscal activities such as financial-sector restructuring, thus further complicating the management of overall public finances. A major step forward in this area was making the public funds subject to parliamentary approval beginning with the 2003 budget process. A number of extra-budgetary funds, excluding those related to financial activities, have also been consolidated and transformed into public funds, making them subject to the same regulations and fiscal discipline. The discretion of the responsible minister in increasing the outlay of a public fund without the consent of the National Assembly was reduced from 50 to 30 per cent.

The government has consolidated or abolished public funds whose objectives are overlapping or have already been achieved. Consequently, their number was reduced from 75 in 1997 to 55 in 2004, of which nine were extra-budgetary financial funds. A key to the consolidation of public funds was the introduction of comprehensive reviews of their operations beginning in 1999. The reviews are conducted by a Fund Operation Evaluation Team consisting of 40 private specialists and the results are reported to the Cabinet Council, which, in turn, submits them to the National Assembly. Public funds are also required to have monitoring standards and procedures comparable to those for the national budget, such as quarterly funding plans, progress reports, preliminary feasibility studies and project ceiling budgeting. In addition, plans to create new public funds will be subject to more scrutiny. In contrast to the decline in public funds, the number of special accounts has remained constant at around 22, as the consolidation or elimination of special accounts was offset by the establishment of new ones. The government is considering legislation to tighten the conditions necessary for the creation of new special accounts.

Improving the efficiency of the broader public sector

Given the important role of public corporations, the government has made a significant effort to improve their efficiency and to introduce accountability mechanisms. One approach has been to reform the regulatory framework in network industries with public monopolies in order to introduce more competitive pressures (see Chapter 5). Another strategy is privatisation; by 2002, the government had sold eight of the 11 state-owned enterprises (SOEs) identified in the 1998 plan and the phased privatisation is continuing for the remaining three enterprises (the Korea Electric Power Corporation, the Korea Gas Corporation and the Korea District Heating Company). At the same time, the government planned to dispose of the 82 subsidiaries of the 18 SOEs, except for five that have a strong public nature, such as nuclear energy. As of December 2002, 50 had been restructured and 16 liquidated or merged, while 11 have remained unsold due to the lack of suitable buyers. A major impediment to privatisation is the concern about the security of public services and the possible impact on employment, which has provoked protests by labour unions. To improve the efficiency of the SOEs, some of their activities have been delegated to the private sector following the management innovation plan adopted in 1998. The number of such cases reached 289 by mid-2002. The governance problems of public corporations have also been improved by requiring them to produce financial statements and audit reports, while bonus payments at the corporations are linked to management performance assessments conducted by a committee at the Ministry of Planning and Budget.

Despite the efforts to accelerate fiscal decentralisation and devolution of power to local governments, poorly designed incentive structures in transfers from central to local governments and ill-defined spending and financing responsibilities across layers of government have resulted in inefficiency in spending and allocation of funds. Such problems are related to the complex rules for distributing equalisation transfers and the continuing dependence on conditional grants, which distort the incentives of local governments. The latter results from the lack of clear rules for co-financing and service provision between central and local governments. The reform plan under discussion by the presidential committee established in April 2003 includes:

- Introducing an across-the-board devolution of functions to local governments.

- Giving local governments more autonomy in fiscal management and expanding their resources.

- Reducing conditional grants (National Treasury Subsidies), and partially replacing them with general tax transfers (Local Share Taxes), which will be simplified.

- Improving the accountability of local governments by strengthening the Local Fiscal Management Evaluation System.

Improving the tax system

The government has introduced measures to broaden tax bases and to promote efficient resource allocation. To improve taxation of the self-employed, the income assessment method was fundamentally changed in 2002 by requiring proof of tax deductions, and a new system for issuing receipts for cash payment is to be introduced by 2005. The government has also broadened the corporate tax base by reducing or streamlining tax incentives deemed to be inefficient, many of which are related to small and medium-sized enterprises (SMEs). For example, the tax deductibility of investment reserves for SMEs has been abolished, while the tax credit ratio for SMEs was lowered from 30 to 15 per cent of the tax base and the eligibility period was shortened. The tax base of the VAT has been significantly broadened by reducing exemptions. The reduction in the threshold for the simplified tax regime for small businesses lowered the proportion of firms under this system from 90 per cent in 2001 to 46 per cent in 2003.

The government has reduced the number of tax incentives from 269 to 254 in 2003. Nevertheless, total tax expenditures, including exemptions and deductions, increased by 15 per cent in 2003 (Table 2.9). The increase is largely attributable to the incentives given to SMEs, investment and R&D. In 2004, the government introduced new incentives aimed at stimulating the economy. In particular, the reduction rate for the corporate income tax for start-ups hiring additional employees will be raised, with the minimum set at 50 per cent and the maximum at 100 per cent in July.

The government announced a plan in 2003 to reform the property holding tax, which consists of separate levies on building and land (Table 2.10). With the tax base for both set at only around 30 per cent of market value, the effective tax rate has been only 0.16 per cent (Cho and Sung, 2003). Moreover, the tax has

Table 2.9.   **Trend of tax expenditure**
Billion won

	2000	2001	2002	2003[1]	Increase (per cent)
Tax expenditure (A)	13 282.4	13 729.8	14 726.1	16 883.0	14.6
Direct taxes	9 514.7	9 718.3	10 167.6	11 726.1	15.3
Indirect taxes	3 629.3	3 902.5	4 432.3	5 044.0	13.8
Tariffs	138.4	109.0	126.2	112.9	−10.5
Related tax revenues (B)	83 221.4	88 602.0	96 408.6	107 220.1	11.2
A/(A + B) (per cent)	13.8	13.4	13.3	13.6	

1. Forecast.
Source: Ministry of Finance and Economy.

Table 2.10. **Changes in the property holding tax**

	2003	2004	2005
Buildings			
Tax Base	Standard construction cost (170 thousand won/m^2)	Standard construction cost (180 thousand won/m^2)	Standard market value[1] (460 thousand won/m^2)
	Adjusted by the size	Adjusted by the market value[1]	
Tax Rate	Between 0.3 and 7 per cent		Lower tax rates
Taxation	Levied on individual building		Introduce comprehensive property tax
Land			
Tax Base	36.1 per cent "Application Ratio" to the standard market value[2]	Raise "Application Ratio" by more than 3 percentage points	50 per cent of the standard market value[2] (enforced by law)
Tax Rate	Between 0.2 and 5 per cent		
Taxation	Comprehensive land tax		Introduce comprehensive property tax

1. Surveyed by the National Tax Service.
2. Surveyed by the Ministry of Construction and Transportation.
Source: Ministry of Finance and Economy and Ministry of Home Affairs and Government Administration.

been regressive as it is adjusted for building size rather than market value. Under the new plan, the effective tax rate will be increased by raising the tax base for buildings to their full market value, while that for land will be raised to 50 per cent. In addition, the size-related adjustment will be eliminated. Finally, comprehensive taxation of an individual's property holdings will be introduced in 2005.

Reducing the number of special accounts and public funds in the government budget requires abolishing earmarked taxes and various quasi-taxes. Four earmarked taxes (Liquor, Transportation, Education and Rural Development) collected nearly 10 trillion won (10 per cent of total tax revenue) in 2002. The government postponed the planned elimination of earmarked taxes for transport and rural development-related special accounts in 2004 due to the difficulty in finding alternative revenue sources in the context of weak economic growth. These two earmarked taxes have been extended for three and ten years, respectively. The basic law on quasi-taxes, which was introduced in 2001, required that the authority responsible for collection and the purpose of the revenue must be clearly indicated. In addition, the law resulted in the consolidation of 12 quasi-taxes and placed restrictions on the introduction of new ones. Nevertheless, the number of quasi-taxes increased from 95 in 1999 to 102 in 2002, boosting the revenue collected from this source by 82 per cent during that period.[7]

Overall assessment and scope for further actions

The economy is on a recovery track led by external demand. The upturn was supported by easy monetary conditions, as the central bank lowered the short-term policy interest rate to a historic low in July 2003 and the effective exchange rate declined in a context of a rapid accumulation of foreign exchange reserves. In contrast, the stance of fiscal policy was contractionary in 2003.

With the economic upturn in 2004, fiscal policy should aim at a neutral stance in 2004. Once the process of bringing the financial-sector restructuring costs into the budget is completed in 2006, the authorities should aim at a balanced budget, excluding the social security surplus, over the business cycle. As for monetary policy, it is likely that some of the monetary stimulus may need to be withdrawn over the business cycle in order to keep inflation in the medium-term target zone of 2.5 to 3.5 per cent. However, the extent of the necessary rise in interest rates will depend to some degree on exchange rate developments. Given the costs and risks associated with intervention, there is no need for continued foreign exchange accumulation now that reserves are almost three times higher than short-term foreign debt. While this may result in some upward pressure on the exchange rate, there are likely to be some offsetting positive effects. Overall, it may promote a more balanced expansion over the medium term.

The rapid pace of population ageing poses the greatest threat to fiscal sustainability over the longer term. Korea has a window of opportunity for fundamental pension reform before the National Pension Scheme begins paying regular pension benefits in 2008. The reform should aim at putting the NPS on a sustainable basis while enhancing the role of private-sector saving for retirement. *First*, the benefits and contributions of the NPS should be brought into balance, primarily by lowering the replacement rate, given the negative labour market consequences of high contribution rates. *Second*, the effective coverage of the NPS should be expanded, as a quarter of the people currently required to contribute to the Scheme do not participate. *Third*, the social benefit system should be expanded to limit poverty among the elderly until the NPS begins paying full pensions. *Fourth*, the financial imbalances in the public-sector occupational pension schemes, which are already in deficit, need to be addressed, while introducing portability with the NPS. *Fifth*, the plan to transform the retirement allowance system, which is generally unfunded by firms, into a corporate pension system should be implemented. Its success, though, will depend on adequate prudential supervision of private pension schemes.

The increased spending resulting from population ageing and the development of the social welfare system, as well as the uncertain cost of economic cooperation with North Korea (Box 2.1), make it important to improve the efficiency of the public expenditure and tax systems. On the tax side, the measures to broaden the tax base for the corporate income tax and the VAT, as well as to raise

Box 2.1. **Economic co-operation between North and South Korea**

The North Korean economy is estimated to have grown 1 to 2 per cent in 2003, its fifth consecutive year of growth, despite continuing shortages of food and energy. Indeed, it has faced a food shortfall each year, estimated at around 2 million tonnes, since the 1990s. Moreover, manufacturing production is estimated to be one-fifth below its 1995 level. Economic reforms in the North are continuing to shift power away from the center and towards factory managers and municipal authorities, thus helping to reduce the reliance on central planning.

Processing-on-commission trade, concentrated in the textile industry, has been boosting trade between the North and South. Two-way trade increased 13 per cent in 2003 to $724 million, with commercial exchanges accounting for a little more than half of the total. Joint projects, such as the Mount Geumgang tourism site, and humanitarian aid accounted for the remainder. For example, the South supplied the North with 0.3 million tonnes of fertilizer and 0.4 million tonnes of food in 2003. Of the commercial trade, textile and agricultural products accounted for about four-fifths of the South's imports from the North, while textiles and electronic products are its most important exports to the North. The expansion of trade in recent years would make the South the second-largest trading partner for North Korea, accounting for a third of its total trade. However, for South Korea, trade with the North amounts to only 0.2 per cent of its international trade. According to the National Statistical Office of South Korea, the South Korean economy is 28 times larger than the North's.

The eighth meeting on Inter-Korean Economic Co-operation in March 2004 focused on the development of an industrial park for South Korean firms in Kaesong, which is just north of the border. This project is of interest to South Korean firms, given the low wage level of $57 per month that will be paid to North Korean workers in the zone. However, many legal and infrastructure problems, including transport and the supply of electricity, must be settled before this industrial park can attract investors. In the second half of 2004, some 3.3 million m^2 is scheduled to be ready for South Korean firms. Road and rail links to Kaesong, financed by the South Korean government, are expected to be completed this year, while infrastructure within the industrial zone is being developed by Hyundai. The zone is eventually expected to cover 66 million m^2, with housing for North Korean workers expected to take more than half of the total. The convenient location of Kaesong may help it to be more successful than earlier attempts to establish special economic zones in North Korea, which were located in remote areas. Meanwhile, work on the Seoul-Sinuiju railroad line and on the Donghae line on the east coast is advancing with test runs expected this year. Direct transport links will help overcome the high cost and inconvenience of indirect trade through third countries.

the effective tax rate on real estate, are commendable. The priority should be to reduce the generous allowances and tax credits in the personal income tax that result in about 50 per cent of all individual income earners not paying income tax.

Although progress has been made in improving the public expenditure system, implementing best practices requires an acceleration of reform to enhance efficiency and transparency. Given the indicative nature of the existing medium-term budget framework, its linkage with the annual budget process needs to be strengthened further. The weakness of *ex post* spending review and performance auditing suggests the necessity of establishing an effective institutional framework for evaluating performance, in particular, by increasing the capacity of the Board of Audit and Inspection. Public funds and special accounts should be consolidated further based on stricter evaluation. There is also a need for tighter controls on the creation of new funds and accounts. Moreover, the ability of the responsible minister to boost the outlays of a public fund by up to 30 per cent without the consent of the National Assembly should be further narrowed. Earmarked taxes and quasi-taxes should be reduced. To improve the governance of public corporations, general accountability mechanisms need to be upgraded further by adopting more output-oriented reporting through activity-based costing and strengthening monitoring mechanisms. The government should proceed toward fiscal decentralisation by improving the incentive framework in transfers from central to local governments, while increasing the autonomy and flexibility of local governments.

Notes

1. Wage data may be over-estimated since the survey is limited to firms with more than five employees and to regular workers. Given the increasing number of lower paid non-regular workers, the actual wage hike may be somewhat less. It is clear, though, that wage growth slowed only slightly in 2003 despite the economic slowdown.

2. A change in the overnight call rate is estimated to begin to influence output two quarters later, reaching its maximum impact four to six quarters later (Yang Woo Kim, 2002). As for inflation, the impact is estimated to be felt from the third quarter, but does not reach its full effect until eight or nine quarters.

3. The main contents of this package are: 1) expanding the supply of housing by constructing new towns in northern Seoul; 2) providing better financial investment opportunities; 3) strengthening the capital gains and property holding taxes; and 4) reinforcing other regulatory measures such as tax audits and limitations on the transfer of parcelling rights.

4. The "housing supply ratio" – the ratio of the number of houses to households – has risen from 86 per cent nation-wide in 1995 to 101 per cent in 2002. In Seoul, in contrast, the ratio, though increasing in recent years, is only 82 per cent.

5. This figure excludes the cost of bringing government-guaranteed borrowing into the budget in 2003 and the impact of privatisation, which is treated as negative net lending in the GFS measure of the government budget.

6. Report by the Executive Agencies Evaluation Committee in 2002, cited in MPB (2002).

7. This reflects the creation of new non-tax payments such as the Electric Power Industry Fund and a surcharge on water usage.

3. Reforming the labour market

The labour market has moved near the top of the policy agenda in Korea. Although there have been profound changes following the democratisation of the country in 1987 and the financial crisis in 1997, it is clear that the current labour market framework is not appropriate, given the large and growing role of high-technology industries and Korea's increasing integration with the world economy. The government's most immediate concern is sluggish *job creation* and the relatively high unemployment rate for young adults. The reluctance of firms to hire is linked to a lack of *labour market flexibility*, resulting from strict employment protection for regular workers. The strong opposition of workers to relaxing constraints on dismissals is due in part to the limited *social safety net* to protect the jobless. Given the high level of employment protection for regular workers, firms have increased hiring of non-regular workers, such as part-time and temporary employees, who are paid less and receive less protection from the safety net, creating concerns about a *dualistic labour market*. The role of *active labour market policies*, which could help promote employment, particularly for disadvantaged groups, is relatively minor in Korea. Overlaying this set of difficult challenges is the problematic state of *industrial relations*, which have weakened the confidence of investors in the Korean economy. Over the longer term, *boosting labour force participation rates* is essential to cope with rapid population ageing.

The concern that labour market problems might seriously damage the country's growth potential and undermine social cohesion led to the agreement on a "Social Pact for Job Creation" in the Tripartite Commission in February 2004. The Commission, which consists of labour, management and government, was established in the wake of the crisis to create social consensus on difficult labour market issues. The Pact, which is summarised in Box 3.1, emphasises promoting job creation by increasing business investment, enhancing employment security in exchange for wage moderation, narrowing income gaps, stabilising industrial relations and assisting disadvantaged persons in finding jobs.

This chapter analyses the key issues in the areas of job creation, labour market flexibility, the development of the social safety net, the dualistic nature of the labour market, active labour market policies, industrial relations and boosting labour force participation. The discussion below leads to the conclusion that a

Box 3.1.   Key recommendations of the Social Pact for Job Creation

1.   **The government will develop a "Comprehensive Programme for Job Creation" that encompasses economic, social and industrial policies.**

2.   **Measures to promote corporate investment by creating a business-friendly environment:**
     - The government will take steps to promote entrepreneurship and to review all regulations that may hinder investment growth.
     - The authorities will expand tax incentives to promote investment and increase financial assistance to small and medium-sized enterprises (SMEs) and venture businesses, while helping them to secure workers.
     - The government will increase assistance for vocational training and improved job-placement services in order to ensure the supply of workers that meet the needs of firms.
     - Businesses will gradually increase investment in job creation.

3.   **Measures to increase employment security and reduce income gaps between working classes:**
     - Firms will minimise dismissals of workers through good-faith consultations with labour unions, while employment will be expanded through job sharing as working hours are reduced.
     - Large companies will support the business stability of their subcontracting firms and support R&D and human resource development in their suppliers and related companies.
     - Firms will not discriminate unfairly against non-regular workers in terms of wages and working conditions.
     - Workers with high wages agree to co-operate in stabilising their wages over the next two years in an effort to create jobs and reduce wage gaps.
     - The government will enhance the income of workers by keeping inflation at around 3 per cent, stabilising housing prices, reducing private education costs and cutting the tax burden.
     - The authorities will expand the social safety net by increasing the scope of social welfare programmes and improving the coverage of social insurance programmes.

4.   **Measures to increase employment of those with difficulty in finding jobs:**
     - The government will create jobs in the public, welfare and social service sectors, while firms and government will make efforts to boost youth employment.
     - The authorities will increase employment of the elderly through subsidy programmes, while labour and management will introduce a wage system that encourages the continuous employment of older workers.

Box 3.1. **Key recommendations of the Social Pact for Job Creation** (*cont.*)

- The government will double the length of paid maternity leave from 30 to 60 days.

5. **Measures to stabilise industrial relations:**
  - Employers will build a basis for trust between workers and management by practicing transparent management and ending illegal political funding.
  - Workers and management will peacefully and autonomously settle their disputes through dialogue and compromise within the legal framework.

---

comprehensive package that balances the interests of labour and management is essential to create a consensus for reform. One essential element should be an end to government intervention in industrial relations problems, forcing labour and management to settle their disputes autonomously. A second element should be measures to achieve adequate employment flexibility, while reducing dualism in the labour market and its inherent equity concerns. This requires relaxing employment protection for regular workers and improving the coverage of the social safety net, especially for non-regular workers. Active labour market policies, notably job-placement services and vocational training for the unemployed, may be useful in boosting employment but all policies should be subject to rigorous cost-benefit analysis. Finally, removing disincentives to work by women and older persons is essential to increase the labour force participation rate. The recommendations are presented in more detail in the final section of the chapter and listed in Box 3.3.

A jobless recovery?

As in some other OECD countries, there is concern in Korea about "jobless growth", a situation in which employment does not increase despite output gains. The *Social Pact for Job Creation* is based on the premise that "The Korean economy's ability to create jobs has sharply fallen". Part of the blame is attributed to the shift of production overseas, leading to the "hollowing out" of the economy.[1] Concern about a jobless recovery was reinforced by the slight fall in employment in 2003, the first decline since 1998, despite economic growth of about 3 per cent (Figure 3.1). In contrast, 2001 – a year with a similarly low rise in output – recorded significant job gains. Moreover, employment fell in the second half of 2003 (year-on-year), although the economy had entered a recovery stage. The brunt of slow

Figure 3.1. **Employment growth**

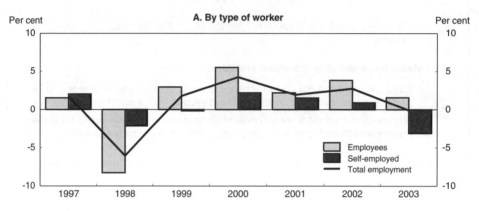

A. By type of worker

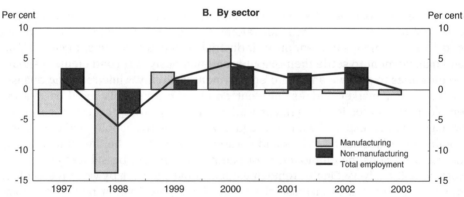

B. By sector

Source: Korea National Statistical Office.

job creation has fallen on young adults in the 15 to 29 age group, whose unemployment rate reached 7.7 per cent in 2003, compared to an overall rate of 3.4 per
cent. This may reflect the fact that a substantial portion of new job offers are for
non-regular positions, which young people tend to regard as a trap that makes it
difficult to be hired later as regular workers. With the working-age population rising by nearly 1 per cent a year, the economy must create more than 300 000 jobs a
year to maintain full employment and even more if the long-run upward trend in
the labour force participation rate continues. The challenge is heightened by
rapid structural change, which has resulted in a decline in the number of manufacturing jobs (Figure 1.10).

Increased overseas production does not appear to have had a major impact on employment in Korea. The stock of outward foreign direct investment (FDI) has remained between 5 and 6 per cent of GDP since 1998, one of the lowest in the OECD area (Figure 3.2). Moreover, the annual outflows have fallen in the past few years. The impact on employment in Korea, therefore, appears limited. It is true that the shift overseas of labour-intensive companies is increasing, helping to make China the largest recipient of Korean FDI since 2002. Indeed, it accounted for nearly 40 per cent of the total outflow from Korea in 2003. Firms are attracted by the low wages in China's manufacturing sector, which are 10 to 20 per cent of Korean wages – and thus below Korea's minimum wage – and the easier industrial relations situation in China (Changwon Lee, 2003). Given the chronic problems of some SMEs in labour-intensive industries in finding an adequate number of employees,[2] the shift to lower-wage countries seems unavoidable. The incentive to shift production elsewhere will become even stronger once the industrial park is opened in Kaesong, North Korea, where workers will be paid $57 per month (3 per cent of the average manufacturing wage in the South). The other alternative to outsourcing abroad is to allow the entry of more foreign workers. Such workers have increased in recent years and now account for about 2 per cent of the labour force.[3]

Disappointing job gains appear to be more closely linked to sluggish domestic demand in 2003 than to overseas investment or any sharp break in the functioning of the labour market. In contrast to 2001, when exports were essentially flat and private consumption led economic growth, the reverse was true in 2003; export growth was buoyant, but domestic demand was flat as private consumption declined. The stagnation of domestic demand explains the sharp fall in self-employment (including family workers) in 2003, which more than offset the rise in dependent employment (Figure 3.1). The unbalanced nature of this recovery is confirmed by the fact that the growth of employment in the non-manufacturing sector, which had averaged 3¼ per cent between 1999 and 2002, fell to zero in 2003 (Panel B). A rebound in domestic demand, which is expected in the second half of 2004, should fuel job gains in the non-manufacturing sector, as well as increasing the number of persons who are self-employed.

The significant rise in labour costs also had a negative effect on job creation. Despite the economic downturn, wages increased 9.2 per cent in 2003, compared to an 11.2 per cent rise in the preceding year. Consequently, unit labour costs rose 6 per cent, or about 2½ per cent in real terms. Econometric evidence suggests that the number of employed would have been about 60 000 higher if there had not been such an increase in real unit labour costs.[4] Buoyant wage growth in 2003 is primarily due to large firms, where the increases were more than double those in the smallest firms (Figure 3.3). This pushed the wage premium for workers at firms with more than 500 employees to more than 40 per cent above the average wage (Panel B). Workers at the largest firms earn about twice as much

Figure 3.2. **Korea's outward foreign direct investment**

A. Evolution of flows and stocks

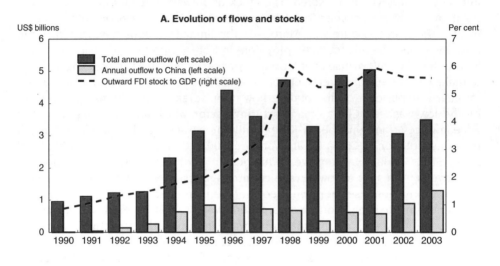

B. Stock as a share of GDP in 2000(1)

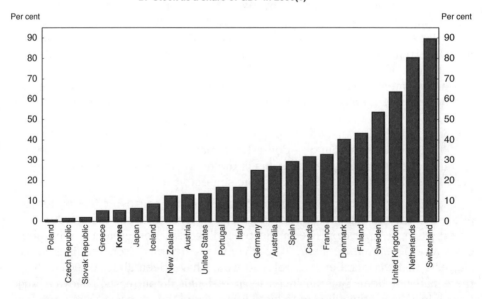

1. For countries where the FDI position data are not available, values of bilateral stocks reported by their OECD part-
    ners were summed to obtain an approximate measure of multilateral FDI stocks.
Source: Export-Import Bank of Korea and OECD.

Figure 3.3. **Wages by size of firm**

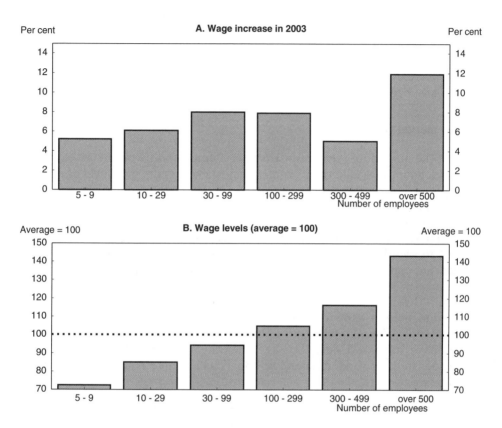

Per cent **A. Wage increase in 2003** Per cent

Average = 100 **B. Wage levels (average = 100)** Average = 100

Source: Ministry of Labour.

as those employed at firms with 5 to 9 employees. Adjusting for the different characteristics of workers at large and small firms, the wage premium for those at large firms is about 20 per cent (Jeong, 2003).

The large wage gains for workers at the largest firms, which tend to be unionised, has limited the scope for job and pay increases at smaller firms. In the February *Social Pact*, labour representatives agreed to two years of "wage stability" for workers who are highly paid in order to create jobs and reduce income gaps. However, the pact has no legal authority and one of the two national labour federations, the Korea Confederation of Trade Unions (KCTU), refused to participate in the Tripartite Commission's negotiations. Moreover, the KCTU includes many of the key exporting industries, where wages are high. In addition, the prevalence of firm-level wage bargaining[5] limits the scope for establishing effective nation-wide wage agreements. Indeed, attempts to establish national wage guidelines during the 1990s had little success and in 1997 the government stopped recommending the appropriate level of wage increase each year. Meanwhile, the corporate sector's commitments to boost job-creating investment, limit employment reductions and assist subcontracting and related firms are also not legally binding.

Labour market flexibility

The number of regular workers in 2003 remained below the level in 1996. One reason for the smaller number of regular workers is the high level of employment protection accorded to such employees. Moreover, regular workers in the large unionised companies also receive protection in collective bargaining agreements. Although the labour code was revised in the wake of the 1998 crisis to allow layoffs for collective dismissals, the conditions – such as having exhausted "all means" to avoid dismissals, having discussions with workers for at least two months and notifying the government – make it difficult to implement in practice. Consequently, it is doubtful whether the 1998 reform has enhanced flexibility as intended. Given the constraints on dismissing regular workers, restructuring firms have relied more on early retirement packages and economic incentives for voluntary dismissals, although this tends to be more expensive. More importantly, companies have improved flexibility by increasing the proportion of non-regular employees in their workforces, although this has negative equity implications, as noted below.

Easing employment protection for regular workers at large unionised firms, which tend to be major exporters, would facilitate the rapid restructuring that is often necessary in a globalised economy driven by technological advancement. Moreover, less strict employment protection can have the positive impact of spurring job creation and allowing unemployed persons to find work more quickly. However, there is no consensus in Korea for reform in this area. While firms argue that a lack of employment flexibility is an obstacle to restructuring and discourages foreign investment, unions demand that collective dismissals be banned altogether. The February 2004 *Social Pact* does not address this issue, aside from calling for employers to engage in good-faith negotiations with labour unions to minimise the number of workers dismissed and to re-employ dismissed workers first when they later increase employment. As for the expert committee on industrial relations established in 2003 (see below), it proposed shortening the consultation period by allowing it to vary depending on the scale of dismissals involved. In addition, the committee suggested exempting, at least in part, companies involved in bankruptcy proceedings from the

Table 3.1. **The minimum wage**

Year	Minimum wages[1]			Minimum wage as a per cent of average wage in manufacturing	Number of workers paid the minimum wage[1]	Workers earning minimum wage as per cent of dependent employment[2]
	Won per month (thousand)	Won per hour	Increase (per cent)			
1996	288.2	1 275	9.0	22.8	103 191	1.9
1997	316.4	1 400	9.8	23.9	127 353	2.4
1998	335.6	1 485	6.1	26.1	123 513	2.3
1999	344.7	1 525	2.7	23.4	22 980	0.4
2000	361.6	1 600	4.9	22.6	53 760	1.1
2001	421.5	1 865	16.6	24.8	141 102	2.1
2002	474.6	2 100	12.6	24.9	201 344	2.8
2003	514.2	2 275	8.3	24.6	215 000	2.9
2004	567.3	2 510	10.3	n.a.	342 000	4.3

1. The minimum wage is set in September of each year. The figure shown for 1997, for example, was in effect from September 1996 until August 1997. Since November 2000, the minimum wage applies to all firms. Previously, it applied only to those with five or more workers.
2. Percentage of regular workers only since time series data is unavailable for non-regular workers. If they are included, the proportion of total workers receiving the minimum wage increased from 6.4 per cent in 2003 to 7.6 per cent in 2004.
Source: Ministry of Labour.

conditions for dismissals. Finally, it recommended a long-term review of alternative dismissal systems.

In contrast to employment, there is considerable flexibility in wages. This reflects the practice of annual wage bargaining at the firm level and the important role of bonus payments, which are more sensitive to economic conditions than other components of employee compensation. Moreover, bonus payments' share of total compensation has been rising. Meanwhile, the minimum wage remains moderate at about a quarter of the average manufacturing wage, although the proportion of the workers paid the minimum wage jumped to 4 per cent of regular workers in 2004 (Table 3.1). Including non-regular workers, who are paid less on average, the proportion of total workers receiving the minimum wage was 8 per cent, a level between France and the United States.

The development of the social safety net

The strong opposition of workers to dismissals is due in part to the limited development of the social safety net, despite some progress in this area. The proportion of wage and salary earners eligible for the Employment Insurance System (EIS) doubled from one-third when it was introduced in 1995 to two-thirds in 1999 (Table 3.2).[6] However, as coverage was extended to small firms, the enforcement of the EIS became even more difficult. Consequently, the share of

OECD Economic Surveys: Korea

Table 3.2. **Coverage of the Employment Insurance System**
Number of workers in thousands and per cent

	1995 July	1998 Jan.	1999 July	2000 Dec.	2001 Sep.	2002 Oct.	2003 Nov.
Wage and salary earners	12 824	12 500	12 603	13 142	13 265	13 932	14 672
Eligible for EIS	4 280	5 190	8 342	8 700	9 269	9 269	9 651[2]
Actually insured	4 204	4 309	5 876	6747	6 884	7 102	7 180
Eligible as a per cent of wage and salary earners	33.4	41.5	66.2	66.2	69.9	66.5	66.0[2]
Insured as a per cent of eligible workers	98.2	83.0	70.4	77.6	74.3	76.6	74.4[2]
Insured as a per cent of wage and salary earners	32.8	34.5	46.6	51.3	51.9	51.0	49.1
Proportion of unemployed receiving benefits[1]	..	..	13.5	..	16.0	..	19.1

1. Annual averages.
2. Estimates.
Source: Ministry of Labour.

employees covered by the EIS has remained around half since 1999. In sum, about a quarter of the employees that should be covered by the EIS at the end of 2003 were not, presumably workers at small companies, particularly in the service sector. This helps to explain why only 19 per cent of the unemployed at the end of 2003 received benefits, although it also reflects the strict conditions necessary to qualify for benefits as well as their relatively short duration. The social assistance system is also quite limited, providing benefits to only 3 per cent of the population, due to tight eligibility conditions.

Although the legal coverage is being further expanded, improving the safety net requires ensuring greater compliance to increase its effective coverage. Worksite-related health insurance and the National Pension Scheme were extended in July 2003 to part-time employees working at least 80 hours a month, with those not eligible remaining in region-based social insurance programmes. In January 2004, the EIS added daily workers employed for less than one month, including construction workers, and newly hired persons over the age of 60. In addition, the threshold for part-time workers was lowered from 18 to 15 hours per week. However, the difficult challenge is to raise the proportion of eligible workers who actually participate in the system. The compliance problems reflect the frequent turnover of non-regular employees, a cumbersome application process and limited administrative capacity (Hur and Kim, 2002). In the Social Pact for Job Creation, labour and management pledged to reduce the number of non-regular workers and employees of small firms who do not participate in the EIS, while the government will expand publicity campaigns to increase public understanding of the system.

Dealing with labour market duality

Firms have responded to the high protection for regular workers by increasing the proportion of non-regular employees in the workforce. In the Labour Force Survey, non-regular employees are defined as those working for a fixed length of time and those who are not entitled to certain allowances, such as the retirement allowance. According to this Survey, the proportion of regular workers has fallen from 54 per cent of total employees in 1997 to 48 per cent in 2002 – less than one-third of all workers – before rebounding to 50 per cent in 2003 with the export recovery. However, this figure overestimates the precariousness of employment since many employees at small companies are not entitled to certain allowances and are thus classified as non-regular in the Labour Force Survey. Moreover, many of those reported to be non-regular workers expect to remain with the same firm on a long-term basis. Adjusting for such workers, the proportion of non-regular workers would be substantially lower at a quarter of employees (Table 3.3). However, even this lower figure remains high compared to other OECD countries and it has increased significantly since 1997. In addition to enhancing employment flexibility, non-regular workers are less expensive, with wages about 40 per cent below regular workers on average. After adjusting for characteristics, such as age, experience and education, non-regular workers are paid 20 to 27 per cent less according to one study (Jeong, 2003). Moreover, they are excluded from some aspects of the worksite-based social safety net. According to the Labour Force Survey, a third of non-regular workers are not covered by any worksite-based social insurance system.[7]

Table 3.3.   **Non-regular workers in Korea**

		As per cent of dependent employment[1] August 2003
	Less than or equal to 1 month	6.7
	More than 1 month to less than 1 year	4.9
	Exactly 1 year	3.3
Workers with a fixed-term contract:	More than 1 year to less than 3 years	1.3
	3 years or more	0.7
	Subtotal	**17.0**
Workers without a fixed-term contract, where employment is not expected to continue for involuntary reasons		2.6
Temporary agency workers		0.7
On-call workers		4.2
Total		**24.4**

1. The total number of dependent workers was 14.1 million.
Source: Korea National Statistical Office.

Figure 3.4. **Trends in earnings inequality**

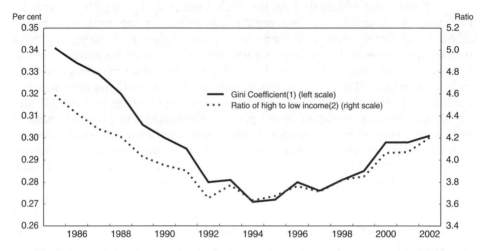

1. A Gini Coefficient of 0(1) indicates perfect equality (inequality).
2. Ratio of top 10 per cent to bottom 10 per cent.
Source: Jeong (2003).

The increasing recourse to non-regular workers creates two important concerns. *First*, the emergence of a dualistic labour market in which one segment is subject to lower wages, less protection from the social safety net and greater job precariousness creates equity concerns. Korea has experienced rising income inequality since the crisis, with a significant increase in the GINI coefficient, although it remains well below its level in the 1980s (Figure 3.4). Similarly, the ratio of the income of the top 10 per cent of households to the bottom 10 per cent rose from 3.7 in 1997 to 4.2 in 2002. While increased inequality presumably reflects higher wages paid to skilled labour in expanding sectors, such as ICT, the rising proportion of non-regular workers is likely to be contributing to this phenomenon. *Second*, it contributes to a high level of turnover, which can have adverse implications for worker training and efficiency. The proportion of workers with tenures of more than 15 years is 12 per cent, even lower than the 18 per cent in the United States, which is a high-turnover country. The share of workers with tenure of less than one year is 34 per cent in Korea compared to 22 per cent in the United States.

Active labour market policies

Public expenditure on labour market policies is one of the lowest in the OECD area (Figure 3.5). While this reflects the relatively low coverage of employment

Figure 3.5.   **Public expenditure on labour market programmes**
Per cent of GDP, 2001

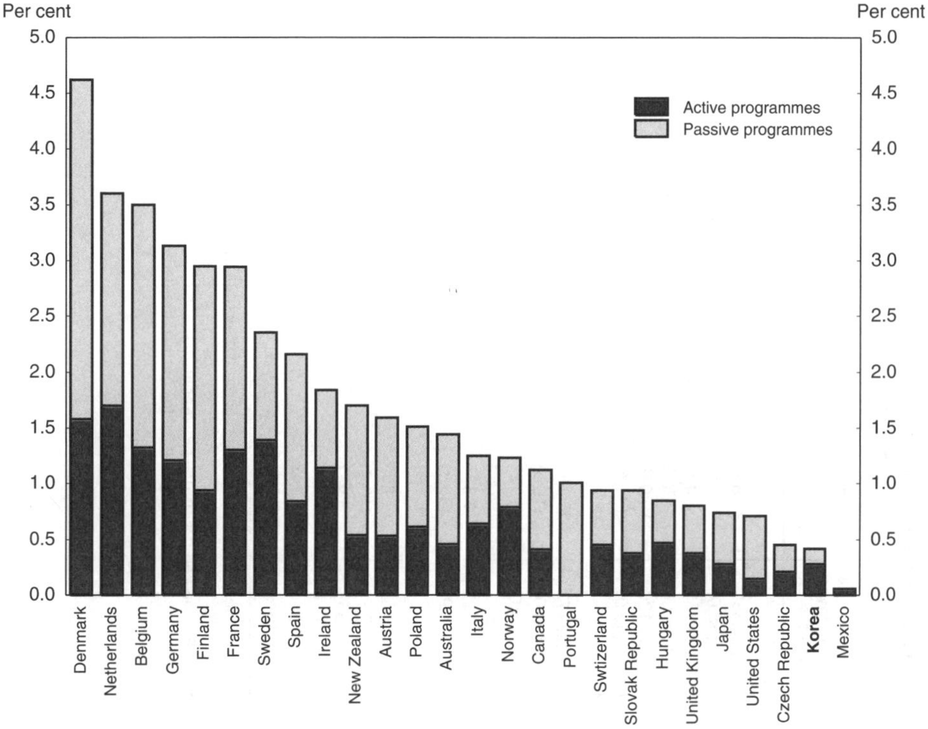

Source: OECD Employment Outlook, 2003.

insurance as noted above, it is also due to the small role of active polices. In the *Social Pact for Job Creation*, the government committed itself to increase public works jobs and vocational training, to improve job-placement services and to use employment subsidies to create jobs.

There appears to be an important role for job-placement services and vocational training for the unemployed as rapid structural change has led to a mismatch between the demand and supply of labour. Korea is one of the few OECD countries in which the unemployment rate for those with a lower secondary school education (at 2.5 per cent at the end of 2003) is lower than for those with an upper secondary school degree (4.6 per cent) or university degree (3.0 per cent). This

Table 3.4. **Training programmes for the unemployed**

	Total	Reemployment training of the unemployed under the EIS	Training programmes not financed by the EIS				
			Employment promotion	Craftsmen	3-D jobs	Business start-ups	New labour market entrants
2001							
Total number of trainees	180 392	104 559	37 657	12 260	9 789	3 195	12 932
	(100.0)	(58.0)	(20.9)	(6.8)	(5.4)	(1.8)	(7.2)
Number of trainees who completed the course	126 318	70 365	26 490	11 047	7 228	2 484	8 704
Completion rate (per cent)	70.0	67.3	70.3	90.1	73.8	77.7	67.3
Found employment[1]	57 696	33 122	10 028	6 435	4 158	561	3 392
	(40.2)	(40.0)	(34.6)	(58.0)	(50.1)	(21.3)	(34.5)
2002							
Total number of trainees	152 301	88 372	25 153	11 578	10 910	–	16 288
	(100.0)	(58.0)	(16.5)	(7.6)	(7.2)	–	(10.7)
Number of trainees who completed the course	103 313	55 802	18 723	10 495	7 613	–	10 680
Completion rate (per cent)	67.8	63.1	74.4	90.6	69.8	–	65.6
Found employment[1]	51 895	29 922	7 335	5 696	4 514	–	4 428
	(43.9)	(44.9)	(36.3)	(54.0)	(51.3)	–	(36.4)
2003							
Total number of trainees	108 187	57 662	11 805	10 760	11 662	–	16 298
	(100.0)	(53.3)	(10.9)	(9.9)	(10.8)	–	(15.1)
Number of trainees who completed the course	40 238	25 354	5 937	2 885	1 226	–	4 836
Completion rate (per cent)[2]	37.2	44.0	50.3	26.8	10.5	–	29.7
Found employment[1]	18 703	12 256	1 244	1 387	1 849	–	1 967
	(39.0)	(40.2)	(19.2)	(47.3)	(88.6)	–	(34.3)

1. The percentage of trainees that found employment equals (early employment + those found employment after training)/(number of trainees who completed course + early employment) x 100.
2. The reason for the relatively low completion rate of 37.2 per cent in 2003, compared with 70.0 per cent in 2001 and 67.8 per cent in 2002, is that it is the rate as of the end of 2003, not including trainees who had not yet completed training courses beginning in 2003. In contrast, the figures for 2001 and 2002 were produced after the completion of all training courses.

Source: Ministry of Labour.

phenomenon is reflected in the chronic shortage of labour experienced by small manufacturing companies. Job-placement services are provided by the Public Employment Service, which has separate networks operated by the central and local governments, and a long-established network of private firms, totalling more than 5 000. Another policy to deal with the mismatch problem is vocational training for the unemployed. In the wake of the crisis, the number of trainees soared to 1½ per cent of the labour force in an effort to cope with the rise in the unemployment rate to 8 per cent. The number of trainees has fallen to about a third of that level, reflecting the improved economic situation. However, the employment rates for those completing training have been low (Table 3.4).

Policies to boost employment through public works jobs and wage subsidies account for more than a third of expenditures on active labour market policies in Korea. The use of public works jobs has declined since 1999, when the number of participants in short-term employment reached 7 per cent of the labour force. Although the number declined to around 2 per cent in 2002, the government plans to create 80 000 public works jobs in 2004. Employment subsidies also play an important role; in 2003, they were used to support jobs for more than half a million workers (Table 3.5). The majority are in "employment promotion programmes", which subsidise jobs in companies that are restructuring. Other programmes support the hiring of certain categories of workers, such as women, the long-term unemployed and the elderly, an area that the *Social Pact* suggests should be increased.

Table 3.5. **Employment subsidies**

	Number of participants (thousands)				Expenditure (billions of won)			
	2000	2001	2002	2003	2000	2001	2002	2003
Total	449.3 (100.0)	568.3 (100.0)	474.6 (100.0)	507.0 (100.0)	113.9 (100.0)	128.8 (100.0)	90.7 (100.0)	92.7 (100.0)
Employment maintenance programmes	148.5 (33.1)	257.4 (45.3)	152.4 (32.1)	119.1 (23.5)	29.4 (25.8)	56.0 (43.5)	32.7 (36.1)	27.4 (29.6)
Of which: Temporary shutdown	130.1 (87.6)	178.4 (69.3)	122.2 (80.2)	107.9 (90.6)	21.8 (74.1)	32.2 (57.5)	19.9 (60.9)	21.1 (77.0)
Employment promotion programmes	300.8 (66.9)	310.9 (54.7)	322.2 (67.9)	387.9 (76.5)	84.5 (74.2)	72.8 (56.5)	58.0 (63.9)	65.3 (70.4)
Of which: Hiring of laid-off workers[1]	62.7 20.8 (9.7)	30.3	–	–	40.8 (48.3)	20.2 (27.7)	–	–

1. Subsidies to encourage the hiring of laid-off workers were abolished as of July 2001.
Source: Ministry of Labour.

The industrial relations system

The government hopes to develop a labour-management culture based on laws and principles and on dialogue and compromise in order to establish more co-operative industrial relations. The number of industrial disputes stabilised in 2003, while the workdays lost as a result of industrial disputes fell by 18 per cent. However, the number of workers involved in strikes in 2003 increased by 46 per cent. Moreover, industrial actions are sometimes accompanied by violence and occupation of work-places. Contentious industrial relations have a negative impact on business confidence and investment; according to a 2003 poll of CEOs of Korean and foreign firms, about half were reluctant to invest in Korea because of labour-management problems. Moreover, labour problems account for almost a third of the complaints made to the Investment Ombudsman by foreign firms operating in Korea, with a negative impact on prospective foreign investors.[8]

Difficult industrial relations problems reflect a long period of adjustment for the social partners following the democratisation of the country in 1987 and the development of independent labour unions. Although there was increased co-oper-ation to overcome the impact of the crisis, confrontational attitudes resurfaced with the economic recovery, in part due to workers' efforts to reverse the deceleration in wage growth. In the past, the government has tended to intervene in on-going dis-putes to facilitate early agreements rather than develop an environment more con-ducive to harmonious industrial relations. However, the government is now making efforts to establish the principle of autonomous agreements between labour and management by refraining from intervening. In particular, the Labour Relations Com-mission will be strengthened to make it an effective tool in settling disputes.

To create the legal and institutional foundations of a more effective labour market, the government established an expert committee in May 2003. Its final report, which is summarised in Box 3.2, was sent to the Tripartite Commission in December.[9] In September 2003, the government announced the "Roadmap for Industrial Relations Reform". The "Reform Measures for Advanced Industrial Relations Laws and Systems", which was included in the Roadmap, was also submitted to the Tripartite Commission. However, there are wide differences between the positions of labour and manage-ment in the Commission that make it difficult to reach a consensus, forcing a delay in the deadline for an agreement until the first half of 2004. Still, the government hopes to send relevant legislation to the National Assembly, based on the results of the dis-cussion in the Tripartite Commission, before the end of the year.

Since the mid-1990s, the focus of the labour unions' collective bargaining agenda has shifted towards labour's right to participate in management, social reforms and labour law issues. The expert committee recommends broadening the range of collective bargaining issues to include collective industrial relations[10] and union activities, but not issues of rights. On the issues of rights, the expert committee made a number of proposals, as summarised in Box 3.2. *First*, replace

Box 3.2.   Key recommendations of the Expert Committee on Industrial Relations

Dismissal of workers for managerial reasons

- Introduce some differentiation in the required consultation period prior to dismissals, based on the scale of dismissals involved, while limiting the maximum period to the current minimum 60-day consultation period.
- Exempt, at least in part, firms in bankruptcy proceedings from the requirements attached to dismissals.
- Conduct a long-term review of alternative dismissal systems.

Rights of association and collective bargaining

- Permit unemployed persons to join unions other than those at the enterprise level.
- Allow the customary practice of firms paying wages to full-time union officials to remain legal up to a ceiling (under current law, it is to be banned from 2007 when multiple unions at the firm level are allowed).
- Preserve the "no work, no pay" principle that bans unions from taking industrial actions to demand the payment of wages lost during a strike.
- Conduct a long-term and in-depth discussion of the criminal penalties attached to unfair labour practices.
- Broaden the range of topics that are allowed to be the subject of collective bargaining – currently limited to the area of working conditions – to include collective industrial relations and union activities.

Industrial action

- Ensure the transparency and fairness of labour unions' voting procedures on strike action, while leaving the minimum requirement for approval at a simple majority of union members.
- Abolish the concept of "essential public service" (*i.e.* electricity, water & gas, railways, hospitals, oil and the central bank) in which arbitration is compulsory. Replace the current system with "public-interest services", which would be subject to special mediation. Workers would have to give one week advance notice of strikes and the use of replacement workers would be permitted to maintain a minimum level of services.

Dispute mediation procedures

- Expand the scope of mediation, which is currently limited to collective bargaining issues (i.e. working conditions), to cover all industrial conflicts, including those concerning rights.
- Provide mediation before and after industrial actions and regardless of whether it has been requested.

Box 3.2.   **Key recommendations of the Expert Committee on Industrial Relations** (*cont.*)

– Improve and expand the Labour Relations Commission to provide high-quality mediation services.
– Foster the development of private, fee-charging mediation services and link them to public organisations.

Labour-management councils

– Broaden the range of topics discussed by the councils to include changes in production lines, performance monitoring methods and change of business activities.
– Provide adequate information in advance on subjects to be discussed to the workers who are members of the council and refer disputes concerning the councils to the Labour Relations Commission.
– Submit agreements reached at the councils to workers for their agreement.

---

the ban on the common practice of companies paying union officials – which is to take effect in 2007 – with a legal limit on the number of full-time union officials that can be paid by a firm. Under current law, multiple unions within an enterprise are to be allowed at the same time that payments to union officials will be banned. *Second*, allow unemployed persons to join labour unions at the regional, national and industrial level, while maintaining the ban on their membership in enterprise-level unions. *Third*, abolish the concept of essential public services, which are subject to compulsory arbitration, and replace it with the requirement to maintain minimum service during strikes in order to protect public interests. The expert committee also proposed expanding the scope of mediation by the Labour Relations Commission,[11] which is currently limited to collective bargaining issues, to cover all industrial conflicts, including those concerning rights, and fostering private mediation services.

Increasing the labour force participation rate

A number of studies suggest that a key to coping with population ageing is to increase, or at least maintain, labour force participation rates. The rate in Korea is below the OECD average, despite the fact that the rate for older workers (aged 55 to 64) is relatively high (Figure 3.6). One reason is that the rate for those in the 15 to 24 age category is exceptionally low, reflecting the high proportion of this age group engaged in higher education or military service. In addition, the

Figure 3.6. **Labour force participation rates**
2002

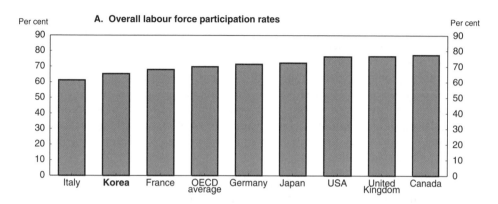

A. **Overall labour force participation rates**

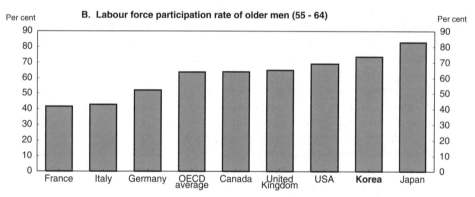

B. **Labour force participation rate of older men (55 - 64)**

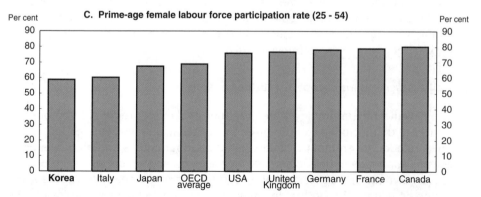

C. **Prime-age female labour force participation rate (25 - 54)**

Source: OECD.

participation rate for prime-aged adults – aged 25 to 54 – is also below the OECD average due to the low participation rate of women (Panel C). Despite a substantial increase over the past few decades, the rate in Korea is still the third lowest in the OECD area after Mexico and Turkey. The low rate is not explained by disincentives in the tax system, which is based on individual incomes. The key explanations are the lack of part-time job opportunities, the absence of adequate childcare facilities and societal attitudes that tend to concentrate female employment opportunities in smaller firms, particularly in the service sector. Another factor influencing female participation is the wage differential by gender, which was about 20 per cent in 2002 for regular workers, after adjusting for workers' characteristics (Jeong, 2003). It is probably larger since only 36 per cent of female workers are regular employees compared to 61 per cent of men, according to the Labour Force Survey. The wage discrimination against non-regular workers may thus discourage female participation.

It will be important to maintain, or even increase, the high participation rate for older workers as the population ages. However, pay scales based on seniority pose an obstacle to continued employment of older workers. The average wage of male workers in the 45 to 49 age group is 70 per cent higher than for those aged 25 to 29. This gap is larger than in other OECD countries for which data are available, including Japan, where seniority-based wage systems are the norm. Firms thus have an incentive to retire such workers at a relatively young age, given their higher expense. Consequently, the typical age for workers to leave employment in firms is around 55, although the majority remain in the labour market, often through self-employment. According to some studies, the importance of age in setting wages has actually increased slightly in recent years despite government efforts to encourage performance-based pay, which would eliminate the bias against older, more expensive workers. A second concern is that the public pension system, under the current rules, would provide a disincentive to employment for those starting to receive their pensions once the system matures in 2028. Indeed, the loss in pension income for a 65-year-old worker with average earnings and a full working career who remains in the labour force would amount to more than a quarter of net-of-tax earnings in 2028.

Overall assessment and scope for further actions

Significantly improving Korea's labour market will require a comprehensive package that includes compromises by both management and labour, as well as a new role for government. The fact that the labour unions and employer associations have already criticised specific elements in the December 2003 report by the expert committee[12] suggests that a negotiated programme that includes some elements demanded by both sides may have the best chance of success in the Tripartite Commission, which has an important role to play in developing a consensus for reform. However, the Commission has had considerable difficulty in the past in reaching a consensus on difficult issues. In some cases, such as allowing labour union pluralism within companies and the ban on firms paying union leaders in 2002, it simply deferred reforms until 2007. Hopefully, the *Social Pact for Job Creation*, which was signed by the Commission in February 2004, marks a turning point away from confrontational power struggles and towards a more co-operative relationship.[13] However, the fact that this *Pact* is not legally binding certainly facilitated its approval.

The underlying principle of industrial relations should be the creation of a partnership between labour and management that forces them to settle their disputes autonomously without government involvement. The pattern of *ad hoc* intervention by the authorities encourages the social partners to push for a favourable decision by the government rather than being forced to compromise with each other. Allowing both labour and management to fully exercise fundamental rights would create checks and balances that would be more effective in limiting the social costs of industrial disputes than artificially restricting strikes. The fact that nearly one-tenth of strikes are illegal is one of the reasons for government involvement in industrial disputes, suggesting a need to bring Korea's industrial relations practices into line with internationally accepted standards.

Employment flexibility is essential in an economy like Korea that is rapidly restructuring and specialising in volatile high-technology industries. However, the equity costs of achieving such flexibility through increasing reliance on non-regular workers is too high as it is creating a dualistic labour market in which one important segment of the population is subject to significantly lower wages, less protection from the social safety net and greater job precariousness. Indeed, it may be contributing to the deterioration in income distribution. Instead, it is necessary to reduce employment protection for regular workers, while enhancing the coverage of the social safety net, particularly the Employment Insurance System. One way to increase compliance with the System may be through enhanced co-operation with other social security administrators and the tax administration to find employees who do not participate in employment insurance.

Given the sluggishness of domestic demand, it may be too early to conclude that the economy's ability to create employment has been permanently weakened. The low level of taxes and social welfare in Korea do not indicate any major disincentives to work. Nevertheless, active labour market policies may help to reduce the extent of mismatch problems and to assist disadvantaged groups to find jobs. However, it is essential to rigorously examine the costs and benefits of each programme. In the area of training, it is important to ensure that programmes are: *i)* targeted on participants; *ii)* small in scale; *iii)* result in a qualification that is recognised and valued by the market; and *iv)* include a strong on-the-job component, which helps to establish close links with employers. The increasing reliance on employment subsidies may not be an efficient approach to boost employment. In other OECD countries using such policies, the deadweight and substitution costs tend to be as high as 90 per cent.

Labour market reforms should also take into account the impact of rapid population ageing. In particular, the practice of most regular workers leaving employment at around age 55 is not appropriate in the context of increasing life expectancy. Reducing the importance of seniority in determining wages would help Korea to maintain the employment of older workers. While wage-setting in the corporate sector is a private-sector decision, introducing compensation systems in the public sector that place more emphasis on performance may encourage the spread of performance-based pay. Moreover, the public pension system should be reformed to eliminate incentives – which will emerge as the system matures – for older workers to leave the labour force. In addition, encouraging greater labour force participation by women would help in coping with rapid population ageing and a declining number of working-age persons. Female participation can be positively influenced by family-friendly polices, notably childcare subsidies and paid maternity and parental leaves (Jaumotte, 2003), and ending wage discrimination against women.

Box 3.3. Summary of recommendations for the labour market

Encourage job creation

- In developing the social safety net, avoid introducing disincentives in the tax and social benefit systems that would discourage employment.

Increase labour market flexibility

- Reduce employment protection for regular workers, in part by shortening the minimum consultation period necessary before dismissal.
- Encourage the continuation of wage-setting practices that promote flexibility in wages.
- Limit any negative impact on employment from the minimum wage system.

Further develop the social safety net

- Continue to expand the coverage of the Employment Insurance System.
- Increase compliance with the Employment Insurance System, in part through enhanced co-operation with other social security administrators and the tax administration.
- Increase the coverage of non-regular workers in social insurance systems based in workplaces.

Limit labour market dualism and the associated negative implications for equity

- Reduce employment protection for regular workers in order to reduce the incentives to hire non-regular workers.
- Increase the coverage of non-regular workers in social insurance systems based in workplaces.

Use active labour market policies effectively to promote employment

- Rigorously examine the costs and benefits of each policy to avoid wasteful spending.
- Ensure the availability of job-placement services, through both the Public Employment Service and the private-sector providers, while avoiding duplication, in order to limit mismatch problems.
- Make certain that publicly-financed training programmes for the unemployed are effective in raising the employment prospects of the participants.
- Avoid wage subsidies, given their generally high deadweight costs.

Develop more co-operative industrial relations

- Resolve remaining labour rights issues such as union pluralism at the firm level, paying full-time union officials and the question of essential public services.

Box 3.3. **Summary of recommendations for the labour market** (*cont.*)

- Allow both labour and management to fully exercise fundamental rights to create checks and balances that would limit the social costs of industrial disputes.
- The authorities should develop an environment more conducive to harmonious industrial relations and avoid getting involved in industrial disputes, thus forcing labour and management to settle their disputes autonomously.

Enhance labour force participation

- Reduce the importance of seniority in setting wages in order to maintain the employment of older workers.
- Reform aspects of the public pension system that will create incentives for older workers to leave the labour force.
- Encourage greater labour force participation by women by introducing more family-friendly policies.

Notes

1. For example, the *Social Pact for Job Creation* stated that "Industrial hollowing out has been taking place with an increasing number of manufacturers moving their production bases overseas".

2. This is reflected in Article 2-6 of the *Social Pact for Job Creation*, which states that "To help SMEs hire professionals or skilled workers, the government will grant a bounty" for such hiring.

3. In 2003, the government changed the "Foreign Industrial Trainee System" to allow one year of training followed by two years of employment. With the legalisation of about 200 000 illegal foreign workers, the number of legal foreign workers reached nearly 400 000 at the end of 2003. The introduction of the "Foreign Workers Employment Scheme" in August 2004 will further simplify inflows of workers from abroad. Under the new system, foreign workers will have the same rights as domestic workers and the maximum work period will be three years.

4. According to one estimate, by Hur (2004), a 1 per cent rise in real unit labour costs reduces employment by 0.1 per cent. This study takes into account the fact that the wage level reported by the official survey is biased upwards because it is limited to regular workers at firms with five or more employees.

5. There are exceptions, such as regional-level bargaining in the transportation sector (buses and taxis) and sectoral level bargaining in textiles.

6. However, some employees, such as public officials, workers over the age of 65 and private-school teachers have remained excluded from the system. Given the large number of self-employed and family workers, only one-third of all workers are covered by employment insurance.

7. This includes Employment Insurance, Health Insurance and the National Pension Scheme. However, non-regular workers would be covered by regional health insurance schemes and could still contribute to the National Pension Scheme.

8. The cost of hostile industrial relations is reflected in recent research that shows that the existence of a union is associated with a worsening performance and greater risk of bankruptcy in Korea (Cho, 2003).

9. The committee, the Research Committee on the Advancement of Industrial Relations, consisting of 15 academic experts, produced an interim report, "Reform Measures for Advanced Industrial Relations Laws and Systems", in September 2003 and a final report in December.

10. This includes such topics as the guarantee of union activities during working hours, matters related to collective bargaining and industrial action procedures.

11. The success rate of the Commission in mediation has risen from 15 per cent in 1997 to 50 per cent in 2003.

12. See for example, "Labor proposal under fire from all sides", *The Korea Herald*, 9 December 2003.

13. By the end of April 2004, social pacts had been signed in 21 local jurisdictions and in one industry. In addition, the "Job Creation Committee", a joint public-private organisation, was created to monitor the implementation of the Pact.

4. Reform of the corporate and financial sectors

The corporate and financial sectors, which lay at the core of the 1997 crisis, have evolved significantly in recent years. The corporate sector is still in the process of restructuring in the wake of several important changes, including stronger competitive pressures, a new corporate governance framework and more independent financial institutions. Of the top 30 chaebol in 1997, seventeen have entered legal bankruptcy procedures or been forced into workout programmes, including Daewoo, which was the second largest group. A number of others lost major subsidiaries. The surviving chaebol have substantially reduced debt; the average debt-to-equity ratio has fallen to 116 per cent from more than 500 per cent at the time of the crisis. The improved financial health of the corporate sector has had beneficial effects on the financial sector. Moreover, the restructuring programme launched in 1997 has been successful in overcoming the impact of the crisis and laying the foundation for a more efficient market-oriented system. The restructuring of the financial sector required large outlays of public funds, the closure of nearly a third of financial institutions operating in 1997 and the upgrading of prudential supervision – notably through the creation of the Financial Supervisory Commission. The positive results are most evident in the banking sector, where the commercial orientation and financial soundness have been strengthened.

Despite considerable progress, the reform agenda remains unfinished. A recent accounting scandal at a large chaebol-affiliated company reflects a continued lack of transparency and caused liquidity problems for the investment trust companies. They were also negatively affected by difficulties in the credit card sector, which has contracted significantly with the end of the household credit boom. The problems in the non-bank financial sector have led to a deterioration in the banking sector's performance as well. More fundamentally, the financial-sector problems reflect insufficient pre-emptive supervision with the result that the government intervenes after the event to stabilise financial markets and reduce systemic risks. Such interventions, in turn, can result in moral hazard problems.

This chapter begins with an overview of the corporate sector, in particular the corporate governance system and the innovation framework. This leads to the conclusion that, while the legal framework for corporate governance is approaching best practices, more progress in implementation is necessary. Reforms to improve the innovation framework would help to increase the return from R&D spending, while care needs to be taken to avoid the potential costs of picking winners in the technology and industrial sectors. The chapter then analyses developments in the banking and non-bank financial sectors. Establishing the autonomy of the banking sector requires continued progress in privatising the state-owned banks, which is also having the beneficial effect of increasing the foreign presence and helping to recover the costs of financial-sector restructuring. However, it is also necessary to address the problems in the non-bank financial sector, notably the investment trust companies and the credit card companies, which are negatively affecting the banks. Fundamentally improving the situation will depend on developing a pre-emptive prudential supervisory framework and strengthening market discipline. The recommendations are presented in more detail in the final section of the chapter and listed in Box 4.1.

The corporate sector

The restructuring of the corporate sector has improved the balance sheets of firms. In the manufacturing sector, the debt to equity ratio has fallen from nearly 400 per cent in 1997 to 123 per cent in 2003 (Table 4.1), a level below that in the United States and Japan. Lower debt, combined with the fall in interest rates, lowered financial expenses to 1.9 per cent of sales. Consequently, the ratio of operating profits to interest expenses has risen from less than 100 per cent in the late 1990s to 367 per cent in 2003. Financial vulnerability has been reduced as the proportion of firms with an interest coverage ratio of less than one declined from 28.6 per cent in 2001 to 26.3 per cent in 2002 (Panel B). Nevertheless, the debt of these firms, which did not earn enough profit to cover even their interest payments, was significant at nearly 16 per cent of GDP. Chaebol restructuring has also led to the spin-off of 76 companies between 1997 and 2001, with employment of almost 70 000. This section will discuss three areas important to the development of the corporate sector; improving corporate governance and transparency, upgrading the innovation framework and policies towards small and medium-sized enterprises (SMEs).[1]

Corporate governance and transparency

The legal framework for corporate governance has improved significantly since the crisis, in part by the introduction of a stronger code of corporate governance in 2003. One study ranked it at 0.8 out of 1.0, not far below the US rating of 0.89 (Table 4.2). The greatest progress has been in increasing the accountability of managers by strengthening shareholders' rights, creating a market for corporate control and establishing the legal responsibility of controlling shareholders. However, the auditing framework was rated as relatively inadequate. Nevertheless, the rise in the foreign ownership share in listed companies to 42 per cent in 2003 –

Table 4.1. **Performance indicators for the corporate sector**

Per cent

A. The manufacturing sector

	1997	1998	1999	2000	2001	2002	2003
Financial indicators							
Debt-equity ratio	396.3	303.0	214.7	210.6	182.2	135.4	123.4
Total borrowings-assets ratio	54.2	50.8	42.8	41.2	39.8	31.7	28.3
Current ratio[1]	91.8	89.8	92.0	83.2	97.9	106.1	109.8
Asset turnover ratio	0.90	0.82	0.82	0.96	0.98	1.08	1.10
Profitability indicators							
Operating profit-sales ratio	8.3	6.1	6.6	7.4	5.5	6.7	6.9
Labour cost-sales ratio	11.4	9.8	9.8	9.7	10.0	10.1	10.3
Ordinary profit-sales ratio	−0.3	−1.8	1.7	1.3	0.4	4.7	4.7
Financial expense-sales ratio	6.4	9.0	6.9	4.7	4.2	2.6	1.9
Average interest rate	10.6	13.5	11.5	10.5	9.4	7.7	6.8
Interest coverage ratio[2]	129.1	68.3	96.1	157.2	132.6	260.3	367.1

B. Firms with interest coverage ratio[2] below one in 2002

Years below one	2002	2001-2002	2000-2002	1999-2002	Total
Number of firms	1 217	583	296	216	2 312
As a percentage of all externally-audited firms	13.8	6.6	3.4	2.5	26.3
Total debt (trillion won)	22.4	41.8	16.7	25.8	106.6
As percentage of GDP	3.3	6.1	2.4	3.8	15.6

1. The ratio of liquid assets to short-term liabilities.
2. The ratio of operating profits to interest expenses.
Source: Bank of Korea for Panel A. Ministry of Finance and Economy for Panel B.

compared to 10 per cent in 1998 when the ceiling on foreign ownership was abolished – suggests greater international confidence in the governance of Korean companies. The foreign share of the top ten chaebol is approaching 50 per cent.

Despite the improvement since the crisis, corporate governance and management transparency remain a serious concern, as shown in the recent accounting scandal at SK Global, the trading unit of the SK Group, which is the fourth largest chaebol. At the end of 2002, the Financial Supervisory Service (FSS) responded to a request from a non-governmental organisation to investigate a secret derivative transaction between two SK Group companies (SK Global and SK Securities) and a foreign financial institution. The FSS revealed that the Group had violated the Securities Transaction Law by failing to disclose the contents of the transaction in its financial statements. In March 2003, the chairmen of SK Corp. and SK Global were indicted on charges of breach of fiduciary duty,[2] insider trading activities and window-dressing the financial statements to inflate the net equity and profit.[3] The prosecutor announced that SK Global had hidden debts so large that its net equity was actually negative. The scandal has resulted in losses

Table 4.2. **Corporate governance and investor protection in 2003**[1]

	Institution index[2]	Enforcement index[2]
Disclosure and audit	0.79	0.50
Disclosure	0.88	0.47
Audit	0.63	0.53
Supervision and litigation by shareholders	0.72	0.39
Independence of supervisory bodies	0.50	0.47
Power of supervisory bodies	1.00	0.51
Litigation by shareholders	0.67	0.19
Accountability of managers	0.90	0.45
Shareholders' rights	0.88	0.34
Market for corporate control	1.00	0.56
Director/controlling shareholders' liability	0.83	0.45
Overall	0.80	0.45

1. Index score ranges between 0 and 1, with 1 being the perfect score.
2. The institution index is constructed by examining the legal framework, while the enforcement index is based on a survey of experts.
Source: Youngjae Lim *et al.* (2003).

for SK affiliates and damages to their shareholders, as well as serious turmoil in the financial market (see below).

The SK Global scandal raised many corporate governance issues, especially related to the chaebol. The divergence between the low level of ownership by the families and their high level of control, which is facilitated by shareholding links, remains the main source of corporate governance problems. The interrelated business activities among the affiliates of a business group, insider trading and "unfair" intra-group transactions have been used to benefit the family owners of chaebol at the expense of minority shareholders. However, the families' low level of ownership is making them vulnerable to attempted take-over bids.

The failure of the external auditing framework and lack of transparency demonstrated the need for additional improvements in this area.[4] Indeed, the FSS fined as many as one-third of the domestic accounting firms in 2003 for sloppy and fraudulent practices. The accounting scandal at *inter alia* SK Global prompted additional steps to improve corporate governance and the accounting system similar to some of the moves introduced in the United States following irregularities in the corporate sector.

– CEOs and CFOs of all publicly-traded companies are now required to personally certify the completeness and accuracy of financial statements.

– At least one member of the audit committee must have professional knowledge of auditing while the new corporate governance code calls for at least two-thirds of the committee to be outside members.

- Outside auditing companies must be changed at least every six years to ensure their independence.

- Outside auditors are banned from providing non-audit services if it is likely to create a conflict of interest or threaten their independence.

- Measures to increase the number of auditors have been implemented.

- Outside directors must account for a majority of board members for all listed companies with assets of more than 2 trillion won.

While the legal framework for corporate governance is tending to con-verge to best practices, particularly with the reforms noted above, actual practice is lagging behind. Indeed, experts evaluate the enforcement of corporate gover-nance, disclosure and audits to be much weaker, with experts ranking it at 0.45 relative to the legal framework (Table 4.2).[5] An important weakness is that many outside directors have had a long association with the company or the con-trolling family, making it questionable whether they are capable of independent judgment. One key to improving enforcement is the introduction of class action suits for large firms (about 80 in total) in 2005 and for all firms listed on the stock exchange in 2007. Thus far, the primary recourse for minority shareholders has been derivative suits, but these have proven difficult to pursue, with less than 20 filed thus far. Class action suits will initially cover only securities-related cases of false disclosure, window dressing and unfair trading, including stock price manipulation. The class action legislation includes good practice provisions to prevent abusive litigation and the development of professional plaintiffs, while setting the threshold for shareholders to initiate a class action suit at a low level. The prospect of facing such suits already appears to be influencing the behavior of management and outside directors. Indeed, it may help eliminate "rubber stamp" outside directors.

Improving the innovation framework

As noted in Chapter 1, Korea has a high level of investment in knowledge, measured as expenditure on R&D and education as a share of GDP. However, there is concern that the absolute size of R&D expenditures – about 8 per cent of the total in the United States and 20 per cent of that in Japan – makes it difficult to compete in high-technology fields. To overcome its size disadvantage, the govern-ment is pursuing a strategy of concentrating resources in specific areas thought to hold the greatest potential for success. Ten strategic industries were identified in August 2003 as future growth engines for the Korean economy (Table 4.3). The National Science and Technology Council, which is responsible for inter-ministerial co-ordination of R&D and science and technology policy within the government, is charged with formulating a plan for the development of the necessary technology, manpower and infrastructure. The authorities plan to invest 400 billion won in 2004 for the development of these areas.

Table 4.3. **The ten strategic industries chosen as growth engines**

Industry	Ministry responsible
Bio-medical products	Ministry of Science and Technology
Next-generation computer displays	Ministry of Commerce, Industry and Energy
Next-generation semiconductors	Ministry of Commerce, Industry and Energy
Next-generation batteries	Ministry of Commerce, Industry and Energy
Future automobiles	Ministry of Commerce, Industry and Energy
Intelligent robots	Ministry of Commerce, Industry and Energy
Digital television and broadcasting	Ministry of Information and Communication
Next-generation mobile communications	Ministry of Information and Communication
Intelligent home networks	Ministry of Information and Communication
Digital content and software solutions	Ministry of Information and Communication

Source: Korean government.

However, the decision to focus limited R&D resources on areas thought to provide the greatest growth potential may risk excessive concentration. The fact that some of the industries picked as new growth engines build on existing strengths in the Korean economy may increase the chances of success. For example, the ten industries include next-generation semiconductors (Korea is the world's largest producer of DRAM chips), next-generation mobile communications (Korea is the largest producer of CDMA phones) and future automobiles (Korea is the sixth largest car producer). However, the risks associated with government policies to promote certain industries are illustrated by the Heavy and Chemical Industry (HCI) drive of the 1970s, which had mixed results, due in part to excessive government-led investment that eventually led to serious macroeconomic problems. Moreover, a policy of picking winners can lead to economic distortions in the economy and the opportunity cost of concentrating on specified sectors can be high. The new growth engine policy looks very similar to the HCI drive of the 1970s in that the government fosters strategic industries, but it differs since the government plays the role of R&D investor, infrastructure builder and promoter. However, the concentration of R&D in certain technologies may further increase the already high degree of R&D concentration in major firms; the top twenty investors in R&D account for half of the total in Korea.

There are also concerns about weak international linkages in the R&D sector, as well as limited interactions between the main domestic actors, and the effectiveness of technological advances in boosting productivity.

- Although universities employ three-quarters of the nation's researchers with doctorates, they account for a surprisingly small share of R&D (Figure 1.3). Indeed, Korea is one of only seven OECD countries in which the government performs more R&D than the higher education sector. Moreover, there is limited interaction between R&D efforts in the private sector, government institutes and universities, reflecting in part a lack of labour mobility.

Table 4.4. **Programmes to assist small and medium-sized enterprises**

Billion won in 2003

Ministry	Outlays	Number of programmes	Selected programmes
Small and Medium Business Administration	3 094	18	– Restructuring support – Start-up support – Stable operation support – Regional SME support – Technology development support – Venture company support
Ministry of Commerce, Industry and Energy	965	23	– Industrial technology development support – Modernisation of distribution network support – Activation of industrial complex support – Energy saving support
Ministry of Agriculture and Forestry	122	3	– Rice processing factory support – Agricultural product processing support – Agricultural machine product support
Ministry of Information and Communication	451	8	– Information and communication technology development support – Leading technology development and distribution support – Multi-media industry support – Software development support
Ministry of Labour	190	7	– Workplace accident prevention support – Workplace environment improvement support – Company nursery facility support
Ministry of Environment	106	5	– Anti-pollution facility support – Environmental technology development support – Recycling industry support
Ministry of Culture and Tourism	223	6	– Film promotion fund support – Sporting goods development support
Ministry of Science and Technology	122	2	– Technology development support – New technology project investment support
Ministry of Maritime Affairs and Fisheries	39	3	– Marine product distribution support – Fishing net support
Ministry of National Defence	14	1	– Defence industry support
Ministry of Construction and Transportation	64	1	– Standardising construction material support – General freight terminal construction support
Ministry of Health and Welfare	12	2	– New drug development support
Total	**5 402**	**79**	

Source: Small and Medium Business Administration.

- Korea is not active in international collaboration in the area of science and technology. In terms of the share of foreign ownership of domestic inventions, Korea ranks second to last after Japan among OECD countries.[6] This may limit the scope for technological progress since international sources of knowledge are increasingly important for innovation, leading to growing co-operation across national borders. One positive sign is that the number of foreign R&D centres located in Korea has doubled to 122 since the crisis.

Small and medium-sized enterprises

The role of SMEs has expanded in recent years. Their share of employment rose from 74 per cent in 1997 to 86 per cent in 2002, while their share of bank credit increased from 20 per cent of GDP to 32 per cent over the same period. Despite the growing role of SMEs, they continue to receive help in a number of ways that may impinge on competition policy (see Chapter 5). In addition, a total of 79 different programmes, supervised by 12 different ministries, provided 5.4 trillion won (0.8 per cent of GDP) of support in 2003 (Table 4.4). Moreover, credit guarantees, amounting to 42 trillion, were provided as of 2002.

The financial sector

The number of financial institutions has fallen by more than one-third since the crisis (Table 4.5), largely due to the closure of weak institutions or their acquisition by stronger institutions. Reform is more advanced in the commercial banks, where the financial-sector restructuring programme was primarily concentrated. In particular, problem loans, as measured by the proportion of loans classified as substandard or below, have fallen significantly to below 3 per cent, less than half of the ratio in the non-bank sector (Table 4.6). Consequently, the banking sector is less vulnerable to shocks. Moreover, the banks remained profitable in 2003, while the non-banks recorded a loss, primarily due to a large loss in the credit card sector. This section will briefly discuss the commercial banks before turning to the non-bank financial sector.

The banking sector

The commercial banking sector has remained profitable since 2001, helping to keep the average capital adequacy ratio of the nation-wide banks above 10 per cent (Table 4.7). Moreover, loans classified as substandard or below fell to a record low 2.4 per cent of total loans in 2002. These favourable conditions facilitated the privatisation of banks that had been re-capitalised using public money in the wake of the crisis. Indeed, the government's ownership share in the commercial banking sector fell from 53 per cent in 1999 to 38 per cent by mid-2003. At present, the government is the principal owner of two of the remaining eight nation-wide banks, with large shares in two of the others, as well as three out of six

Table 4.5. **Number of financial institutions**

A. Changes between 1997 and 2003

	1997 (A)	Exit (B)	Mergers (C)	Newly established	End of 2003 (D)	(B + C)/A (per cent)	D/A (per cent)
Banks	33	5	10	1	19	45.5	57.6
The non-bank sector	2 068	641	153	70	1 344	38.4	65.0
Merchant banks	30	22	7	1	2	96.7	6.7
Securities	36	7	3	18	44	27.8	122.2
Investment trusts	30	6	1	9	32	23.3	106.7
Insurance	50	11	6	17	50	34.0	100.0
Credit unions	1 666	482	107	9	1 086	35.4	65.2
Saving banks	231	102	27	12	114	55.8	49.4
Lease	25	11	2	4	16	52.0	64.0
Total	**2 101**	**646**	**163**	**71**	**1 363**	**38.5**	**64.9**

B. Concentration in the financial industry (HHI*1 000)

	1997	2000	2002	Sep. 2003	USA (2000)	Japan (2000)
Banks	569	822	1 185	1 291	287	700
Life insurance	2 393	2 696	2 694	2 642	364	1 116
Securities/investment trust	1 267	689	637	556	640	2 065
Overall financial industry[1]	**405**	**535**	**744**	**800**	**400**	**335**

1. Based on financial groups. A rising number indicates increased concentration.
Source: Financial Supervisory Commission for Panel A. Bank of Korea for Panel B.

local banks (Table 4.8). Privatisation is advancing further with the listing of the holding company of Woori Bank on the domestic stock market and the New York Stock Exchange in 2003, while the government is seeking strategic investors. The authorities are also mapping out plans, contingent on management and stock market conditions, to sell its remaining stakes in some of the other banks.

The privatisation of the banks has provided an opportunity to increase the share of foreign ownership in the banking sector from 7 per cent in 1997 to 27 per cent in 2002. Foreign investors are the largest shareholders in three commercial banks, and four of the other banks have a substantial foreign presence (Table 4.8). Foreign investors tend to improve governance by pushing banks to concentrate more on shareholder value. The growing role of foreign banks should have a beneficial impact on competition and efficiency as they appear to have comparative advantages in risk analysis and management, loan project assessment, credit analysis, portfolio management and computerisation.

However, the nation-wide banks' balance-sheet quality and profitability in 2003 were negatively affected by problems in the non-bank sector, notably the

Table 4.6. **Performance of financial institutions by sectors**

	Total			Banks[3]			All non-banks		
	2001	2002	2003	2001	2002	2003	2001	2002	2003
Loan quality (in trillion won)									
Total loans (A)	769.6	897.0	949.1	551.2	648.2	709.0	218.4	248.8	240.1
Substandard loans or below (B)[1]	41.6	30.4	33.9	18.7	15.1	18.6	22.9	15.3	15.3
B/A (per cent)	5.4	3.4	3.6	3.4	2.3	2.6	10.5	6.1	6.4
Net profit (in billion won)[2]	9 480	10 252	-1 606	4 684	5 013	1 859	4 796	5 239	-3 465

	Non-bank lending institutions			Insurance companies			Securities/investment trusts[4]		
	2001	2002	2003	2001	2002	2003	2001	2002	2003
Loan quality (in trillion won)									
Total loans (A)	164.3	191.2	178.7	45.2	50.7	54.4	8.9	6.8	7.0
Substandard loans or below (B)[1]	15.8	10.6	11.0	2.5	2.1	2.2	4.6	2.6	2.1
B/A (per cent)	9.6	5.5	6.2	5.4	4.1	4.1	51.6	38.4	29.2
Net profit (in billion won)[2]	2 221	2 939	-10 385	1 943	3 151	6 281	632	-851	640

1. Includes loans classified as substandard, doubtful and estimated loss at the end of each calendar year.
2. Based on fiscal years, which vary by type of institution. Net profit through September 2003 for some non-bank lending institutions and between April and November 2003 for the insurance companies. Net profit for securities/investment trusts sector includes only securities firms.
3. Includes all domestic banks (nation-wide banks, local banks and specialised banks).
4. Lending is not the main business for the securities/investment trusts. The high ratio of substandard loans is due to acquiring loans through merging merchant banks and bridge loans to Daewoo-affiliated companies.
Source: Financial Supervisory Service.

Table 4.7. **Indicators of bank profitability**
Nation-wide banks, in billion won

	1998	1999	2000	2001	2002	2003
Before-tax profits						
Net profits	-3 244.6	1 625.1	7 794.1	8 997.8	9 018.6	10 698.1
Net profits minus loan loss provisions	-10 346.8	-5 523.5	-1 420.4	3 888.9	3 836.0	982.4
Net profits minus all provisions	-10 077.6	-5 523.5	-1 863.8	3 630.3	3 669.8	497.8
After-tax profits	-10 130.0	-5 953.7	-2 399.9	3 391.5	2 898.2	425.0
Return on equity (per cent)	-48.63	-24.73	-10.81	16.30	10.95	1.50
Return on assets (per cent)	-2.99	-1.42	-0.53	0.79	0.56	0.07
Total loans	263 940.4	305 524.9	337 927.5	353 211.0	432 161.5	463 789.7
Substandard loans or below[1]	18 971.0	42 367.6	29 847.2	11 726.1	10 564.3	12 989.1
Ratio to total loans (per cent)	7.2	13.9	8.8	3.3	2.4	2.8
Loan loss reserves	12 102.5	18 873.6	18 523.7	8 445.0	8 816.0	–
Reserves to substandard loans or below[1] (per cent)	63.8	44.5	62.1	72.0	83.5	–
Capital adequacy ratio (BIS ratio)	8.22	10.79	10.52	10.81	10.46	10.40
Number of branches	4 164	4 040	3 977	4 052	4 304	4 345

1. Includes loans classified as substandard, doubtful and estimated loss.
Source: Financial Supervisory Service.

Table 4.8.   **Government and foreign ownership of the commercial banks**

End of 2003, per cent

	Government ownership	Foreign ownership
A. Nation-wide banks		
Choheung	–	2.27
Woori[1]	Woori Financial Group – KDIC[2] (86.84)	–
Korea First	KDIC (48.49), Government (2.95)	48.56 (New Bridge Capital 48.56)
Korea Exchange	Ex-Im Bank (14.00), Bank of Korea (6.18)	71.04 (Lone Star 51.0, Comerz Bank 14.8)
Kookmin	–	73.56 (ING Bank NV 3.78)
Shinhan	–	–
KorAm	–	89.59 (Carlye Consortium 36.7, Standard Chartered Bank 9.76)
Hana	KDIC (21.66)	43.16 (Allianz 8.16)
B. Local banks		
Daegu	–	31.31 (SSB-SMALL Capital 5.00)
Pusan	–	38.46 (Capital Research & Management Co. 10.40)
Kwangju	Woori Financial Group – KDIC[2] (86.84)	–
Cheju	KDIC (31.96)	–
Jeonbuk	–	0.25
Kyongnam	Woori Financial Group – KDIC[2] (86.84)	–

1. Formerly known as Hanvit Bank.
2. Woori (100 per cent), Kwangju (99.99 per cent) and Kyongnam (99.99 per cent) are owned by the Woori Financial Group. The KDIC owns 86.84 per cent of Woori Financial Group.
Source: Financial Supervisory Service.

accounting scandal at SK Global and the financial distress in the credit card sector. Loans classified as sub-standard or below rose to 2.8 per cent in 2003, forcing a rise in loan loss reserves that reduced profits to 0.4 trillion won, compared to 2.9 trillion won in 2002 (Table 4.7).[7] Although the delinquency rate on bank loans to the household sector has remained relatively low, there is a risk that the rise in credit card delinquency (see below) could be an indicator of a broader decline in the quality of household credit in 2004. This could negatively affect the banks when a large portion of their household loans come due.[8] The risk would be heightened if financial distress in the credit card business is not resolved quickly.

The non-bank sector

The progress of restructuring within the non-bank sector has been uneven, particularly regarding asset quality. For example, in the savings banks and credit unions, which have large exposures to the households and SMEs, the ratio of loans substandard or below has remained high (Table 4.9).[9] In addition,

Table 4.9. **Performance indicators of non-bank lending institutions**

	Savings banks			Merchant banks			Credit unions			Mutual credits		
	2001	2002	2003	2001	2002	2003	2001	2002	2003	2001	2002	2003
Loan quality (in trillion won)												
Total loans (A)	15.9	19.6	24.9	2.9	1.9	0.6	10.7	10.1	11.1	–	79.2	90.2
Substandard loans or below (B)[1]	3.1	2.2	2.9	1.0	0.2	–	1.0	0.6	0.7	–	2.0	2.1
B/A (per cent)	19.5	11.3	11.7	34.5	7.9	–	9.8	6.0	6.3	–	2.6	2.3
Net profit (in billion won)[2]	123	130	88	16	–44	15	–144	96	100	–	–	–
Capital adequacy ratio (per cent)[2]	11.1	10.5	8.8	14.0	11.6	–	–	2.0	2.3	–	–	–

	Credit card companies			Leasing companies			Finance companies			Venture capital companies		
	2001	2002	2003	2001	2002	2003	2001	2002	2003	2001	2002	2003
Loan quality (in trillion won)												
Total loans (A)	39.4	53.0	29.4	9.6	7.7	5.7	15.5	18.9	16.2	0.6	0.8	0.6
Substandard loans or below (B)[1]	0.5	2.1	3.2	3.9	2.6	0.8	3.4	0.9	1.3	0.1	–	–
B/A (per cent)	1.3	4.0	11.0	40.6	33.5	13.5	21.9	4.7	7.8	16.7	–	–
Net profit (in billion won)[2]	2 594	236	–10 474	–608	321	205	211	2 292	–303	29	–93	–15
Capital adequacy ratio (per cent)[2]	13.3	12.4	–5.5	1.5	8.8	–	–19.3	11.5	–	39.2	38.3	–

1. Includes loans classified as substandard, doubtful and estimated loss at the end of each calendar year.
2. Follows the fiscal year. Net profit through September 2003 for the leasing, finance and venture capital companies.
Source: Financial Supervisory Service.

there are substantial variations in capital adequacy between sub-sectors. Finally, the number of merchant banks and small institutions, such as savings banks and credit unions, has fallen sharply, while the number of insurance companies, investment trust companies and securities firms remained relatively unchanged (Table 4.5). However, the performance of the latter two groups suggests that there may be a need for further consolidation. This section discusses the investment trust companies and securities firms after first examining the credit card industry, which recorded a huge loss of 10.5 trillion won in 2003.

The boom in household credit and the impact on financial institutions

Historically, consumer credit was relatively undeveloped in Korea, reflecting the emphasis on investment in the industrial sector. However, it has risen rapidly since the crisis, accompanied by a sharp run-up in real estate prices (Table 4.10). Between 1998 and 2002, total household credit increased by 2.4 times, rising from 38 to 62 per cent of GDP. A large part of this increase was due to structural changes in the financial sector, particularly in the banks and credit card companies. Following the crisis, banks became increasingly aware of the risks of lending to chaebol-affiliated firms, which at the same time have focused on reducing their debt. This led to intense competition between banks to increase lending to the high-profit and low-risk household sector. The rising share of households in bank lending was accompanied by the expansion in total lending by

Table 4.10. **Household credit trends**

	1998	1999	2000	2001	2002	2003
A. Amount (in trillion won)						
Banks	52.9	76.3	107.2	156.7	222.0	253.8
Credit card companies	16.1	23.4	47.2	67.2	84.1	51.8
Savings institutions[1]	45.3	44.6	44.0	46.1	52.7	66.9
Others[2]	47.9	46.2	41.4	39.0	41.6	32.2
Insurance	21.5	23.5	27.1	32.6	38.7	42.9
Total	183.6	214.0	266.9	341.7	439.1	447.6
B. Sources (per cent)						
Banks	28.8	35.7	40.2	45.9	50.6	56.7
Credit card companies	8.8	10.9	17.7	19.7	19.1	11.6
Savings institutions[1]	24.7	20.8	16.5	13.5	12.0	14.9
Others[2]	26.1	21.6	15.5	11.4	9.5	7.2
Insurance	11.7	11.0	10.2	9.5	8.8	9.6
Total	100.0	100.0	100.0	100.0	100.0	100.0

1. Includes savings banks, credit unions, community credit cooperatives and mutual credits.
2. Includes finance companies, bank trust accounts, postal savings, sales credits and the National Housing Fund.
Source: Bank of Korea.

Table 4.11. **The use of credit cards**

Trillion won

	1998	1999	2000	2001	2002	2003
Number issued (in millions)	42.0	39.0	57.9	85.0	104.8	95.2
Amount of sales using credit cards	30.8	42.5	79.9	175.5	268.0	240.7
Per cent of private consumption	12.9	15.5	25.6	51.1	70.3	62.0
Amount of cash loans from credit cards	32.7	54.3	157.3	304.9	412.8	276.6
Total amount of credit card use	63.6	96.8	237.3	480.4	680.8	517.3
Net profit[1]	**0.0**	**−0.3**	**0.9**	**2.6**	**0.2**	**−10.5**

1. Includes only non-bank credit card companies.
Source: Financial Supervisory Service.

banks, based on the success of the restructuring programme in restoring their financial health. Moreover, rising real estate prices raised the value of households' loan collateral, allowing them to borrow more money.

A second factor increasing household credit was the expanded use of credit cards, which was encouraged by deregulation and tax advantages. In 1999, the government introduced a deduction from taxable income for purchases made using credit cards, as well as a lottery for credit card users, in order to increase the share of retail sales that is captured in the value-added tax net and thereby limit the number of transactions escaping tax.[10] In addition, the government removed the ceiling on monthly cash advances, which had been set at 700 000 won. These policies helped trigger phenomenal growth in the credit card sector (Table 4.11). Between 1998 and 2002, the number of cards issued more than doubled to over 100 million, an average of 4.6 cards for every working-age adult, and total turnover increased about eleven-fold. This had a positive impact on the growth of consumption, as well as the enforcement of the tax system. In contrast to credit cards, the use of debit cards has not expanded, despite tax advantages similar to those offered for credit cards.[11]

- The rise in delinquency rates

Between 2000 and January 2004, the number of individual delinquent borrowers almost doubled, reaching 3.8 million or 16 per cent of the working-age population (Table 4.12).[12] However, the delinquency rate for bank loans to households has been relatively stable (Table 4.13), reflecting the fact that about half of them have been used to finance house purchases, which has contributed to rising prices in the real estate market.[13] The risk to banks from such loans is limited because their loans to households are usually backed by collateral such as real estate. Moreover, the customary loan to value ratio is around 60 per cent, lower than in

Table 4.12. **Individual delinquent borrowers**

A. Trend of delinquent borrowers

	2000	2001	2002				2003				2004
	Dec.	Dec.	Mar.	June	Sep.	Dec.	Mar.	June	Sep.	Dec.	Jan.
Delinquent borrowers											
(in millions)[1]	2.08	2.45	2.46	2.26	2.46	2.64	3.00	3.23	3.50	3.72	3.77
Related to credit cards[2]	0.44	1.04	1.11	1.12	1.30	1.49	1.77	1.98	2.20	2.40	2.45
Per cent	21.2	42.4	45.1	49.6	52.8	56.4	59.0	61.3	62.9	64.5	65.0

B. Delinquent borrowers by age

	Teens	20's	30's	40's or over	Total
Delinquent borrowers (in thousands)					
2000	3	267	655	1 159	2 084
2001	12	409	704	1 326	2 450
2002	7	488	759	1 382	2 636
2003	4	732	1 133	1 851	3 720
Jan. 2004	4	727	1 154	1 883	3 768
Per cent of total delinquent borrowers	0.1	19.3	30.6	50.0	100.0
Per cent of population	0.1	8.9	13.0	10.4	9.0

1. The registration threshold for delinquency was raised in July 2002, from 50 thousand won for three months to 300 thousand won.
2. Includes those who are delinquent to other financial institutions in addition to the credit card campanies.
Source: Korea Federation of Banks.

many other countries, thus providing some buffer against corrections in collateral values.

The rapid increase in the number of delinquent borrowers was largely due to the lack of risk management practices at the credit card companies and the sluggish economy (Shin, *et al.*, 2003). In contrast to the banks, the delinquency

Table 4.13. **Delinquency rates for household credits**

Per cent

	2000	2001	2002	2003			
	Dec.	Dec.	Dec.	Mar.	June	Sep.	Dec.
Banks[1]							
Household loans	2.5	1.3	1.5	2.1	2.0	2.3	1.8
In-house card operations	7.5	7.3	8.4	12.0	12.0	10.2	7.8
Credit card companies							
Delinquency rates	5.2	5.8	6.0	9.4	9.6	11.2	14.0
Rescheduled loans[2]	–	–	7.1	11.2	16.3	26.3	29.2

1. Includes all banks.
2. Rescheduled loans divided by total credits.
Source: Financial Supervisory Service.

ratio of the credit card companies has nearly tripled from 5 to 14 per cent since 2000. Moreover, it would be even higher if it were not for the marked increase in rescheduled loans, which rose from 7 to 29 per cent of the companies' total credits in one year.[14] The proportion of credit card companies in the total number of delinquent borrowers rose from 21 to 65 per cent between 2000 and early 2004 (Table 4.12), indicating that the delinquency problem is closely linked to credit cards.[15]

During the past several years, the credit card companies discounted the risks of increased lending and competed vigorously for market share to the extent that they issued cards without proper background credit checks of potential customers.

- The ease of obtaining credit cards made them available to some people with low incomes and savings, little access to bank loans and limited previous experience with financial transactions. Indeed, two-thirds of the new delinquent borrowers in 2002 were new customers during the preceding two years.

- Credit cards are widely available to young people. About 40 per cent of the new delinquent borrowers in 2002 were under the age of thirty.

- About two-thirds of credit card turnover consists of cash loans, with purchases of goods and services accounting for the remainder, a pattern that is the reverse of most other OECD countries. The delinquency rate on cash loans has been almost twice as high as that on sales credits.

- The ceiling on cash loans set by the credit card companies was 2.3 million won on average in April 2002 (more than triple the government-set ceiling that was abolished in 1999).

- The credit card companies require borrowers to settle their balance in full every month.

- The lack of an integrated credit information system allowed borrowers, who had five different cards on average, to revolve credit by shifting debts from one credit card company to another.

The household credit boom came to an end in the third quarter of 2002, and the sharp decline since then contributed to the fall in private consumption in 2003.[16] In addition to the rising delinquency ratio, there were other factors that ended the boom. *First*, the government tightened provisioning and other prudential regulations by the end of 2002, forcing the credit card companies to cut credit lines. This included changes in asset classification and minimum provisions.[17] *Second*, credit bureaus began accumulating information about the debts of consumers holding multiple credit cards, thus restricting the scope for borrowers to revolve credit between companies. These measures helped bring the latent delinquency problems to the surface, thus limiting the scope of the problem and improving the soundness of financial institutions.

• Impact on the financial institutions and the government's response

The government has introduced credit rehabilitation programmes, although there is a risk that they will aggravate the moral hazard of borrowers. *First*, individuals indebted to a single financial institution are to seek assistance through a programme offered by their creditors. *Second*, for individuals with multiple debts, financial institutions are encouraged to participate in a joint debt rescheduling or collection programme. Meanwhile, individual workout programmes have been implemented through the Credit Counselling and Recovery Service, a non-profit organisation. *Third*, delinquent borrowers with little likelihood of repayment will be subject to the Consumer Rehabilitation Law, a new legal framework enacted in 2004. Under this law, relief is to be provided to debtors with expected future income through court mediation without the debtor having to declare bankruptcy. *Fourth*, the government announced a plan in March 2004 to establish a bad bank for more efficient resolution of problem loans to the household sector. The bank will be a temporary paper company owned by financial institutions and the Korea Asset Management Corporation (KAMCO).

The impact of the deterioration in asset quality on the credit card sector depends on their ownership structure. Before the crisis, there were fourteen in-house credit card operations run by banks and nine non-bank credit card companies.[18] The major financing source for the banks' card operations is bank deposits, and the total credits extended, including sales credits, amounted to only 5 per cent of total bank loans. Thus, the impact on the banks from the deterioration in the asset quality of their in-house credit card operations is manageable. However, the situation is very different for non-bank credit card companies, whose main financing source is debt, such as bonds and commercial paper. The loss of confidence of their creditors and investors has made it difficult for them to survive the credit card bust.

The situation was further aggravated when the accounting scandal of SK Global in 2003 triggered a sharp drop of liquidity in the fixed-income market. The scandal caused problems for the investment trust companies (ITCs), which held SK Global paper as part of their investment portfolio. The ITCs attempted to meet their investors' demands for redemption by selling their holdings of credit card company bonds. However, the simultaneous fall in asset quality of these bonds made them illiquid, leaving the ITCs with liquidity problems.

The loss of market confidence in the credit card companies made it difficult for them to roll over their debt. The government intervened to assist the credit card companies by asking financial institutions to roll over the debt, notably the banks and the ITCs, which each held more than 25 trillion won of credits (4 per cent of GDP). However, given the weaknesses of the ITCs, they rolled over only half of their credit card company debentures maturing in the April to June quarter of 2003 – 10 trillion won in total – with the other 5 trillion borne by banks, securities firms and insurance companies. While this resolved the temporary liquidity problem, the credit card companies also promised to secure new capital through self-rescue efforts. However, the underlying problem proved to be far worse as the delinquency ratio rose to 14 per cent by the end of 2003 despite the rapid increase in rescheduled loans (Table 4.13).

In particular, the largest credit card company, LG Card, lost access to the capital market and stood on the brink of collapse by the end of 2003. Creditors balked at assuming control of the company, which was found to have liabilities exceeding its assets. The authorities were concerned about possible systemic risks from the failure of LG Card, which is the largest company in this sector, accounting for 40 per cent of assets, 41 per cent of credits, 21 per cent of turnover, and 26 per cent of cards issued as of September 2003. They argued that it could set off a wave of downgrading, triggering repayment clauses and possibly a liquidity crisis at the other credit card companies, causing turbulence in the bond market and perhaps jeopardising the still fragile economic recovery. Consequently, the government played a co-ordinating role in a plan to save LG Card, which required the support of sixteen creditor financial institutions, including ten banks and six insurance companies. Under this plan, the Korea Development Bank (KDB), a government-owned institution, took over the key role in restructuring the company.[19]

The authorities tried to minimise the moral hazard from the LG Card rescue plan by replacing the management, writing down the shareholders' equity and converting bank loans into equity. The penalty imposed on management failure makes this case different from past episodes of restructuring. As part of a debt-equity swap with creditors, the family ownership of LG agreed to give up its own equity, as well as that of the group, in LG Card, and to sell another non-bank financial company (LG Investment & Securities), with the proceeds to be injected into LG Card. The family ownership also agreed to provide 75 per cent of any additional liquidity needed for the restructuring of LG Card, by offering its equities in other affiliates of the group as collateral. Such an outcome between a creditor and the shareholder family may go beyond the provisions of the insolvency laws.

Investment trust companies

A well developed collective investment sector is crucial in providing long-term saving vehicles for expanding pension funds as households prepare for retirement. However, the experience of the investment trust sector in the late 1990s revealed that the system in Korea, which is based on investors acquiring fixed-income claims on the corporate sector, was basically unsound, as it was unable to withstand the collapse of Daewoo in 1999. Indeed, the fixed-income market has still not recovered fully from the shock. The ITCs remain vulnerable to liquidity pressures following the SK Global accounting scandal. Public awareness of the financial difficulties and the negative capital ratios of some large ITCs is increasing,[20] raising the risk of a loss of market confidence that would lead to contagion in other segments of the securities market, which remains generally weak.

The government has taken steps to restructure this sector. After injecting 2.2 trillion won in public funds, 80 per cent of the government's share in Hyundai ITC, the third largest, was sold to Prudential Financial in February 2004. As for the two largest, Korea (KITC) and Daehan (DITC), the government announced that they would be sold by the end of 2004 after the injection of additional public funds.[21]

The Korean financial market still tends to be limited to domestic operations, especially in the asset management sector. Few foreign securities are listed on the stock exchange and foreign ownership in the fixed-income market is only 0.6 per cent. As a further spur to the asset management sector, the government is planning to establish a Korean Investment Corporation (KIC).[22] This move may help create a regional financial hub by attracting asset management firms to the country. However, more important than direct business promotion is the establishment of conditions that will attract foreign asset management firms, in particular by bringing the regulatory framework into line with global standards.

The securities firms

The Korean securities industry is dominated by relatively small companies that are limited to a narrow range of operations and rely mainly on brokerage commissions.[23] The industry is under pressure from declining income due to strong competition in brokerage fees, and the capital levels of some companies are low. In most other financial markets, there have been structural changes to favour a small number of investment banks who put capital at risk in a number of operations and participate in innovative techniques. Korean institutions have been relatively slow to develop skills in these areas.

Recovering public funds used for financial restructuring

From 1997 to 2003, a total of 161 trillion won of public funds – 22 per cent of 2003 GDP – was spent to restructure the financial sector (Table 4.14). As the amount of public funds approved by the National Assembly has been virtually exhausted, any significant future injections will either require additional legislative approval or the use of funds recovered through the sales of non-performing loans (NPLs) and the proceeds from privatisation. Public funds totalling 63 trillion won were recovered by 2003, a 39 per cent recovery rate. However, it has been

Table 4.14. **The financial-sector restructuring programme**
November 1997 to December 2003 in trillion won
A. Outlays by type of financial institutions

	Equity participation	Capital contributions	Deposit payoffs	Asset acquisition	NPL purchases	Total
Banks	34.0	13.8	–	14.4	24.6	86.8
The non-bank sector	26.3	3.4	29.2	1.0	12.0	71.9
Merchant banks	2.7	0.2	17.2	–	1.5	21.7
Securities/investment trusts	7.7	–	–	–	8.5	16.2
Insurance	15.9	3.0	–	0.4	1.8	21.0
Credit unions	–	–	4.7	–	–	4.7
Saving banks	–	0.2	7.3	0.6	0.2	8.3
Foreign institutions	–	–	–	–	2.4	2.4
Total	**60.3**	**17.2**	**29.2**	**15.4**	**39.0**	**161.1**

B. Outlays by source of financing

	Equity participation	Capital contributions	Deposit payoffs	Asset acquisition	NPL purchases	Total
Bond issuance	42.2	15.2	20.0	4.2	20.5	102.1
Recovered funds	3.9	1.9	6.3	4.8	17.4	34.3
Public money	14.1	–	–	6.3	–	20.4
Others	0.1	0.1	2.9	0.1	1.1	4.3
Total	**60.3**	**17.2**	**29.2**	**15.4**	**39.0**	**161.1**

C. Recovery of expenditure

	KDIC	KAMCO	Government	Total
1998	–	2.4	–	2.4
1999	4.3	9.7	–	14.0
2000	6.1	8.9	–	15.0
2001	4.1	5.3	–	9.4
2002	2.6	3.8	6.6	13.0
2003	5.6	2.4	1.1	9.1
Total	**22.7**	**32.5**	**7.7**	**62.9**

Source: Public Funds Oversight Committee.

estimated that 69 trillion won in public funds is not recoverable, with the burden to be spread out over 25 years.[24]

Between the end of 1997 and November 2002, the Korea Asset Management Corporation (KAMCO) purchased NPLs with a face value of 110 trillion won for the price of 40 trillion won on behalf of the government. Thus far, KAMCO has recovered 33 trillion won through the sales of NPLs, with most of these funds recycled for further restructuring of the financial sector. KAMCO still holds almost 40 per cent of the NPLs that it purchased.[25] While KAMCO's role as a government agency responsible for resolving NPLs is over, it is focusing on restructuring its remaining assets with the aim of raising corporate value. KAMCO's use of new techniques to extract value from impaired credits, by using loan sales, securitisation and foreclosure, has advanced the development of domestic financial markets. As noted above, KAMCO will begin to play a role in the restructuring of household debt.[26]

The Korea Deposit Insurance Corporation (KDIC) has played a key role in re-capitalising financial institutions and in meeting the claims of depositors in failed institutions. KDIC still has 28 trillion won of equity participation in eleven financial institutions. With the reinstatement of the partial deposit insurance system in 2001, KDIC's role has broadened from deposit insurance provider to include expanded responsibilities in monitoring and safeguarding the financial stability of insured deposits and the Deposit Insurance Fund. To safeguard the Fund, it is considering the introduction of risk-based premiums. However, their adoption has been delayed for fear of a negative impact on weaker institutions.

Overall assessment and scope for further action

The financial health of the corporate sector has improved markedly since the crisis, while the legal framework for corporate governance and auditing has been upgraded. However, as the SK Global scandal demonstrated, there is still a lack of enforcement of the new framework and transparency is weak. To overcome these weaknesses, it is essential to stress the implementation of the corporate governance and auditing frameworks. For example, companies should be required to publicly disclose to what extent they adhere to best practices, as defined in the Code of Corporate Governance, so that investors can make informed decisions. The long-awaited introduction of class action suits in 2005 – a topic debated over the past five years – provides a key tool to help shareholders fight fraud. Its coverage should be extended beyond the 80 largest companies and its scope expanded beyond the issue of securities fraud to include the important areas of related party transactions and inter-company transfers. The increased power of shareholders, combined with stronger and more independent financial institutions, increased international competition and strengthened competition policy, are becoming increasingly effective in disciplining chaebol behaviour. As noted in Chapter 5, this allows the phasing out of the regulatory controls that have been used with mixed success in an effort to control the large business groups. Finally, there is a need for rationalisation of policies to assist small companies, whose relative position has strengthened significantly in recent years.

Economic growth will be determined to some extent by the return on Korea's large investment in knowledge. One objective should be to get the university system more involved in the R&D effort. This should be accompanied by more interaction and labour mobility between the three main sectors – government research institutes, business and academia. Deepening international linkages is another key to improving R&D. Another important goal is to incorporate the new ICT technology – an area where Korea is a leading producer – in ways that boost productivity. Finally, it is necessary to avoid the risks inherent in concentrating R&D efforts in the ten key sectors identified as future growth engines.

The improved financial health of the corporate sector has had a positive impact on the financial sector. However, there are other risks to this sector. In particular, it is important to ensure that the health of the commercial banks is not endangered by the adverse developments in the non-bank sector, which already caused a sharp dip in profits in 2003. Privatisation of the banks should be pursued continuously, in part to recover some of the funds used to restructure the financial sector. Moreover, a strong, privately-owned banking sector is essential to establish the autonomy of bank management and to advance corporate restructuring. Full divestiture would eliminate potential conflicts of interest arising from the government's role as both regulator and owner of banks. The privatisation process also offers an opportunity to further increase the foreign presence in the banking sector and strengthen competition. Foreign banks have a number of comparative advantages that can upgrade practices at domestic banks.

Considering the uncertainties about the strength of the economic recovery and the high unemployment rate for young adults, the delinquent borrower problem and financial distress in the credit card companies are unlikely to be resolved quickly. Nevertheless, addressing these issues should be a top policy priority, as they have important implications for the macroeconomic situation as well as the financial sector. All of the credit card companies should be required to secure sufficient equity to cushion themselves against continuing defaults, with those that fail to do so subject to prompt corrective action. They also need to develop their capacity to recover loans. Moreover, it is essential to improve credit risk management practices. Credit bureaus, or rating agencies, should provide complete information on borrowers' credit histories and obligations. Given the fact that one-sixth of the working-age population is classified as delinquent borrowers, it is essential to implement effective credit rehabilitation programmes. The recent improvement of the legal framework is an important step in this regard. However, success will depend on the attitude of creditors and debtors to the new regime, and whether they will use these programmes effectively to improve the financial health of delinquent borrowers.

The problems in the credit card sector underline the need for a more developed forward-looking regulatory scheme. The supervisory framework should emphasise a pre-emptive and risk-based prudential approach rather than focusing on compliance with rules. One new concern, for example, may be the exclusion of credit unions from the deposit protection system in 2004. It is important that the private insurance system that is established be monitored closely by the authorities. Moreover, the criteria for prompt corrective action measures should be re-examined and stiffened, thus reducing the need for *ex post* punitive measures and government bailouts.

The weakness of pre-emptive regulation leads to problems that prompt government intervention to maintain stability, thus weakening market discipline and creating moral hazard problems. The enormous size of the problems in the credit card sector makes it difficult for the government to adopt a hands-off approach, given the risk to financial stability and to economic growth. However, the government's efforts to resolve the LG Card problem could risk signalling to investors a return to the pre-crisis approach of "too big to fail". It should be clear that the bail-out of LG Card was an exceptional case. The treatment of the ITCs, which, in an effort to boost their profitability, bought high-yield, high-risk debt issued by the credit card companies, raises similar questions. The fact that unrelated banks and insurance companies had to bear the cost of this strategy weakens market discipline. Moreover, this reduced the pressure on credit card companies, who are the underlying cause of the problem, to take painful restructuring measures, thus slowing efforts to resolve the crisis. Finally, the moral hazard may extend to households, who feel less pressure to pay back their debts.

Improving the health of the ITCs should be a priority as part of developing the asset management sector. Increased participation by foreign institutional investors in Korea's securities market would greatly enhance its stability and development. The development of a strong group of institutional investors, which could play the role of strategic investor, would promote long-term savings, enhance productivity and innovation and emphasise trust and corporate governance.

Box 4.1. **Summary of recommendations in the corporate and financial sectors**

The corporate sector

- Ensure that class-action suits become an effective tool for minority share-holders to prevent abuses by management and controlling shareholders. Expand the scope of suits gradually to include more firms and perhaps more types of abuse, such as related party transactions and inter-company transfers.

- Further strengthen corporate governance, the financial sector and prudential supervision in order to discipline chaebol behavior.

- Ensure the full Implementation of the most recent changes to the corporate governance and auditing frameworks to improve transparency and prevent fraud.

- Improve the R&D framework by better utilising the universities and by enhancing the links between government research institutes, business R&D centres and the universities.

- Avoid undue emphasis on the ten industries identified as future growth engines, which could lead to distortions and high opportunity costs.

- Consolidate assistance to small and medium-sized enterprises.

The financial sector

- Continue the privatisation process of banks.

- Monitor the soundness of household loans and introduce steps to ensure that problems in the credit card sector do not spread to other sectors including banks.

- Restore the financial health of the credit card companies by requiring them to obtain new capital and strengthen risk management.

- Improve the health of the investment trust industry, in part through restructuring and privatising the largest two companies.

- The Financial Supervisory Commission should enforce the supervisory framework to promote the stability of the non-bank financial sector, especially in the non-bank lending institutions, and shift to a more pre-emptive and risk-based approach to deal with emerging risks.

- Strengthen market discipline and eliminate moral hazard problems, both for financial institutions and consumers.

Notes

1. The Korea Fair Trade Commission's policies to regulate the chaebol are discussed in Chapter 5.

2. Following a guilty verdict in June 2003, the accused appealed the case to a higher court.

3. Later examination by the FSS revealed that in 2001 window-dressing in the financial statement of SK Global amounted to 7.7 trillion won, which inflated its net equity and profit by 2.0 and 0.2 trillion won, respectively. The FSS also found another accounting fraud at SK Shipping.

4. Related auditing firms and CPAs, who had neglected their roles as external auditors, received heavy penalties. Meanwhile, nine banks and two securities firms were reprimanded for issuing fabricated loan documents, thus circumventing the external audit process.

5. This conclusion is consistent with that of the CLSA corporate governance indicator, which rates Korea at 7.0 for its rules and regulations and 3.5 for enforcement. Singapore, the highest ranking Asian country in the index, is rated at 8.5 and 7.5, respectively.

6. For the inverse – domestic ownership of inventions made abroad – Korea is the third lowest.

7. The domestic banks set aside 2.8 trillion won in provisions for loan losses due to SK Global and LG card, in addition to 8.2 trillion won for household loans, of which 5.3 trillion won was related to banks' in-house credit card business. Moreover, equity losses due to credit card subsidiaries amounted to 0.7 trillion won.

8. The IMF (2003) concluded that Korean banks are resilient to the direct impact of interest and exchange rate shocks, but that household debt and its implied feedback effects on non-performing loans and capital could be significant. In a stress test for household credit, a 50 basis-point increase in interest rates, combined with a 5.8 per cent decline in disposable income, was found to boost the default ratio to 8.9 per cent (from 1.2 per cent) and reduce the capital adequacy ratio by 1.5 percentage points. However, this would be an unprecedented shock; even in the wake of the crisis when output fell 7 per cent in 1998, household income rose by 6.5 per cent. The relatively large expected impact on banks is due to the higher credit risk of new lending and the way that most household loans are structured. Three-year bullet loans, with only interest due in the interim, are common, and this may lead to an understatement of problem loans. In March 2004, the newly established Korea Housing Finance Corporation launched a state-run mortgage system that will replace some of current short-term housing loans with long-term mortgage loans.

9. Despite the problems in the credit card sector, the substandard or below loan ratio for these companies has remained rather stable because the ratio does not reflect the sharp increase in rescheduled loans.

10. For consumers, 20 per cent of credit card purchases in excess of 10 per cent of gross income is deducted from taxable income, with the maximum deduction set at 5 million won. For merchants, 1 per cent of credit card sales is deducted as a tax credit from the value-added tax.

11. Purchases using debit cards are only 0.04 per cent as large as those using credit cards and the proportion of merchants who accept debit cards is less than 2 per cent. In order to promote their use, the tax advantages of debit cards were expanded from 20 to 25 per cent of card purchases, their scope was expanded to include check cards, and the lottery system was divided into different pools for credit and debit cards.

12. The threshold for delinquency is 300 thousand won (one-fifth of the average manufacturing wage) for three months. Credit information is collected by the Korea Federation of Banks and passed on to financial institutions. Information on delinquent borrowers is kept for a maximum of two years after repayment and can have a broad impact on the individual (*e.g.* their employment and financial transactions).

13. The Bank of Korea surveyed all new bank loans to households between January 2001 and March 2002 (350 thousand in all). House purchases accounted for about half, while only 2 to 3 per cent were used for consumption. The survey also found that banks' lending practices were not too risky; only 11 per cent of the borrowers were not home-owners, and 90 per cent of the loans were secured by collateral or guarantees.

14. Rescheduled loans are given to already delinquent borrowers, who repay 10 to 20 per cent of the previous loans when receiving them. Rescheduled loans are automatically classified as impaired assets, because without them, the borrowers would remain delinquent. Moreover, delinquency rates on such loans have been consistently high, at around 30 per cent.

15. Moreover, of the 1.08 million persons registered as delinquent during 2003, 0.9 million had unpaid debt to the credit card companies.

16. It is estimated that the contraction of the credit card sector since 2002 lowered private consumption growth by 1.2 to 2.5 percentage points and real GDP growth by 0.7 to 1.6 percentage points during the first three quarters of 2003 (Park, 2004).

17. The minimum provision ratios for banks' household loans were raised from 0.5 to 0.75 per cent for normal loans, 2 to 8 per cent for precautionary loans and from 50 to 55 per cent for doubtful loans. For credit card companies, the ratios were raised from 0.5 to 1 per cent, 2 to 12 per cent and 50 to 60 per cent, respectively. The ratios for the substandard and estimated loss categories remained at 20 and 100 per cent, respectively, for banks' household loans and credit card companies. In July 2002, the authorities limited cash loans to a maximum of 50 per cent of total turnover, and required that past loans exceeding that amount be repaid by the end of 2004. However, declining sales credit and increasing rescheduled loans forced the deadline to be extended twice – to the end of 2007.

18. The primary owners of these nine companies were banks (five) and chaebol (four).

19. The key points of the agreement are as follows. *First*, creditors will swap 3.65 trillion won of loans into equity. The creditors provided 2 trillion won of this amount in 2003. KDB would become the largest shareholder of LG Card once the proposed restructuring plan is implemented. *Second*, the proceeds from selling the family and group ownership in LG Investment & Securities (21.2 per cent), which is expected to total 350 billion

won, will be injected in LG Card. Third, LG Group will inject an extra 800 billion won, with 500 billion won converted into preferred shares. Fourth, the funding requirement in excess of the bailout plan – up to 500 billion won – will be shared by the LG Group and creditors at a ratio of 75 to 25. In the event, the family ownership was burdened with 220 billion won (out of a possible 375 billion won) in excess funding requirements. Two of the creditor banks, Korea Exchange Bank and KorAm Bank, later withdrew from this agreement.

20. Partly as a result of concerns about the soundness of the asset management industry, investors prefer to establish their own funds and roll over investment annually. Consequently, there were 5 625 funds at the end of 2002, a number that makes it hard to benefit from economies of scale. According to the Investment Company Institute in the United States, the total asset size of funds in Korea was 15th out of 35 countries, while the average asset size per fund was 31st.

21. Despite the injection of 7.7 trillion won in public funds after the Daewoo crisis in 1999, KITC and DITC have suffered from financial difficulties. By June 2003, their net equity capital declined to negative 800 billion won and 300 billion won, respectively.

22. The KIC will be launched in 2005 with an initial $20 billion transferred from the Bank of Korea. The KIC will be guaranteed independence and commercial orientation, and management will be outsourced to reputable asset management firms regardless of nationality.

23. In 2002, 87 per cent of operating income in the securities companies came from brokerage of securities and funds. Meanwhile, in the United States, 47 per cent of operating income came from investment banking services, with brokerage accounting for only 17 per cent.

24. This indicates an ultimate recovery ratio of 56 per cent. As for the 69 trillion won that is not recoverable, 20 trillion won will be shouldered by financial institutions, on the grounds that they have benefited from public fund injections to stabilise the financial sector. This amount will be raised by imposing a special deposit insurance fee set at 0.1 per cent of deposits. The remaining 49 trillion won will be covered by the government budget, costing an annual average of approximately 2 trillion won based on the present value.

25. The recovery ratio as of January 2004 was 116 per cent, which means that KAMCO's operations have been successful in selling NPLs for more than their purchase price. However, the ratio is expected to decline due to the lower quality of the remaining NPLs.

26. As of January 2004, KAMCO had purchased household NPLs, with a face value of 7 trillion won, from 1 million delinquent borrowers. Moreover, KAMCO is expected to be responsible for the asset management of the newly established bad bank.

5. Product market competition and economic performance

The OECD *Growth Study* and other empirical work demonstrate that competition in product markets plays a significant role in the process of economic growth. Korea has succeeded in transforming itself from one of the poorest countries in the world in the 1960s to an important industrial nation over the period of one generation (Figure 1.1). This has been accomplished despite government measures over the past forty years to accelerate growth, focusing on export-oriented manufacturing industries in which scale economies are important, which tended to weaken competition to some extent. The outstanding economic performance suggests that there may have been some positive results from these policies, perhaps because they enabled Korea to overcome various negative externalities prevalent at an early stage of development. However, they have also left a negative legacy that includes distortions in resource allocation, high concentration in product markets, barriers to entry and exit, an important role for trade associations, government ownership, and the formation of business conglomerates, called chaebol. Moreover, the development strategy resulted in a dualistic economy, divided between highly competitive, export-oriented manufacturing and a much less dynamic, domestic demand-oriented sector. As noted in Chapter 1, the productivity gap between the manufacturing and service sectors in Korea is the largest in the OECD area. These various negative factors may prove detrimental to Korea's growth prospects, which are likely to be increasingly linked to a knowledge-based economy.

Korea's labour productivity (per hour worked) was about half of the OECD average in 2002, suggesting considerable scope for further convergence. As noted in Chapter 1, inputs of labour and capital have played a key role in its economic development, while total factor productivity has accounted for less than one-third of growth (Table 1.2). However, slowing inputs of labour and capital during the coming decade, reflecting declining working hours and the falling trend of business investment, may significantly reduce the growth potential. According to one study, the contribution to growth from labour and capital inputs will fall by half from 4½ percentage points a year in the 1990s to 2¼ in the coming decade (Han *et al.*, 2002). Economic growth will thus depend increasingly on total factor productivity gains. Structural reforms, including measures to strengthen product market competition, are essential to realising such gains and sustaining Korea's growth potential. This is particularly true in the service sector, where competition is relatively weak at present and productivity is low, due in part to the fact that it is less exposed to international competition. The authorities have introduced measures aimed at strengthening market forces, although the legacy of past policies is difficult to dismantle and progress has been uneven.

This chapter begins by presenting some indicators to gauge the strength of competitive pressures, as well as the implications of barriers to trade and foreign direct investment. This is followed by an overall assessment of the competition policy framework and its role in promoting competition. The chapter then analyses a number of sectors where policies to strengthen competition can be expected to have particularly large benefits. The chapter concludes with a set of policy recommendations.

Indicators of competition

Although measuring the extent of competition is not straightforward, it is useful to examine available indicators that may convey some information on the strength of competitive forces. Available indicators include concentration ratios, price mark-ups and barriers to trade and investment. While these indicators suggest that competition has strengthened gradually over the past twenty years, the degree of competition may still be weak relative to other countries.

The concentration ratios show several interesting trends (Table 5.1). *First*, ratios at the industry level (Panel A) and the market level (Panel B) have been declining since the 1980s, suggesting that the economy is moving toward a more competitive structure.[1] However, the downward trend was temporarily reversed in the wake of the 1997 crisis, reflecting the exit of non-viable companies or their merger with stronger firms.[2] *Second*, the general concentration ratio (Panel C), measured as the shares of the largest 50 and 100 firms in terms of turnover and employment, has also fallen significantly since the crisis. *Third*, concentration diminishes as market size increases (Panel D). However, for markets larger than 1 trillion won, concentration goes up instead, reflecting the importance of economies of scale in leading industries, such as semiconductors and cars, and the fact that the high level of initial investment required acts as an entry barrier.[3] However, these highly concentrated industries are part of a larger competitive global market.

International comparisons of concentration show that the average share of the three largest firms in Korea is comparable to those in Japan and the United States (Table 5.1, Panel E). However, compared to the latter two countries, the HHI shows a significantly higher degree of concentration in Korea.[4] The HHI in "segmented" industries, which are characterised by large firms and significant entry barriers, is particularly high in Korea (Table 5.2).

Table 5.1. **Concentration ratios**

A. Industry concentration ratios

	1980	1990	1997	1998	1999	2000	2001
Share of top 3 firms (per cent)							
Simple average	62.4	52.8	48.6	50.0	45.4	44.0	43.4
Weighted average	55.1	52.6	51.7	53.6	54.2	52.5	51.5
HHI × 1 000[1]							
Simple average	263.8	221.3	179.4	190.5	158.6	152.5	153.1
Weighted average	180.6	187.8	177.8	188.0	194.5	183.5	182.1

B. Market concentration ratios

	1980	1990	1997	1998	1999	2000	2001
Share of top 3 firms (per cent)							
Simple average	81.7	73.9	73.1	73.0	72.5	69.9	68.0
Weighted average	67.1	62.6	65.4	67.3	67.1	65.6	64.0
HHI × 1 000[1]							
Simple average	473	393	388	388	389	357	331
Weighted average	288	262	283	289	295	285	267

C. General concentration ratios (per cent)

	1980	1990	1997	1998	1999	2000	2001
Turnover:							
50 largest enterprises	30.0	30.0	37.1	38.4	38.0	38.1	36.8
100 largest enterprises	39.0	37.3	44.2	45.9	45.1	44.8	43.7
Employment:							
50 largest enterprises	13.3	13.6	16.5	16.6	14.7	13.9	13.2
100 largest enterprises	18.6	18.4	20.1	20.1	18.1	17.0	16.0

D. Industry concentration ratio by market size

Size (billion won)	Less than 1	1-10	10-50	50-100	100-500	500-1 000	1 000-5 000	Higher than 5 000
Number of Industries	2	18	42	34	179	92	96	21
Total turnover (billion won)	10	926	11 354	26 021	470 057	646 040	2 055 946	2 640 110
Share of top 3 firms (per cent)	100	80	52	49	37	37	39	68
HHI × 1 000[1]	674	483	182	155	121	105	127	255

E. International Comparisons

Market Concentration	Japan (2000)	Korea (2001)
Top 3 firms (per cent, simple average)	72.0	68.0
HHI × 1 000 (simple average)	269.3	331.0

Industry concentration	US (1997)	Korea (2001)
Top 4 firms (per cent, simple average)	42.8	48.6
HHI × 1 000 (simple average)	75.8	149.3

1. The Hirschman-Herfindahl Index combines elements of both firm numbers and inequality. For an industry with N firms, it can be defined as:

$$HHI = \sum_{i=1}^{N}\left[\frac{X_i}{\sum_i X_i}\right]^2$$

where i indexes firms 1, 2,..., N and Xis an appropriate measure of firm size (*e.g.* gross output). When an industry is occupied by only one firm (a pure monopolist), the index attains its maximum value of 1 (1 000 in this table since the index is multiplied by 1 000).

Source: Korea Fair Trade Commission and Korea Development Institute.

Table 5.2.   **International comparison of concentration ratios**[1]
Based on establishment data[2]

	Korea	Japan	United States
	1997	1999	1997
MANUFACTURING			
Fragmented, low R&D			
Food products	18.8	1.5	3.3
Textiles	12.0	3.3	6.5
Wearing apparel	73.0	4.0	8.6
Leather products	86.2	45.6	65.1
Footwear	72.2	32.1	n.a.
Wood products	109.2	5.0	3.7
Paper and pulp products	76.1	23.0	14.4
Publishing and printing	60.9	17.9	3.0
Plastic products	50.7	6.8	5.0
Non-metallic products	29.3	8.8	6.6
Fabricated metal products	232.7	9.9	1.6
Furniture	70.6	13.2	7.6
Unweighted average	74.3	14.3	11.4
Segmented, low R&D			
Beverages	177.8	39.8	191.5
Tobacco products	1 225.5	386.4	n.a.
Refined petroleum products	1 988.9	236.9	n.a.
Rubber products	490.3	75.3	n.a.
Glass products	377.3	105.2	n.a.
Basic metals	195.5	46.4	29.0
Iron and steel	344.5	71.8	n.a.
Non-ferrous metals	293.0	64.9	n.a.
Shipbuilding and repairs	1 096.9	178.4	n.a.
Unweighted average	687.7	133.9	110.3
Fragmented, high R&D			
Machinery and equipment	42.5	7.5	7.5
Medical appliances	112.4	47.7	n.a.
Other manufacturing	45.7	34.2	11.1
Unweighted average	66.9	29.8	9.3
Segmented, high R&D			
Coke and petroleum products	1 919.1	220.1	76.4
Chemicals products	54.3	14.9	14.4
Drugs and medicines	91.8	50.9	n.a.
Office and computing machinery	1 301.8	84.2	17.9
Electrical machinery	51.6	21.6	13.9
Radio, TV and communication equipment	144.6	18.6	n.a.
Optical and photographic equipment	1 919.5	137.9	n.a.
Watches and clocks	762.9	1 173.9	n.a.
Motor vehicles	226.7	49.4	23.9
Other transport equipment	585.3	109.2	n.a.
Railroad equipment	3 305.3	805.0	n.a.
Aircraft	2 675.8	593.1	n.a.
Unweighted average	1 086.6	273.2	12.2

1.   The Hirschman-Herfindahl Index * 10 000.
2.   No data is available for Korea for the non-manufacturing sector.
Source: OECD.

Industries with high market concentration ratios show significantly higher price mark-ups according to one study (Jeong *et al.*, 2002). Moreover, the relationship becomes more powerful as firms' export ratio (export/shipment) increases, which may indicate that exporting companies have a relatively high degree of dominance in domestic markets. As for R&D expenditures, there is a weak positive correlation with industry concentration ratios. However, in monopolistic market structures, R&D expenditures fell. This suggests that, beyond a certain point, market power tends to reduce incentives to adopt and develop new technology, thus discouraging dynamic efficiency gains.

Import penetration has risen from around 10 per cent at the beginning of the 1990s to 17 per cent a decade later (Figure 5.1). The rate in Korea is in line with those in other OECD countries after controlling for country size, per capita income and transportation costs (Panel B). However, a breakdown by type of manufacturing industry reveals a particularly low import penetration rate for segmented industries with high R&D intensities (Table 5.3). This may reflect the fact that this category includes many of Korea's leading industries, such as cars and communication equipment, where it has a strong comparative advantage. However, industries which have few domestic competitors and low imports, such as petrochemicals, oil refineries and cement, are more problematic from the perspective of competition.

Explicit *trade barriers* in terms of tariff rates are higher than in other OECD countries due primarily to the protection granted to the agricultural sector. The average tariff rate in 2001 was 8 per cent, compared to around 3 per cent in the United States, the European Union and Japan (Table 5.4). However, the average rate for non-agricultural products in Korea was 4½ per cent, much closer to the rates in major OECD countries. The proportion of imports affected by non-tariff measures (defined as quantitative controls, finance measures and price control measures) is low at 2.4 per cent compared to more than 5 per cent in Korea's major trading partners (Panel B). However, imports are hindered by regulatory and administrative procedures in some areas, especially sanitation and safety, which are not consistent with international standards. For example, the Korean list of permitted food additives differs from the one agreed to within the FAO/WHO Expert Committee, and there are differences in cosmetic standards.

As noted above, the level of protection is much higher for agriculture. The overall level of support for farmers, as measured by the Producer Support Estimate, remains one of the highest in the OECD area and double the OECD average (Figure 5.2). The net effect is to boost farm income by nearly three times (Panel B). Over 90 per cent of this assistance is provided through market price supports, which distort trade and production, compared to an average of 66 per cent in the OECD area. For example, quotas remain in place for 190 agricultural products, and for 114 of these products, domestic producer cooperatives have exclusive rights to

Figure 5.1. **Indicators of market openness**

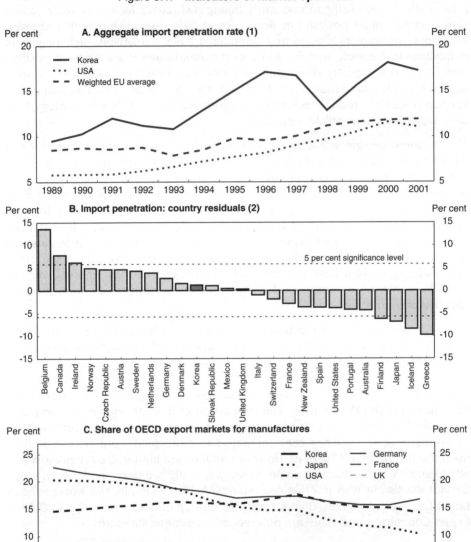

1. Manufacturing imports relative to manufacturing imports plus GDP, excluding intra-EU trade.
2. Average residuals for the period 1995 to 2000 after controlling for effects of country size, GDP per capita and transportation costs.
Source: OECD, Monthly Trade Statistics and OECD calculations.

Table 5.3.   **International comparison of import penetration**
by type of manufacturing industry[1]

	High R&D		Low R&D	
	Segmented	Fragmented	Segmented	Fragmented
Austria	51.9	42.6	27.9	29.5
Belgium	54.7	63.9	26.6	37.1
Czech Republic	43.3	41.3	25.8	25.7
Denmark	55.2	34.3	30.7	35.5
Finland	38.4	26.5	18.7	10.8
France	31.1	32.0	18.6	20.6
Germany	28.8	22.2	20.3	21.7
Italy	35.0	19.8	19.3	12.3
Netherlands	–	39.4	27.9	33.3
Spain	39.7	36.8	17.5	15.3
Sweden	34.9	30.0	25.2	17.8
United Kingdom	39.3	32.4	21.7	23.2
United States	26.4	22.7	10.2	14.4
Canada	44.2	55.9	21.0	22.9
Japan	8.0	7.2	8.4	8.7
Korea	**20.0**	**38.5**	**14.4**	**13.7**
Mexico	34.0	51.9	19.2	24.6
European average	39.9	34.1	22.3	22.9
OECD average	36.6	35.1	20.8	21.6

1. Segmented market structures are characterised by large firms and significant entry barriers associated with high
    costs, while fragmented market structures are characterised by small firms and low sunk costs and entry barriers.
Source: See Oliveira Martins, J., T. Price and N. Mulder (2003) "A taxonomy of market structure cluster", OECD Economics
Department, mimeo.

import or distribute import quantities within the quota limit, thus further limiting
benefits from competition. The total support provided to farmers by Korean consumers and taxpayers amounted to 3½ per cent of GDP in 2003, according to the
OECD. In addition to this direct cost, the high protection of agriculture is a major
obstacle to the success of multilateral trade negotiations, as well as Korea's participation in regional free trade agreements, which would allow it to benefit more
fully from the economic dynamism of Asia.[5]

  Foreign direct investment (FDI) inflows had played a minor role in Korea prior
to the crisis in 1997, reflecting a generally hostile attitude toward foreign investors
and legal restrictions such as ownership and screening requirements, which were
relatively restrictive compared to other OECD countries (Figure 5.3). However,
since 1998, the authorities have adopted sweeping measures to promote FDI,
beginning with the Foreign Investment Promotion Act in 1998, which focused on
creating an investor-friendly environment. At present, 99.8 per cent of all business
lines (out of a total of more than 1 100) are open to foreign investment, a level on a

Table 5.4. **International comparison of trade protection**

A. Tariff rates in 2001 (per cent)

	Simple average			Weighted average[1]		
	Total	Agriculture	Manufacturing	Total	Agriculture	Manufacturing
Korea	**12.7**	**44.2**	**7.3**	**7.9**	**64.1**	**4.5**
United States	5.4	9.7	4.4	3.1	2.7	3.1
European Union	4.8	9.4	3.9	3.1	6.0	2.9
Japan	5.0	10.5	3.6	2.5	7.1	1.7

B. Coverage of non-tariff measures[2]

	Japan	Korea	United States	European Union
Primary products	7.49	9.29	4.69	1.98
Agricultural products	7.69	10.76	4.56	2.30
Mining products	6.31	0.60	5.44	0.47
Manufactures	5.08	0.37	5.23	10.77
Iron and steel	0.48	0.00	42.44	51.94
Chemicals	1.15	1.25	3.35	4.18
Other semi-manufactures	0.64	0.16	4.59	0.86
Machinery and transport equipment	0.05	0.00	5.18	2.41
Textiles and clothing	23.06	0.38	1.13	87.21
Other consumer goods	0.68	0.00	0.92	4.82
Other products	0.00	0.00	0.00	0.00
All products	5.61	2.37	5.08	5.79

1. Weighted by imports.
2. Coverage as a per cent of total imports in latest year available.
Source: World Trade Organisation for Panel A. UNCTAD for Panel B.

par with that of other OECD economies.[6] The amendment to the Foreigner's Land Acquisition Act in 1998 removed restrictions on foreign ownership of real estate. Perhaps even more importantly, the negative attitudes toward direct investment have been largely changed, as reflected in the creation of Invest Korea[7] and the Office of the Investment Ombudsman to provide "one stop" service for potential investors and assistance after investment.

The reforms to attract FDI and the restructuring of the corporate and financial sectors in the wake of the crisis, which caused a surge of cross-border M&As, resulted in a sharp rise in FDI inflows (Figure 5.4). Indeed, the $35 billion in actual inflows between 1998 and 2002 was more than double the amount received during the previous 35 years. This surge boosted the stock of FDI in Korea from 2 to 9 per cent of GDP. Nevertheless, Korea still ranks among the lowest of the OECD economies in this regard. Moreover, since 2001, the annual inflow of FDI has fallen below $5 billion on an arrival basis, less than half of the amount in 1999 and 2000. The decline may be attributed to internal as well as external factors, such as the

Figure 5.2. **An international comparison of agricultural support**

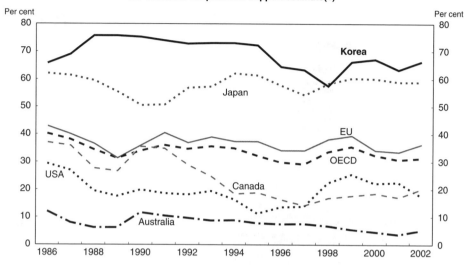

A. **Trends in the producer support estimate(1)**

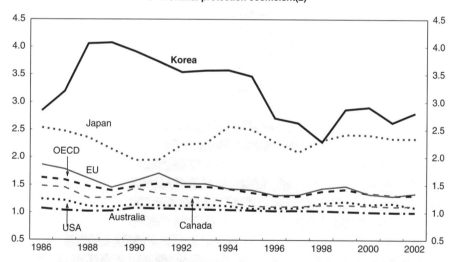

B. **Nominal protection coefficient(2)**

1. An indicator of the value of monetary transfers to agriculture resulting from agricultural policies. It is presented as a share of the total value of production at domestic producer prices.
2. The NPC is a measure of market protection defined as the ratio between the average prices received by producers and border prices.
Source: OECD, *Agricultural Policies in OECD Countries.*

Figure 5.3. **Foreign direct investment restrictions,**[1] **1998**
By type

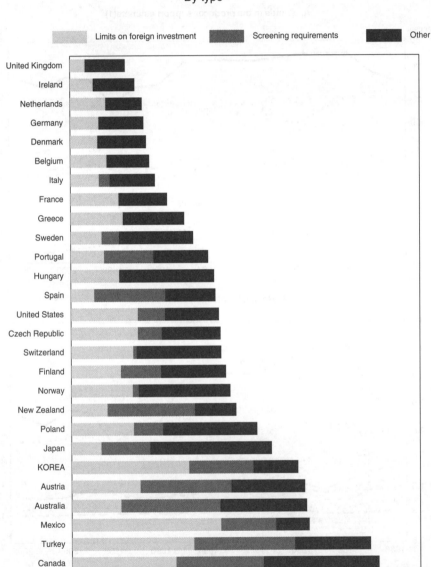

1. The indicator ranges from 0 (least restrictive) to 1 (most restrictive).
Source: OECD.

general slowdown in the world economy and in global FDI flows since 2001. Other external factors include economic weakness in Japan, the largest foreign investor in Korea, the North Korean nuclear issue and the attractiveness of China as an investment site. The major internal factor has been labour problems (see Chapter 3), though it may also suggest that the liberalisation and promotional efforts by the Korean government have reached a threshold. The authorities have taken additional steps, notably by designating Incheon, Busan, and Gwangyang as "Free Economic Zones" (FEZs) in 2003. These zones, which offer a variety of advantages, are intended to make Korea an economic hub for Northeast Asia.

In summary, these indicators of concentration, import penetration and inflows of FDI suggest that competition has strengthened in recent years, particularly since the crisis. Nevertheless, the level of competition indicated by concentration and FDI inflows appears to be somewhat weak compared to other OECD countries.

Enforcement of competition law

The role of the competition enforcement body in Korea is unusually broad. Application of the 1990 Monopoly Regulation and Fair Trade Act (MRFTA) by the independent Korea Fair Trade Commission (KFTC) concentrates on horizontal constraints and unfair practices. The KFTC also applies laws to protect small businesses and consumer rights, and it is heavily involved in direct regulation of the structure, governance and operations of the chaebol. The KFTC systematically monitors industry structure in manufacturing, but most of the targets of its priority-setting "Clean Market Project" have been in services. In the last three years, these targets have included telecoms and broadband internet service, medical services and pharmaceuticals, wedding and funeral services, construction materials, apartment and office rents, media, school uniforms, private instructional institutions, liquid natural gas, credit cards and insurance, internet shopping, real estate agents and services, home maintenance services, job referral, electric power, instalment finance and banking, advertising, and professional certification. The sectors were chosen for monitoring by the competition authority because they have a direct and visible impact on consumers and because many have been significantly deregulated in recent years. The KFTC emphasises a law-enforcement approach along with its important advocacy and reform roles, and it is perceived as an aggressive prosecutor. Recent amendments to the law strengthen its enforcement tools.

In competition law enforcement, the KFTC pays most attention to horizontal collusion. The KFTC has tried to establish a *per se* rule against price fixing. The legal foundation for that approach, which treats such agreements as illegal in themselves without the need to show their effects in the particular case, is still uncertain in Korea. Nonetheless, the KFTC has scored several successes in price

Figure 5.4. **FDI inflows in Korea**

A. Annual inflows in US$ billions

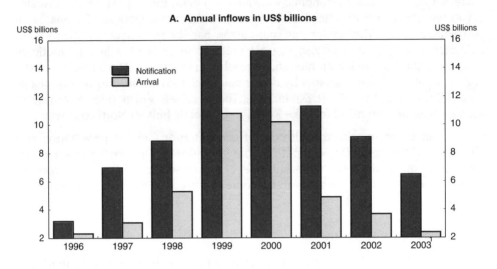

B. Stock as a share of GDP in 2000

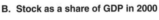

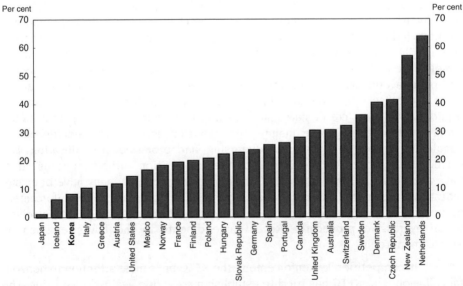

1. Amount arrived through September 2003.
Source: Ministry of Commerce, Industry and Energy for Panel A. OECD for Panel B.

fixing and boycott cases. In two investigations in 2003, Korea's major cement firms and their trade association were fined 26 billion won ($22 million) and manufacturers of iron bar were fined 79 billion won ($69 million), and several of the parties were also referred for criminal prosecution.

Enforcement and sanctions

The basis for computing administrative fines, or "surcharges", was expanded in 1999. That change, combined with stepped up enforcement, greatly increased the sanctions actually imposed against competition violations. Fines against cartels in 2003 totalled 108 billion won ($93 million) and the total against competition violations over the period 1998 to 2003 – about 455 billion won ($393 million) – greatly exceeds the 234 billion won over the previous decade. Yet provisions for financial sanctions are still less stringent than in most other member countries. The ceiling on the administrative fine is 5 per cent of turnover related to the violation (or 1 billion won), and the level actually imposed is typically about 2.5 to 3.5 per cent. The KFTC has asked the National Assembly to double the ceiling for fines, which would make the multiplier comparable to that used in most of Europe (10 per cent). However, that level could still be effectively lower than it is in countries where sanctions are based on total firm turnover, not just the turnover related to the violation. Individual executives may also face criminal punishment in Korea. There have been a few prosecutions, but no one has actually gone to jail because sentences have typically been suspended. That may change, though. A trial court recently sentenced several defendants to up to a year in prison and the case is on appeal to the Supreme Court. Making the threat of individual sanctions credible will make it a more effective deterrent.

The KFTC has a leniency programme, which has produced enforcement results in about a half dozen cases. In addition to the prospect of a lower penalty, the KFTC programme offers a positive inducement to encourage individuals to come forward: a whistleblower may be awarded a substantial bounty of up to 100 million won ($86 000). A reduction of criminal penalty may also be an incentive for participants in the corporate leniency programme. Nonetheless, the KFTC's investigative powers should be increased. Although stronger sanctions now apply to non-compliance with orders and investigations, information gathering powers remain designed for voluntary investigations. For example, the KFTC cannot search premises and take possession of evidence. Administrative law enforcement bodies that deal with labour, tariff, environment, and tax compliance have such powers, as does the prosecutor. To make the KFTC's administrative enforcement more effective and obviate the need to resort to criminal processes for inappropriate reasons, the KFTC needs such compulsory investigative powers. To supplement public enforcement, the right to bring a private lawsuit independently is being expanded. Private suits would no longer have to wait for the KFTC to decide first. The KFTC has also considered "public interest" suits to deal with damages to groups of individuals.

Market dominance and merger policies

In dealing with dominant firms and mergers, the KFTC focuses principally on structure, while showing increasing sensitivity to economic analysis of particular market situations. In characterising dominance, it uses three-firm concentration as its basic market structure test, while acknowledging that high concentration (by its measure, over 75 per cent) can be consistent with strong competition if the three large firms are all healthy. By defining dominance at a higher level of concentration than in many other member countries, the KFTC in effect permits more latitude to large-firm market conduct. The KFTC no longer maintains a listing of dominant firms subject to particular scrutiny. Claims about predatory low pricing are subjected to the sceptical "recoupment" test, that the predator be able to recover its losses by raising prices free from the challenge of competitive re-entry. The relatively permissive conception of dominance also means that merger control is more likely to permit large combinations. The structural test in the merger guidelines is slightly different, setting a basic threshold at a three-firm concentration of 75 per cent, but permitting some exceptions (based upon factors such as rank or relative market shares). Often large mergers may be efficient, especially if markets are international in scope. When the tests have been relaxed, such as when the KFTC approved restructuring transactions following the financial crisis (the so-called Big Deals), the KFTC has imposed behavioural restraints to deal with risks of market power. Recent merger decisions show reliance on structural as well as behavioural remedies. Modifications in the merger review system are planned, to expand the scope of required pre-notification and provide more time for investigation, while eliminating the notification requirement for small acquisitions. In 2003, rules were issued about the notification of foreign acquisitions with limited effect in Korea. These changes would bring Korea's system more closely into line with merger review systems in most other member countries. Some in the business community have unsuccessfully urged even more radical changes to the law, on the same grounds that they would bring Korea's law into line with the laws of other countries, namely eliminating its concern over aggregate concentration and its restrictions on the structure and conduct of the chaebol conglomerates.

Policy toward the chaebol[8]

Regulating the chaebol is a significant KFTC function. The KFTC designates the firms that are subject to special regulation because of their size, enforces rules governing the structure of holding companies, limits total shareholdings outside a designated group and cross-holdings within it, limits loan guarantees within a group, restricts how financial affiliates in a group can vote shares, and polices "undue" transactions within a group. The KFTC considers these functions to be as important as competition law enforcement, and the KFTC is just as stern in enforcing these rules, periodically announcing enforcement campaigns to check for undue transactions and other violations. Since 1998, nearly half of the financial sanctions imposed (341 billion won out of a total of 752 billion won) were against violations of the chaebol rules. The KFTC refined its approach in 2002, in part because reforms since 1997 have changed chaebol structure and conduct. Rather than list the top 30 groups in total assets and apply uniform controls to all of them, the KFTC now differentiates them according to their total assets. In the 2003 designation, there are 17 "type A" chaebol that are subject to a ceiling on total shareholding of other domestic companies (a limit that can be lifted if the group corrects its excessive debt-equity ratio), and 49 "type B" chaebol that are subject to controls on cross-shareholdings and debt guarantees; all of the "type A" groups are also "type B." The KFTC plans to ask the National Assembly to delete provisions about the debt-equity ratio, which exempt some chaebol from the ceiling on shareholding, and to extend the KFTC's powers to demand financial information from financial institutions concerning their customers' "undue" transactions.

The investigation of "undue" intra-group transactions is the chaebol regulation that is most closely related to conventional conceptions of competition law. Subsidies in the form of transactions within a group on more favourable terms are conceived to present competition problems analogous to state aid subsidies. For example, the KFTC contends that if a firm should be liquidated according to market standards, but an affiliated firm props it up, the result is anti-competitive because entrenching inefficient large firms bars entry of potentially more competitive small ones. The analogy to anti-competitive state aid was more apt when it appeared that the chaebol, or some of them, would be treated as too big to fail. In the absence of implied government support for the supposed subsidies, there should be a stronger presumption that transactions will be subject to the discipline of market forces, even within a group – although controlling shareholders may nonetheless try to escape that discipline. KFTC monitoring in the absence of any such implicit guarantee is reminiscent of older styles of regulatory intervention, such as control over firms' investment decisions and adherence to consensus price levels. Suspicious intra-group transactions may involve unfairness or something like predation, but more often the real problem is misappropriation, breach of fiduciary duty, or embezzlement. KFTC enforcement actions against clearly identifiable threats to market competition are of course necessary, but actions may fail where they aim at corporate misconduct that is not actually anticompetitive. Meanwhile, the new laws and institutions for dealing with corporate misconduct could remain underdeveloped as long as the KFTC is occupying the field.

The KFTC contends that the other aspects of its unusual enforcement agenda are consistent with reliance on markets for growth and efficiency, because transparent structures and fair competition support confidence in market transactions, thus encouraging the flow of resources into productive uses. That general "dynamic efficiency" motivation is undermined by some of the rules' constraining effects. For example, concerns have been expressed that the ceiling on chaebol shareholdings may make it more difficult to set up large-scale projects that require teaming substantial Korean firms as strategic investors with substantial foreign investors; however, the KFTC has not found any instances of projects that could not be done for this reason. The KFTC also defends its continued attention to corporate governance and investment matters on the grounds that corporate, financial, and securities laws and regulatory institutions are not yet established well enough to do the job adequately. Meanwhile, it is relaxing the requirements for forming holding companies, a structure that would increase transparency. Although holding companies were first allowed in 1998, the conditions attached have meant that only a handful have been created thus far. In addition, the KFTC has proposed a "Three-Year Market Reform Roadmap" that would offer chaebol incentives to improve their corporate governance practices and ownership structure. This proposal, which is under consideration by the National Assembly, would set specific criteria that would allow companies to graduate from the regulations on equity investment. At the same time, the KFTC intends to provide more information on corporate governance and ownership structure to investors and stakeholders.

Opaque corporate structures needed to be cleared up, because they allowed financial leverage at a scale that undermined stability. To do that task, the KFTC was more independent and effective than the existing financial regulators, although they failed to prevent the problems that led to the 1997 crisis. But there have been numerous reforms to improve corporate governance, financial soundness, and transparency since 1997. Other enforcement agencies, notably the Financial Supervisory Commission and the Financial Supervisory Service, which were created in 1998, are in place to deal with problems related to corporate financing. Supervisory functions related to internal cross-holdings and guarantees and intra-group transactions that amount to misuse of corporate assets should be concentrated in regulators responsible for financial and securities matters. Transactions that have an exclusionary or distorting effect on product market competition in particular cases should still be subject to competition-law control.

Exemptions from the competition law

The scope of exemptions from competition law is now limited. Government entities are subject to the same rules as private enterprises. Equal treatment applies to chaebol regulation too, as large government entities are now designated as groups whose transactions are regulated, and the KFTC has fined several of them for undue transactions and abuse in relationships with contractors.

Claims that anti-competitive conduct is authorised by official action are treated sceptically. The KFTC has intervened against several cartels whose members claimed they had acted pursuant to administrative guidance. But some sectors are still protected or controlled to some extent. Notably, liner shipping conferences are exempted by special legislation on the grounds that they are "internationally recognised" cartels. Many exemptions were eliminated by the Omnibus Cartel Repeal Act of 1999, which eliminated statutory authority for 17 cartels, thus prohibiting fee-setting arrangements for a number of professional services. However, some of the changes were delayed (see below).

Several programmes to favour small and medium-sized enterprises (SMEs) appear to distort competition. The most significant of these – preventing entry by larger firms in as many as 88 business lines – is to end in 2004. The most pervasive programme, permitting wide-ranging cooperatives, is subject to a competition test, but these groups should be watched carefully, as their self-regulatory codes of unfair practices could impair competition. The government planned to cut back a system of small-business "cartels" in government procurement, reducing them to 154 items in 2000 and intending to cut further to 103, but the National Assembly rejected the second stage. This system does not prevent buyers from seeking sources other than the cartel, and permitting a degree of co-ordination among very small firms could be efficient. But efficient collaboration should not need legislative exemption from competition law.

Unfair competition and consumer protection roles

The KFTC protects small business interests directly, through rules about unfair practices, particularly in dealing with suppliers and subcontractors. And it protects consumers directly too, through rules about unfair marketing practices and misrepresentation. These functions can complement competition enforcement, although some "fair trade" rules that limit promotional offers could risk dampening market competition. In other cases, the KFTC is concerned that rules imposed by others to protect consumers may limit competition. For example, in dealing with the credit card problems, which some saw as the result of excessive competition for customers, the FSC wanted companies to control premium offers because they threatened financial stability. At the same time, the KFTC was concerned about the anti-competitive effects of self-regulation. On the grounds that changing rules and eligibility without notice was unfair to consumers, the KFTC ordered the card issuers to make clearer disclosures of the terms of their offers.

Regulatory policies at the sectoral level

Korea's government-driven growth policy has included regulations on over-investment that resulted in various *entry barriers*, such as licensing, permission, nomination, government monopoly and reporting requirements. According to a

Table 5.5.   **Entry barriers in Korea**
Number of industries

	Total industries	Strong barriers	Weak barriers	Total industries with barriers	Per cent of all industries
1992					
Manufacturing	585	103	85	188	32.1
Non-manufacturing	610	249	104	353	57.9
Total	1 195	352	189	541	45.3
2001					
Manufacturing	585	42	73	115	19.7
Non-manufacturing	610	147	165	312	51.1
Total	1 195	189	238	427	35.7

Source: Jaehong Kim (2002).

government study, 63 per cent of all industries – 205 out of 325 – had regulations controlling market entry (KDI, 1997). A private-sector study in 2002, which used more detailed industry categorisation, found that 36 per cent of all industries were subject to entry barriers (Table 5.5). The non-manufacturing sector is subject to more barriers, and those barriers are stronger compared with the manufacturing sector. Entry barriers in specific sectors, such as retail trade, professional services, and network industries, will be discussed below. As for the exit mechanism, it appears to have been improved. In particular, the disappearance of about half of the top thirty chaebol in 1997 has demonstrated that no firm is "too big to fail". However, the widespread use of workout or private restructuring programmes, rather than the revised bankruptcy procedures, reflects weaknesses in the Composition Act and the Company Reorganisation Act. This may tend to delay liquidation and third-party takeovers.

Regulatory policies in service sectors vary widely in scope. Although retail distribution and professional services are inherently competitive sectors, entry controls and self-regulation hamper competition. Strengthening competition requires applying the competition law forcefully in these sectors. On the other hand, network industries have segments with "natural monopoly" where competition is difficult – or even impossible – to introduce. In such areas, regulators should ensure non-discriminatory access to networks for third parties and open potentially competitive segments to competition. International experience has shown that the gains from regulatory reform in network industries are potentially very large if reforms are carefully designed.

The use of land

One factor having an important impact on competition is land-use regulation. The extensive controls on land use, combined with government policies that limit the available supply and drive up its price, can act as entry barriers (see the 2000 Survey). The concern about land use reflects its relative scarcity; Korea has the third highest population density in the world (excluding city-states) at 487 inhabitants per square kilometre. Moreover, two-thirds of the country is mountainous and nearly half of the population is concentrated in the capital region.

The use of land is directed by 315 zoning regulations, established by 112 different laws, which are administered by 13 different ministries (see Jung, 2003). As a result, 5.7 zoning regulations are applied on average to each parcel of land, and sometimes many more. In some cases, zoning regulations contradict each other, and co-ordination between ministries is difficult. A new framework for policy co-ordination requiring that any changes in zoning be discussed with the Ministry of Construction and Transportation was introduced in 2003. While this is a positive step towards a more coherent land policy, the new law covers only 69 of the zoning regulations. Transparency is further reduced by the limited database on land, which provides information on only 33 zoning regulations, thus making it very difficult for a landowner to be aware of the restrictions imposed on a specific plot.

Another problem is the limited amount of land available for development in the face of growing urbanisation. Although the share of the urban population reached 88 per cent in 2000, only 5.8 per cent of total land is allocated for urban development, compared to 13 per cent in the United Kingdom and 7 per cent in Japan. The government has tended to favour preservation over development through extensive restrictions on land use, resulting in high prices. Developing land or transferring it to other uses is an extremely difficult and time-consuming process, thus frustrating the efficient use of land.

The land-use problem is also related to the intensity of concentration in the capital region, which includes the cities of Seoul and Incheon and Kyonggi Province. The region, which only has 12 per cent of the national territory, contains 47 per cent of the total population. The related annual social costs are estimated to be 10 trillion won for congestion and 4 trillion won for environmental effects, amounting to 2 per cent of GDP. Despite policies during the past twenty years to limit the growth of the capital region, concentration has continued to increase, while leaving remote regions relatively under-developed.[9] The continued growth of the capital region indicates that congestion costs have been outweighed by the benefits of locating in the region. Among these benefits, proximity to the nexus of business activities and availability of better educational facilities seem to be important to firms and households. In 2003, the government announced a plan to move the administrative capital from Seoul to Chung Cheong Province, which is located in the middle of the country (Box 5.1).[10] The Special Act on Construction of the New Administrative Capital was enacted in December 2003, and the site for the new administrative capital will be determined by the end of 2004. The actual relocation will start from 2012, after a five-year construction period.

Box 5.1. **Building a new administrative capital city**

The relocation schedule is composed of four stages; preparation in 2003, planning between 2004 and 2007, construction between 2007 and 2011, and actual relocation beginning in 2012. The new administrative capital will be an independent city located at some distance from major towns. The optimal size of the city is suggested to be around 76 km^2, with the population to increase in line with its development. The first phase is to be finished by 2020 with a projected population of 300 thousand. It should rise to ½ million by the end of the second phase in 2030. Most central government institutions will be relocated to the new capital. However, it has not been decided whether to move the legislative and judicial branches.

The estimated cost of constructing the new capital city is 45.6 trillion won (6 per cent of GDP) through 2030. The public sector will bear 11.3 trillion won of that amount for constructing government buildings and highways, while the private sector will cover the remaining 34.3 trillion won for other facilities such as housing and city infrastructure. The budgetary burden would be reduced by utilising the proceeds from the sale of existing government buildings in the capital region and encouraging private participation in infrastructure projects.

The projected impact on the population is a decrease of 513 thousand people in the capital region by 2030, with an increase of 651 thousand people in Chung Cheong Province. The net annual saving in congestion costs is estimated to be 1.2 trillion won. In addition, there is expected to be downward pressure on real estate prices in the capital region (1.5 per cent for land and 1.0 per cent for housing). Some immeasurable benefits are also expected, such as more balanced territorial development and a reduction in regional disparities.

Retail distribution

Korea's retail industry has been evolving, driven by more efficient formats such as large discount stores, whose market share rose to 10 per cent in 2000 from only 1 per cent five years before. The growing foreign presence, which started in 1996, is also an important factor in driving structural change.[11] However, compared to other OECD countries, the sector is still dominated by small, family-run establishments (Table 5.6). Labour productivity in Korea's retail industry is reported to be around 30 per cent of that in the United States, making it the lowest among OECD economies.[12] Regulations aimed at protecting small mom-and-pop stores and promoting investment in manufacturing industries have long impeded the development of the retail industry and have contributed to the low productivity in this sector. Indirect regulations, such as zoning, and a cumbersome application process to open large-scale stores have also had a significant effect on

Table 5.6. **Key structural features of the retail distribution sector**
2000

	Outlet density[1]	Employees per enterprise	Wholesale and retail distribution, total value added per employed person	Non-specialised stores[2] — Share of total output in retail distribution (per cent)
Austria	43	7.7	90	20
Belgium	80	3.5	114	35
Denmark	47	8.1	79	39
Finland	46	5.0	82	44
France	64	4.2	87	37
Germany	35	9.0	75	23
Italy	130	2.2	101	31
Netherlands	54	8.5	81	
Portugal	150	2.5	66	31
Spain	133	2.8	71	32
Sweden	65	4.3	79	34
United Kingdom	36	14.2	68	43
European Union	71	6.3	83	35
Japan	111	5.7	74	16[3]
Korea[4]	**132**	**2.3**		**25**

1. Number of outlets per 10 000 inhabitants.
2. Includes large-format outlets such as hypermarkets and department stores.
3. Share of large stores only.
4. As of 2001.
Source: Eurostat, New Cronos, Japan Statistics, National Statistical Office in Korea.

the retail market (Figure 5.5). Indeed, regulations on the establishment of retail outlets have been judged to be the most restrictive in the OECD area.[13]

Special regulations – over and above general urban planning rules – apply to retail outlets in most OECD countries, thus posing a risk to market entry and competition. Moreover, the influence of established retailers on local authorities may make entry particularly difficult for outsider companies (OECD, 2001b). In Korea, retail outlets of more than 1 000 m² are prohibited in residential and industrial areas (Table 5.7). While there are no regulations on building large-scale stores in commercial zones, such zones account for only 0.2 per cent of the nation-wide land area. Moreover, most of this area is already occupied by other businesses, making available locations too small for large-scale stores. Re-development requires long and complex negotiations to get agreement from multiple owners. Since 1996, the construction of discount stores of up to 10 000 m² in area has been allowed in the "natural green areas" located in urban districts. However, regulations, such as limits on building- and volume-to-land ratios, have hindered the construction of large-scale retail outlets in these zones.[14]

Figure 5.5. **Regulatory indicators in the retail industry**[1]

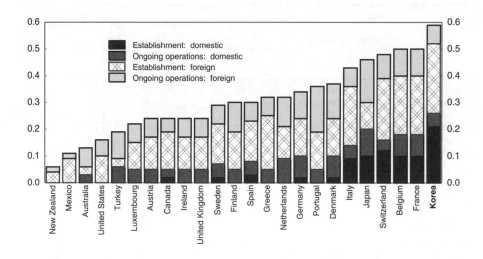

1. The restrictive index scores range from 0 to 1. The higher the score, the greater the restrictions.
Source: Kalirajan (2000).

The cumbersome process to receive permission to open a new large-scale store has been an important barrier in the retail sector. Agreement from the local government is required in the process of transport impact evaluation and construction approval. As in some other OECD countries, the devolution of authority to local governments may be problematic for achieving greater competition in the retail sector since local authorities tend to be even more susceptible than national governments to pressure by incumbent firms and other vested interests. In some cases, local authorities levy additional burdens, such as quasi-taxes.[15] However, there are no regulations on operational issues such as shop opening hours and price controls.

In 1996, Korea eliminated most of the restrictions on the size and number of retail stores that a foreigner could open. Since then, there have been further liberalisation steps such as abolishing remaining restrictions on retailing by foreigners in department stores and shopping centres. Meanwhile, an economic needs test applies to retail outlets for used cars and gas fuels. However, the barriers noted above, such as zoning regulations and the complicated and time-consuming application process, are probably more cumbersome to foreign investors, given their lack of knowledge concerning the local regulatory environment.[16]

Table 5.7. **Zoning regulations applied to retail stores**

	Zones	Area in km²[1]	Allowed retail stores	Exceptions
Urban area				
Residential	Exclusive	14.5	Total sales floor less than 1 000 m²	2 000 m² by municipal ordinance
	General	1 430.6	Total sales floor less than 1 000 m²	No limitation by municipal ordinance
	Quasi	85.1	Total sales floor less than 1 000 m²	No limitation by municipal ordinance
Commercial	Central	23.0	No limitation	
	General	215.3	No limitation	
	Neighboring	9.1	Total sales floor less than 3 000 m²	No limitation by municipal ordinance
	Distribution	4.8	No limitation	
Industrial	Exclusive	73.9	Total sales floor less than 1 000 m²	Stores operated by the plants in the area
	General	511.5	Total sales floor less than 1 000 m²	Stores operated by the plants in the area
	Quasi	145.7	Total sales floor less than 1 000 m² and stores operated by the plants in the area	No limitation by municipal ordinance
Green	Reservation	835.4	No	500 m² by municipal ordinance
	Production	1 267.1	Total sales floor less than 1 000 m²	Agricultural/fishery stores by municipal ordinance
	Natural	10 095.1	Total sales floor less than 1 000 m²	Large discount stores, designated by MOCIE, by municipal ordinance
Management area	Reservation	26 273.2	No	1 000 m² by municipal ordinance
	Production		Total sales floor less than 1 000 m²	Agricultural/fishery stores by municipal ordinance
	Planning		Total sales floor less than 1 000 m²	
Agricultural area		51 018.4	No	1 000 m² by municipal ordinance
Environmental reservation area		7 048.7	No	1 000 m² by municipal ordinance

1. As of 2003.
Source: Ministry of Construction and Transportation.

Professional services

All OECD countries regulate the activities of professional services, either directly or by delegating regulatory powers to professional associations, as a means to protect consumers by alleviating information asymmetries and ensuring high-quality services. In Korea, regulations in accounting are highly restrictive compared to other OECD countries, while those in the legal, architectural and engineering services are relatively moderate (Figure 5.6). These regulations typically govern matters such as entry into the profession, the conduct of members of the profession, the granting of exclusive rights to carry out certain activities, and the organisational structure of professional firms. However, such regulation can have the direct or indirect effect of restricting competition, raising prices and limiting variety and innovation in professional services.

Deregulation of professional services

In 1998, the Regulatory Reform Committee (RRC) launched a reform programme covering 155 trade associations that were performing regulatory functions based on legislation.[17] For example, the law had established 48 trade associations, giving them a monopoly in their fields and requiring all professionals to join. The RRC's reform programme examined such compulsory requirements, the delegation of powers (*e.g.* registration and discipline), training requirements, and regulations concerning establishment and operation. As a result, the compulsory establishment and membership in 36 trade associations was abolished, allowing more than one association to be established, and giving professionals the choice of whether to join the associations (Table 5.8). However, the target of the reform plan was not fully achieved since some of the planned changes for professional associations, including lawyers and certified public accountants (CPAs), were modified or discarded in the National Assembly, thus allowing those associations to maintain their regulatory schemes.

In 1999, the Omnibus Cartel Repeal Act (OCRA) was enacted to abolish or reduce the scope for concerted activities that had been granted exemption from the Monopoly Regulation and Fair Trade Act by sectoral legislation. For example, fees in nine professional services – lawyers, CPAs, architects, certified tax accountants, patent attorneys, customs brokers, certified labour services, administrative recorders and veterinarians – had been set by professional associations and approved by the relevant ministries. The OCRA made restrictions on fee-setting illegal and addressed a number of other non-competitive practices.[18] Following the enactment of the OCRA, the KFTC has closely monitored information on prices to respond to potential problems that could result from the introduction of price competition. A survey by the KFTC reported a significant decline in the fees in the affected sectors (see the 2001 *Survey*). In 2003, five professional services (lawyers, CPAs, architects, certified tax accountants, and judicial recorders) were included in the Clean Market Project for close scrutiny.

Figure 5.6.   **Regulations of professions: restrictiveness indices for OECD countries**

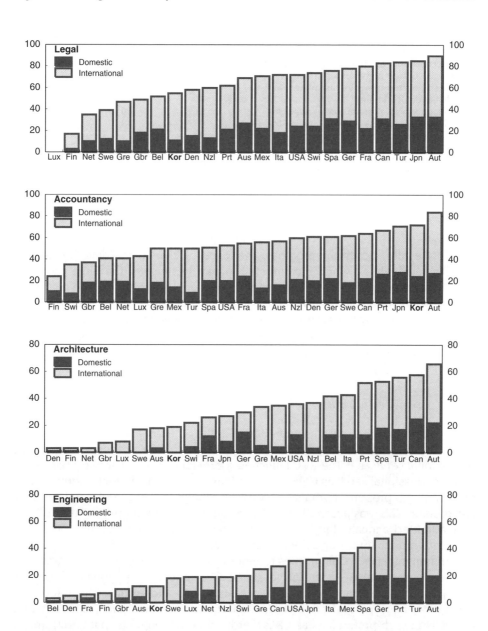

Source: Nguyen-Hong (2000).

Table 5.8. **Deregulation of professional associations**
Number of associations

Planned reform	Target	Implemented	Modified or discarded
Abolish compulsory establishment and membership	48	36	12
Withdraw delegated power for registration	5	2	3
Withdraw delegated power for discipline	5	3	2
Abolish mandatory training	70	54	16
Abolish authority for performance evaluation	6	6	0
Abolish authority for certification of foreign trade	19	19	0
Reform exam management	13	9	4
Reform other delegated authority	31	29	2
Deregulate requirements for entry	82	68	14
Deregulate requirements in operation	112	97	15

Source: Regulatory Reform Committee.

Despite significant progress, the pace of change in some professions remains relatively slow and incremental, in part because of the large economic rents at stake and the intense interest of professional associations. The restriction on fee-setting for architects was reintroduced in 2001, although it took the form of direct notification by the government rather than delegating the power to the professional association. In addition, regulations, rather than market competition, set fees for notaries and engineers. The KFTC is planning a second OCRA to eliminate remaining overly-generous exemptions.

Lowering entry barriers

Entry barriers, such as quantitative limits on entry and unnecessarily high entrance requirements, may hinder competition and allow economic rents in the professional services.[19] The RRC launched a programme to lower entry barriers in seven professional services (CPAs, certified tax accountants, patent attorneys, customs brokers, property appraisers, certified labour services, and administrative recorders).[20] This was accomplished by raising the ceiling on the number of persons admitted annually (and eventually abolishing quantitative limits), reducing the qualifications for taking selection exams, and limiting the advantages given to government officials.[21] Committees to monitor selection policies were established in the relevant ministries, and professional associations are no longer allowed to exercise exclusive control over entrance standards and exams. The reforms to lower entry barriers resulted in at least a doubling in annual entry between 1997 and 2002 in such professions as CPAs, certified tax accountants, patent attorneys, custom brokers and judicial recorders (Table 5.9). Lower entry barriers in these areas are expected to provide better and more diverse services. Entry into

Table 5.9. **Number of entrants per year in the selected professional services[1]**

	1997 (A)	1998	1999	2000	2001	2002	2003 (B)	B/A
Lawyers	604	700	709	801	991	998	905	1.5
CPAs	453	511	505	555	1 014	1 006	1 003	2.2
Certified tax accountants	306	301	354	451	603	699	717	2.3
Patent attorneys	71	80	81	121	200	202	204	2.9
Customs brokers	18	62	60	74	94	77	140	7.8
Property appraisers	101	100	100	135	183	117	135	1.3
Judicial recorders	0	30	52	80	101	100	60	2.0[2]
Certified labour services	43	37	n.a.	n.a.	n.a.	n.a.	61	1.4
Administrative recorders[3]	0	0	0	0	0	0	0	–

1. Covers only those who passed regular entrance exams (excludes those allowed to enter due to experience in the field).
2. Compared with 1998.
3. The examination for selection will be introduced in 2005.
Source: Ministry of Justice, Ministry of Finance and Economy, National Tax Service, Korean Intellectual Property Office, Korea Customs Service, Ministry of Construction and Transportation, Supreme Court of Korea, Ministry of Labour, Regulatory Reform Committee.

accounting is constrained, though not prevented, by the requirement of membership in the professional association and the rule that only a CPA can establish an accounting corporation.

Of the remaining exemptions and regulatory constraints on competition, those involving the legal profession may be the most important. Limits on the admission of new lawyers and unnecessary restraints on forms of practice undermine the development of stronger legal oversight of corporate governance and hamper foreign investment. Foreign lawyers have requested permission to set up branch offices, form joint ventures with Korean law firms, and employ Korean and foreign lawyers (see Office of Ministry for Trade, 2003). However, foreign licenses are not recognised in Korea, and foreign lawyers can only be employed as "legal assistants" in local firms.[22] Limitations regarding commercial presence and the recognition of qualifications of other countries restrict the availability of international professional services, such as legal and accounting services. Since these are factors that encourage foreign investors, failure to open the market can act as an indirect barrier to FDI. The WTO's service negotiations provide an opportunity to further reinforce competition in the professional services market.

Network industries

The liberalisation of network industries in a number of OECD countries during the past decade has generally resulted in substantial price reductions. However, there are examples of less successful reforms or outright failures, although these are mostly related to design problems of deregulation rather than liberalisation *per se*. This section will discuss the electricity, gas and telecommunication sectors in Korea. In electricity and gas, ambitious long-term restructuring programmes have become stalled and these sectors remain dominated by state-owned monopolies. The most progress has been made in telecommunications, though the dominance of the leading companies in some markets raises concern.

The regulatory scheme

Multiple regulators are involved in the network industries, which are subject to the competition laws and regulations enforced by the KFTC. The competition law does not apply to practices that are allowed by other laws, although the Monopoly Regulation and Fair Trade Act states that a ministry must consult with the KFTC when enacting a law that could have anti-competitive implications. In practice, the KFTC and relevant ministries have shared responsibility, with the former accountable for competition issues and the latter for technology and economic issues. This raises concern about consistency in implementing regulations. In some areas, including mergers, business transfers, and access to essential facilities, the relevant ministry and the KFTC are required to consult in order to avoid potential conflicts.

Along with its regulatory function, each ministry has broad powers to promote the development of the relevant industry, in contrast to regulatory bodies in other OECD countries that are charged with protecting consumer interests and promoting competition.[23] Given that fair and transparent regulatory supervision requires that the regulator distance itself from interested parties, there is a large risk of conflict between ministries' industry promotion role and their regulatory functions. Sector-specific regulators, such as the Korea Communication Commission (KCC) and the Korea Electricity Commission (KOREC), were established in response to privatisation and deregulation in the network industries.[24] Although they have the potential to become independent regulatory bodies, they operate within the ministries, and lack autonomy regarding both crucial regulations, such as licensing and pricing, and their own staffing and budgeting.

Tariffs of network industries are basically based on rate of return (ROR) regulation, which is not sufficient to provide an incentive to reduce costs and improve efficiency.[25] Information asymmetries between regulator and business hamper the scheme to find optimal prices, and deregulation in the network industry will raise costs of implementing ROR regulation. The industry promotion role of the regulator may also bring about distortions in tariff structure as shown, for example, in the electricity sector. A more transparent pricing scheme such as a price cap may be an alternative. The implementation of a price cap would prevent non-sector specific considerations from distorting the process of building competition and improving efficiency, and would ensure a smooth and rapid adjustment to a cost-reflective pricing structure.

The electricity sector

The Korea Electric Power Corporation (KEPCO), which is the largest business group in Korea, completely dominates the electricity market. It is the only licensed corporation in transmission and distribution and its six generating subsidiaries produce 96.7 per cent of all electricity generated.[26] Although 45 per cent of KEPCO's shares are held by private investors, government influence over tariffs is strong. Tariffs, which have to be approved by the Ministry of Commerce, Industry and Energy (MOCIE), have been held down by regulating the return on equity, which fell from 11.5 per cent in 1980 to around 5 per cent in 2001 and 2002. The government retains the right to appoint all board members and the chief executive. Entry to and exit from the electricity business is controlled by MOCIE through a licensing process.[27] Given that there are no interconnections with other countries, there is no possibility of foreign competitive pressures. As for the price of electricity, Korea is among the lower group in OECD countries when measured at current exchange rates (Figure 5.7).

In 1999, the government released the Basic Plan for Restructuring the Electricity Industry, which aimed at introducing competition in four phases (Table 5.10). According to the plan, the generating capacity and distribution facilities would be separated from KEPCO and privatised, leaving KEPCO as the only transmission company in Korea. The ten-year reform plan has been advancing, though it is somewhat behind the original timetable. Competition was introduced to power generation in 2001 with the spinning off of KEPCO's power-generating capacity into six subsidiaries and the establishment of the Korea Power Exchange (KPX) as a cost-based trading pool. Large consumers (those with capacity of over 50 000 kVA) were allowed to buy electricity from the KPX directly in 2003. Of the six subsidiaries, five thermal power-generating companies are to be privatised, while the sixth, the Korea Hydro and Nuclear Power Co., will remain a subsidiary of KEPCO due to security reasons.[28] A regulated third-party access system for transmission, which is consistent with practices in the majority of OECD countries, was put in place to facilitate electricity trade between generators and large customers. The terms and conditions of access are required to be non-discriminatory by law, and rate of return regulation is applied to determine the transmission fee level. However, the first attempt to privatise one of the generating subsidiaries through an international bidding process failed in 2003, and the government is now considering gradual privatisation through initial public offerings. The design of a two-way bidding pool has been completed, and mock cyber-operations have been conducted since July 2003.

There are some weaknesses in the plan. *First*, the timetable for liberalisation for consumers, which is very vague, appears to offer choice to most consumers only a decade after the reforms began. *Second*, there is considerable uncertainty about the plan's details, which reduces confidence. For example, the extent of

Figure 5.7. **Electricity prices**
In US dollars/kWh in 2002

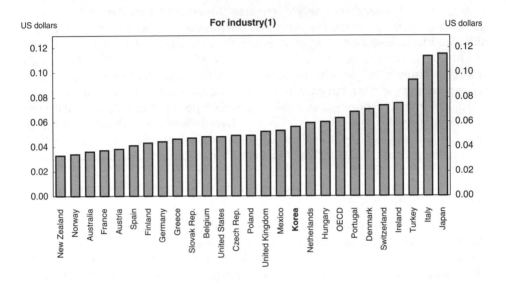

For industry(1)

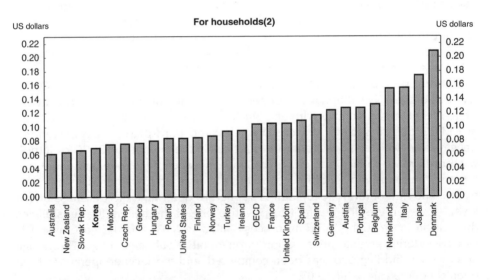

For households(2)

1. Price excluding tax for Australia and the United States. Data is for 2000 for Austria, Belgium and total OECD.
2. Prices excluding tax for the United States. Data is for 2000 for Belgium and total OECD.
Source: OECD.

Table 5.10. **The original plan for reforming the electricity sector**

Phase 1: *Status mid*-1999	– KEPCO is a vertically-integrated utility (generation, transmission, distribution) with 5.5 per cent of power purchased from independent power producers
Phase 2: *Power Generation Competition* (2000-2002)	– KEPCO's power generation capacity is separated into six competing subsidiaries that are to be privatised in stages • Distribution subsidiaries created to distribute power to captive customers • A cost-based pool electricity market established • An Electricity Commission created within MOCIE
Phase 3/Phase 4: *Wholesale Competition* (2003-2008)/ *Retail Competition* (2009-)	– KEPCO becomes principally a transmission and nuclear power business • Distribution subsidiaries are privatised • Open access to power transmission grids • Bid-based generator pool electricity market commences in Phase 3 • Independent brokers of electricity will be permitted in Phase 3 • Consumers select power providers in Phase 4 • Electricity Supervisory Board established

Source: Ministry of Commerce, Industry and Energy.

privatisation and the method of achieving it are uncertain, and it was announced that the privatisation of the distribution subsidiaries would be reconsidered later, which has a direct impact on the value of the generating companies that are supposed to be privatised. However, probably the most significant obstacle to reform is the lack of consensus between the parties concerned, including consumers and labour unions. By early 2003, the reform process had lost its momentum and the subsequent timetable had become unclear. In September 2003, the government set up a Tripartite Joint Study Group to consider how to split the distribution function; the government is awaiting the report from this Group before announcing its position.

There are two other potential obstacles to creating competition in the electricity market that are related to pricing. One is that the tariff structure is characterised by significant distortions between sectors that offer the scope for cross subsidisation (Figure 5.8). According to MOCIE estimates, industry paid 80 per cent of the average sales price of electricity and farmers paid only 57 per cent, while households and commercial customers paid substantially more than the average. However, the difference in prices between sectors has been reduced gradually.[29] Meanwhile, consumers pay higher costs because of "quasi-governmental" functions. In 2001, the Electric Power Industry Fund was established to take responsibility for some of these functions. Although the new approach is more transparent, electricity consumers bear the final burden since the Fund is financed through a surcharge on electricity bills.[30]

Figure 5.8. **Electricity charges by sector, 2002**
As a per cent of average sales price[1]

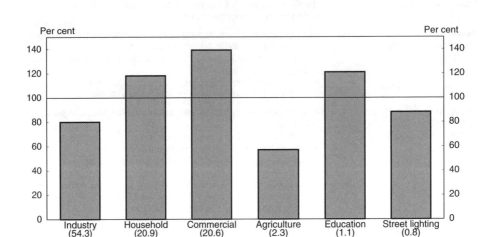

1. The numbers in parentheses show the share of total sales in each sector.
Source: Ministry of Commerce, Industry and Energy.

The natural gas sector

Currently, there is no competition in any area of the Korean gas industry. The Korea Gas Corporation (KOGAS), the state-owned monopoly, manages the import, storage, transmission, and wholesale distribution of natural gas, which exceeded 18 million tons in 2002. Korea has no indigenous production of natural gas, and thus depends entirely on liquefied natural gas (LNG) imports.[31] Besides performing the role of facility operator, KOGAS also supplies natural gas for retail city gas companies and for power generation, which is provided directly without passing through a retail distribution network.[32] As for the local distribution and retail market, there are 32 private city gas companies, all but four of which purchase natural gas from KOGAS and supply it to end users through their own distribution pipelines.[33] Competition in those markets is impossible, since the city gas companies are granted territorial monopolies and have no obligation to allow access to their distribution pipelines.

In 1999, the government announced the Natural Gas Industry Restructuring Plan, which aims at restructuring the industry to introduce competition, and then privatising KOGAS (see IEA, 2002b). The government's share has been reduced to 61 per cent. The reform underway in the electricity industry also necessitates changes in the gas industry, because KEPCO is both the largest customer and major owner of KOGAS. According to the plan, KOGAS will spin off its gas import and wholesale units into three affiliated companies, while keeping the facility sector a state-owned company using an Open Access System. The retail supply businesses will be separated into facility operation and gas sales, as in the wholesale sector, in order to spur competition, which will require interconnection among rival pipelines.

However, implementation of the plan has been delayed. KOGAS has not yet been split, and the three restructuring-related laws, which were submitted to the National Assembly in 2001, have not been approved.[34] The main problems lie in the characteristics of LNG imports[35] and the challenge of restructuring KOGAS (see IEA, 2002b).[36] In 2003, the government decided to revise the original plan. As for the import and wholesale sectors, the decision will be made after thorough debates on how to spin-off the three subsidiaries and whether to allow new entry. Even if new entry is permitted, it is likely to be subject to certain restrictions, at least in the early stage of competition, due to the inflexibility of existing long-term import contracts.

Wholesale natural gas tariffs are subject to approval by MOCIE, while the supply terms and conditions, including the retail gas tariffs, of city gas companies require approval from the local government.[37] The basic approach used in deriving supply costs is rate of return regulation, while "yardstick regulation" is used for some city gas companies. Where several city gas companies exist in a city or province, a single retail price is applied to all the companies. Thus, a company that has relatively high costs cannot fully recover them under the allowed rate of return.

There is some cross-subsidisation for policy purposes. KOGAS gives financial incentives for gas-operated cooling systems in the hope of smoothing seasonal fluctuations in demand by promoting gas sales during the summer season. Tariffs for public welfare facilities and compressed natural gas for buses are also discounted in an effort to reduce air pollution.[38] The government is planning to finance such obligations on a transparent basis as the restructuring proceeds. However, there is no obligation for retail companies to provide services to any customers below cost.

The telecommunication sector

Korea's telecommunication sector has been advancing at a remarkable pace, thanks to the rapid spread of high-tech services and the introduction of competition in this sector.[39] Telecommunication prices for both residential and business-sector users are among the lowest in the OECD area (Figure 5.9). As for broadband, penetration is the highest in the world, while charges are low compared to other OECD countries (Figure 1.4). However, Korea's telecommunication industry is struggling to handle a series of destabilising developments, and

Figure 5.9.   **Telecommunication charges in the OECD**
US dollars, November 2003

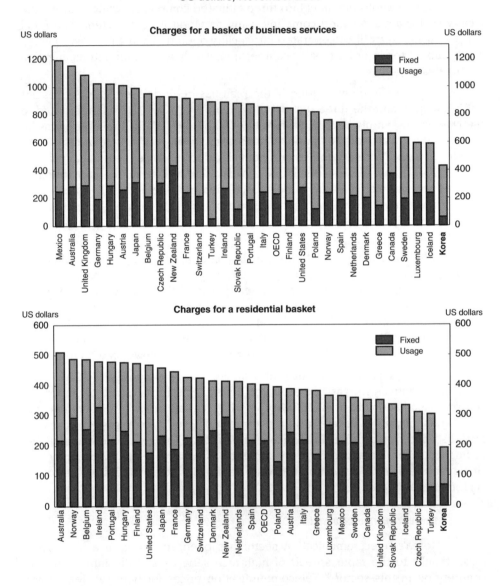

Note: Composite basket includes international calls and calls to mobile networks.
Source: OECD and Teligen.

concerns over Korea Telecom (KT) and SK Telecom's market dominance are growing (Table 5.11). Some competitors are faced with financial difficulties. In 2003, Hanaro was taken over by a foreign consortium, and Onse Telecom and Thrunet Co. were forced to seek protection from creditors.

Market entry was liberalised during the 1990s and there is no longer an *a priori* limit on the number of market entrants in any of the designated license categories. The current license classification system requires authorisation for facility-based providers, registration for special service providers and notification for VAN providers.[40] Licenses for fixed facility-based services are differentiated by the type of service offered (local, long distance or international). A prospective licensee thus needs to apply for multiple licenses. Moreover, requests for licenses for facility-based services are accepted only two weeks during the year. However, entry barriers were lowered by abolishing the up-front contribution fee for new fixed-line providers in 2002, while the mandatory annual contribution from service providers for R&D was also lowered from 3 per cent of sales to 0.5 per cent.

Interconnection charges are a difficult issue in Korea, as in other OECD countries. The "essential facilities doctrine", which was introduced to the Monopoly Regulation and Fair Trade Act in 2001, makes the failure to allow access to essential facilities an abuse of dominant position. Interconnection arrangements between operators with no market power are regarded as commercial matters to be decided by agreements between them, which must be notified to the Ministry of Information and Communication (MIC). In contrast, interconnection agreements involving operators with "significant market power", *i.e.* KT and SK Telecom, are

Table 5.11.   **Competition in the telecommunication sector**

2003

	Market size (trillion won)	Number of major operators	Market share
Local telephone	5.6	2	KT 95.6%, Hanaro Telecom 4.4%
Domestic long distance	1.3	4	KT 76.7%, Dacom 19.5%, Onse Telecom 3.8%, Hanaro Telecom 0.0%
International telephone	1.1	4	KT 39.5%, Dacom 18.0%, Onse Telecom 12.7%, SK Telink 3.5%, Special Service Providers 26.3%
Broadband Internet	3.6	7	KT 53.4%, Hanaro Telecom 27.1%, Thrunet 10.5%
Mobile telecommunication	16.0	3	SK Telecom 59.7%, KT Freetel 26.3%, LG Telecom 10.9%
IMT-2000	–	3	SK Telecom, KT Freetel, LG Telecom

Source: Ministry of Information and Communication.

subject to authorisation by the MIC. In the case of fixed interconnection charges, KT's charge is applied as a "standard" for other operators. Mobile interconnection charges have been set asymmetrically for cellular and PCS operators, taking into account the different nature of frequencies and other cost factors.[41]

Korea is relatively behind other member countries in local loop unbundling (LLU). In 2002, the MIC issued a public notification of unbundling requirements, standards and full implementation, which led to the opening and sharing of KT's copper line network and the broadband network of Internet service providers. However, a weak response led the MIC to revise the notification in 2003 by reducing fees and minimising access refusals. About 1 000 loops were in use for LLU as of March 2004, and the number is expected to increase further.

The method for spectrum planning and allocation should be more competitive and transparent. Previously, MIC would provide information on the detailed allocation of spectrum bandwidths, select the operators and allocate the spectrum within the given bandwidth. For example, in the case of Broadband Wireless Local Loop (B-WLL), the MIC granted spectrum (which was later withdrawn) to KT and Hanaro Telecom without an open bidding procedure and without a contribution fee. Under a new approach, the MIC decides the number of operators for available bandwidths and announces the number of licenses to be issued and the application procedures. Licenses are allocated through a competitive tender procedure, so-called "beauty contests". For example, in 2001, three 3rd generation (3G) licenses were sold for $2.9 billion through beauty contests. While ten OECD countries have used beauty contests to allocate 3G licenses, fourteen used auctions, which generally achieved the objective of allocating licenses in a competitive and transparent manner (see OECD, 2003a).

Numbering policy is important in the context of enhancing local competition and reducing lock-in effects. Not only do new entrants require adequate access to number resources to expand their services, but they also need to be assured that number portability will be allowed to support competition. For local calls, number portability will be extended to the entire country by 2004. As for mobile services, 2nd generation (2G) number portability is being gradually introduced from January 2004 at six-month intervals,[42] and 3rd generation (3G 2GHz IMT-2000) number portability will be introduced within six months after the start of business by more than two service providers. Moreover, the identification numbers for the 2G and 3G phones will be gradually merged.

Current rate of return regulation on the tariffs of the dominant carriers, KT for local telephony and SK Telecom for mobile telephony, should be improved to promote competition and efficiency. The MIC has been exploring the introduction of a price cap on local telephony. By contrast, the rationale for imposing price controls on a cellular mobile company, which is rarely done in OECD countries, is not clear. The MIC justifies its regulation of SK Telecom's prices on the grounds that there are concerns about unfair pricing practices by the dominant firm. However, the need for any type of price control in the mobile sector should be re-considered, given that the market is competitive and prices are declining. The MIC has considered the introduction of a notification system in which tariffs filed by a carrier would take effect after a specified grace period, when they are judged not to pose any concerns for competition. However, in light of recent developments in the telecommunication industry and concerns over further market dominance, the MIC became more cautious about liberalising price regulations, and plans to maintain the current system until effective competition is established.

Overall assessment and scope for further action

The recommendations for strengthening competition are shown in Box 5.2. In summary, Korea has inherited a legacy of state intervention as a result of the government-led development strategy. The focus on creating world-class manufacturing industries, characterised by economies of scale, made competition a secondary consideration during much of its history. The economic reform process, which was accelerated by the 1997 crisis, is helping to reduce government intervention and regulation of the economy. The conflict between industrial development and competition, which still exists in the ministries responsible for network industries, should be resolved by the establishment of sectoral regulators that are independent of ministries. This process should continue by removing remaining entry barriers and further increasing openness to international trade and investment. At the same time, the KFTC should be strengthened and should focus on competition policy. Chaebol-regulating functions such as controlling internal cross-holdings and guarantees and probing misuse of corporate assets that are related to finance and corporate governance should be concentrated in regulators responsible for financial and securities matters. Transactions that have an exclusionary or distorting effect on product market competition in particular cases should remain subject to competition-law control.

The scope for gains is large, given that labour productivity (per hour worked) in Korea is only about half of the OECD average. As the growth of factor inputs slows, increasing total factor productivity growth will become increasingly important in sustaining the convergence process. The gains are likely to be largest in the service sector, which currently faces more extensive regulation. Indeed, labour productivity in this sector is only 62 per cent of that in the manufacturing sector. One economic study found that reforms in five key sectors – electricity, telecommunications, distribution, construction and road transport – could boost GDP by 8½ per cent (OECD, *Regulatory Reform in Korea*, 2000).

Box 5.2.   **Summary of recommendations to strengthen competition**

Overall

  − Reduce entry barriers and regulations that limit competition.

Promoting international competition

  − Reduce tariff levels and harmonise standards with international norms to avoid negative effects on imports.
  − Lower the high level of agricultural protection to contribute to the success of multilateral trade negotiations, as well as facilitate Korea's participation in regional free trade agreements that would enable it to benefit from the economic dynamism of Asia.
  − Establish conditions that will encourage inflows of foreign direct investment, in particular by bringing the economic framework into line with global standards and improving labour market conditions.
  − Extend the special incentives in the Free Economic Zones to the rest of the country.

Strengthen competition law

  − Grant the KFTC compulsory investigative powers to make its administrative enforcement more effective.
  − Make the threat of individual sanctions more credible to ensure that it is an effective deterrent.
  − Concentrate chaebol-regulating functions that are related to finance and corporate governance in regulators responsible for financial and securities matters. Transactions that have an exclusionary or distorting effect on product market competition in particular cases should remain subject to competition-law control.
  − Eliminate remaining unnecessary special-interest exemptions, such as the small-business "cartels" for government procurement.

Retail distribution

  − Deregulate zoning laws to facilitate the development of large retail outlets.
  − Simplify the complex application process for opening large-size retail stores and make it more transparent. The arbitrary imposition of additional costs should be prevented.

Professional services

  − Eliminate unnecessary constraints on entry and the form of practice in key professional sectors, particularly law and accounting.
  − Abolish restrictions on competition, including fees, between members of the same profession, while encouraging competition between professional associations.
  − Minimise the delegation of powers from the government to professional associations. They should not be granted exclusive jurisdiction to make decisions about entrance requirements and other issues.

Box 5.2.   **Summary of recommendations to strengthen competition** (*cont.*)

The electricity sector

- Strengthen the government's commitment to a realistic reform programme that includes more detailed time schedules, while specifying the degree and method of privatisation of the generating and distributing subsidiaries, as well as the final market structure.

- Implement the plan to create independent generation and distribution companies to ensure that they do not have links to KEPCO, which will run the transmission system, nor significant common ownership.

- Ensure cost-reflective pricing, such as a price-cap system, and eliminate cross subsidisation between sectors to provide incentives for the efficient use of electricity.

- Establish an independent regulator. Given MOCIE's policy and industry promotion responsibilities in the electricity sector, and its role as "owner" in voting the government's shares in KEPCO, it will be important that MOCIE play no direct regulatory role.

- Strengthen competition law enforcement in the energy sector, particularly with respect to market access and anti-competitive conduct, by enhancing co-operation between the sector regulator and the KFTC.

The natural gas sector

- Establish a firm timetable for reform in order to prevent further uncertainty and delay, while balancing the goal of introducing competition with concerns about the security of energy and KOGAS's existing contracts with LNG producers.

- Provide incentives for efficient use of gas by ensuring cost-reflective pricing such as a price-cap system.

- Establish an independent regulator and separate it from the policy functions to be retained by MOCIE. Strengthen competition law enforcement in the energy sector by increasing co-operation with the KFTC.

The telecommunication sector

- Use auctions to allocate spectrum for all wireless licences.

- Impose a price cap system in markets where KT remains dominant, while refraining from interfering in all other markets.

- Take more comprehensive measures to promote competition in the local loop.

- Transform the KCC into an independent communications sector regulator, clearly differentiating MIC's policy responsibilities from regulatory responsibilities.

- Reduce barriers to entry by introducing a general approval system.

- Implement number portability extensively to minimise the transaction costs of changing service provider.

Notes

1. Industry concentration is based on the 491 industries in the Korean Standard Industrial Classification (KSIC) 5-digit categorisation, while market concentration is based on the 3 056 markets in the KSIC's 8-digit categorisation. The degree of concentration in each is measured by the combined market share of the top three firms and by the Hirschman-Herfindahl Index (HHI). The Monopoly Regulation and Fair Trade Act (MRFTA) defines a concentrated industry or market as one in which the top firm has a market share of more than 50 per cent or in which the top three firms have a combined share of more than 75 per cent.

2. However, the weighted averages of the concentration ratios and the HHI measure have fallen less than the simple averages and in some cases have risen since the crisis. This reflects the fact that growth in recent years has been driven by the ICT sector, which has become more concentrated. It is also due to the business swaps, the so-called "Big Deals", which were implemented following the crisis in an effort to reduce excess capacity and high debt to equity ratios (see the 1999 *Survey*). The Big Deals covered major industries such as semiconductors, power-generating equipment, petrochemicals, aerospace, railroad vehicles, ship engines and oil refinery. For example, LG Semiconductor was combined with Hyundai Electronics, and later re-named Hynix Semiconductor.

3. The market share of the three largest companies in major industries in 2001 was 92.0 per cent for cars, 88.0 per cent for electronic integrated circuits, 78.5 per cent for ships, 78.1 per cent for petroleum refineries and 70.6 per cent for communication and radio/television broadcasting equipment. This was considerably above the simple average of 43.4 per cent in the manufacturing and mining sectors and the weighted average of 51.5 per cent.

4. Comparisons of HHI are limited by the fact that data are only available for nine OECD countries. Moreover, the HHI is based on firm-level data, except in Korea, Japan and the United States, where it is based on establishment data.

5. The free trade agreement with Chile provoked severe opposition from farmers even though there is little agricultural trade between the two countries. This opposition delayed passage of the agreement by the National Assembly until February 2004 – 18 months after negotiations were completed.

6. Two business lines, radio and television broadcasting, are still closed to direct investment, while 27 are partially restricted. However, 78 firms are designated as defence-related companies in which foreign investment requires prior approval.

7. In 2003, the previous Korea Investment Centre was replaced by Invest Korea with newly adopted project manager (PM) system, which provides customised service to the foreign investors.

8. See Chapter 4 for a description of the evolution of the chaebol.

9. In the capital region, development activities have been highly regulated by the Act on Consolidation Planning for the Capital Region and the Consolidation Plan. Construction of large facilities is restricted by imposing quotas on manufacturing industries and universities, or by levying "congestion charges" on business buildings and government facilities. The development of large sites for residences, factories and sightseeing requires approval from the government. Meanwhile, tax measures are aimed at discouraging concentration and encouraging firms to move away from the capital region.

10. In the mid-1990s, units of ten central government agencies moved to Daejeon, the largest city in Chung Cheong Province.

11. Three (Carrefour, Wal-Mart, and Costco) of the top twenty retailers are now foreign-owned, and a partnership between Samsung and Tesco was formed in 2002.

12. McKinsey (1998) estimated Korea's labour productivity in the retail industry at 32 per cent of the US, and 59 per cent of Japan. Meanwhile, a recent analysis estimated labour productivity in the distribution industry to be 29 per cent of the United States, 34 per cent of Japan and France on the basis of PPP (see Suh et al., 2002).

13. This result differs from another study (OECD, 2000c), which ranked Korea as one of the countries with less stringent regulation. This study considered general restrictions on access, regulations on operations, and price regulations, but did not take account of other regulations governing the location of sales outlets, such as zoning and promotional activities.

14. Ceilings of 20 per cent for the building-to-land ratio and 100 per cent for the volume-to-land ratio are applied in the natural green area, thus making large shopping malls unprofitable (see Suh et al., 2002).

15. There have been seven administrative litigation cases concerning unreasonable rejection of proposals for large-scale stores. Moreover, additional costs, such as quasi-taxes and coerced contributions, are normally 7 to 8 per cent of total construction costs (Dong-Whan Kim, 2003). In 2002, MOCIE issued a ministerial order asking local governments to avoid levying too heavy a burden on new large-scale entrants for such expenses as land and construction costs to build entrance roads.

16. Complaints from foreign retailers to the Office of the Investment Ombudsman indicate that they have serious concerns about the transparency of government administration and lack confidence in it (Kim and Choo, 2002).

17. This was part of the extensive deregulation accomplished following the 1997 crisis. The RRC, established in 1998, led to the elimination of 48.9 per cent of the 11 095 existing regulations, while 42.5 per cent of the remaining regulations were reformed (see the 2000 Survey).

18. The provision allowing premium-fixing by insurance companies was revised, the number of products in which SMEs are allowed to conduct group negotiations for contracts was reduced, co-ordination directives by the government were limited to cases in which they are required to comply with inter-governmental agreements or in the export of military equipment, government co-ordination of bidding competition for overseas construction projects was abolished, and territorial allocation in the supply of unsterilised rice wine was abolished.

19. The RRC stated, "According to the National Tax Service's material submitted to the National Assembly in 1998, the average annual revenues of patent attorneys, lawyers, and certified tax accountants were 400, 250, and 190 million won, respectively" (Maeil Business Newspaper, 21 October 1998). The average annual wage for all workers was 17 million won in 1997.

20. As for lawyers and judicial recorders, reform was implemented by the professions and the related ministry.

21. In some professional services, government officials with long experience (generally at least ten years) in related fields had been exempt from examinations. According to the RRC, the ratio of retired government officials in 1998 was 100 per cent for administrative recorders, 94.2 per cent for judicial recorders, 85.6 per cent for customs brokers, 62.1 per cent for certified labour services, 29.0 per cent for patent attorneys, and 24.5 per cent for certified tax accountants. Limiting the advantages given to government officials will provide more open and fair competition for entry.

22. Korea's "Initial Offer submitted to the WTO in March 2003" is somewhat limited. Foreign lawyers without domestic licenses will be allowed to supply "advisory services" on the law in the jurisdiction where they are qualified as lawyers and on public international law. Moreover, commercial presence in the form of a representative office will be required and lawyers have to stay in Korea at least 180 days a year.

23. For example, the Telecommunications Basic Act provides MIC with the power to "advise" facility-based carriers on where to invest, a provision that is used to justify the mandatory contributions imposed on carriers to contribute to R&D.

24. A law submitted to the National Assembly in 2001 would establish an Energy Commission that would absorb KOREC and regulate both the electricity and gas sectors. However, the law is still pending due to the delays in reforms in the gas sector. Creating such a combined regulator responsible for both sectors may have some advantages, such as limiting the scope for regulatory capture (see OECD, 2004).

25. A study, which recommended adopting price caps and introducing an independent regulator, pointed out the lack of incentives as the most serious problem of ROR regulation. In contrast, over-investment has not been problematic in Korea (Nam *et al.*, 2001).

26. Although each is completely owned by KEPCO, they are run as legally separate companies. In addition, there are 19 independent power producers, which account for 3.3 per cent of total electricity production.

27. However, small power plants with generating capacity of less than 3 000 kW are licensed by local governments, with advice from KOREC.

28. As of 2002, the generating capacity and actual generation of the Korea Hydro and Nuclear Power Co. were 36.4 and 40.6 per cent, respectively, of those of KEPCO's six subsidiaries combined. Therefore, it is expected that the generation market will remain more concentrated than in some other OECD countries. It draws attention to the risk and advantages of having a single publicly-owned company holding nuclear plants and giving it a mandate to construct new base load plants. This could distort competition (see IEA, 2002a).

29. In 2003, prices for industrial use were raised by 3 per cent, while prices for household and commercial uses were lowered by 2 per cent. In 2004, prices for household, commercial and educational uses were further lowered by 3 per cent.

30. The Fund is financed by an earmarked charge of 4.6 per cent of the electricity bill. The Fund is expected to spend 1.2 trillion won (about $1 billion) in 2003.

31. Korea is the second largest importer of LNG next to Japan, and KOGAS is the world's largest LNG importing company. There is no import of pipeline natural gas (PNG). However, the possibility and viability of PNG imports from eastern Siberia are currently being explored.

32. The gas industry relies heavily on the electricity industry as a swing consumer to flatten out seasonal fluctuations in demand, which is due to heating. In 2002, KOGAS supplied

7 million tons of LNG (36.8 per cent of total consumption) to ten power-generating companies, including five subsidiaries of KEPCO.

33. The remaining four companies use liquefied petroleum gas (LPG) as feedstock.

34. The three new laws include the revision of the KOGAS *Law* and the *City Gas Business Law* and the enactment of the *Energy Commission Law* to establish a sector regulator.

35. LNG import contracts have long terms of 20 to 25 years, and commit buyers and sellers to strictly defined obligations, including take-or-pay clauses that require the buyer to pay for a certain amount of gas whether taken or not, as well as an obligation on the part of the seller to make available defined volumes of gas. Such contracts provide a firm basis for both buyers and sellers to finance a highly capital intensive infrastructure. Project financing is normally used for the construction of LNG carriers. Conditions in case of a default on loans that are imposed on the charter agreement for the carrier require a certain level of government ownership, including local governments. In the case of KOGAS, it ranges from 30 to 51 per cent.

36. *First*, splitting KOGAS's import contracts among three affiliated companies is extremely difficult, because suppliers will not agree to have their contracts reassigned without solid guarantees. *Second*, KOGAS will no longer be the world's largest, most powerful LNG importer, and the three new importing companies may find themselves bidding against each other, resulting in higher import prices. *Third*, privatising KOGAS is not consistent with the default provisions for LNG vessels. *Fourth*, the scope for competition is limited by the unchangeable conditions of existing long-term import contracts.

37. The gas tariff consists of feedstock cost and supply costs such as re-gasification, storage, and transmission. The feedstock cost changes automatically bimonthly (monthly for power generation customers) according to fluctuations in oil prices and exchange rates, while the supply costs are approved on an annual basis.

38. In 2001, the amount of support for air conditioning use was 42 billion won, while support for the last two were 1.1 and 0.3 billion won, respectively.

39. The formerly monopolistic market, dominated by KT in fixed-line telephony service and SK Telecom in mobile service, shifted to a more competitive structure during the 1990s. For local service, Hanaro entered in 1999, while Dacom and Onse entered the long distance and international markets during the 1990s. For mobile service, Shinsegi entered in 1994, followed by three Personal Communication Service (PCS) operators in 1996. For International Mobile Telecommunication (IMT-2000) service, SK IMT and KTicom were selected as asynchronous (W-CDMA) providers in 2000. In 2003, SK IMT was merged into SKT, while KTicom was merged into KT. For balanced development of synchronous and asynchronous transmission, LG Telecom was approved as a synchronous CDMA provider in 2001. Asynchronous (W-CDMA) service started in the Seoul area in 2003, while synchronous service will be provided by 2006.

40. Facility-based services cover wire telephony, cellular telephony, PCS, TRS, CT-2, radio paging, and leased line services, while special services cover Internet telephony, international call-back, premises communications, and voice resale. Value-added services provide PC online, Internet, E-mail, and voice mail services.

41. For land to mobile (LM) calls, SK Telecom, KT Freetel, and LG Telecom receive 41.0, 48.0, 52.9 won per minute respectively. SK Telecom, which is a cellular service provider, is providing better quality services due to the characteristics of its frequency. PCS providers insist that SK Telecom is able to cut costs by 40 to 50 per cent using low frequency 800 MHz, while PCS providers use 1.8 GHz.

42. With an aim to assist the late entrants, mobile number portability will be introduced in three phases; SK Telecom in January 2004, KT Freetel in July 2004, and LG Telecom in January 2005.

Bibliography

Bank of Korea (2003), *Report on Financial Stability*, Seoul (in Korean).

Cho, Dongchul and Hyeon Park (2003), "Economic Impact of the Construction of a New Capital", 2003 *Annual Report*, Korea Development Institute, Seoul (in Korean).

Cho, Dongchul and Myung-Kee Sung (2003), "Low Interest Rates and Real Estate Prices; Implications on Monetary and Tax Policy", Korea Development Institute, No. 166, Seoul (in Korean).

Cho, Joonmo (2003), "An Economic Analysis of the Effect of Korean Labor Unions on Corporate Bankruptcy Threat", in *Empirical Evaluation of Corporate Restructuring*, Stijn Claessens and Dongsoo Kang (eds.), Korea Development Institute, Seoul.

Claessens, Stijn and Dongsoo Kang (eds.) (2003), *Empirical Evaluation of Corporate Restructuring*, Korea Development Institute, Seoul.

Haggard, Stephan, Wonhyuk Lim and Euysung Kim (eds.) (2003), *Economic Crisis and Corporate Restructuring in Korea*, Cambridge University Press.

Han, Chin Hee *et al.* (2002), "Prospects for the Korean Economy's Potential Growth Rate: 2003 to 2012", Korea Development Institute Policy Study 2002-07, Seoul (in Korean).

Hur, Jai-Joon (2004), "Labor Demand in Korea", Korea Labor Institute Issue Paper No. 27, Seoul.

Hur, Jai-Joon and Hokyung Kim (2002), "Employment Insurance and Work Injury Insurance as a Social Safety Net", in *Labor in Korea*, Wonduck Lee (ed.), Korea Labor Institute, Seoul.

IEA (2002a), *Energy Policies of IEA Countries: The Republic of Korea 2002 Review*, Paris.

IEA (2002b), *Flexibility in Natural Gas Supply and Demand*, Paris.

IEA (2003), *Energy Prices & Taxes: Quarterly Statistics*, Paris.

International Monetary Fund (2003), *Financial System Stability Assessment*, IMF Country Report No. 03/81, Washington.

Jaumotte, Florence (2003), "Female labour force participation: past trends and main determinants in OECD countries", OECD Economics Department Working Paper No. 376, Paris.

Jeong, Jin-Ho (2003), "Wages in Korea", Korea Labor Institute Issue Paper No. 25, Seoul.

Jeong, Kap-Young *et al.* (2002), "Mid-&-Long-Term Vision of Competition Policies: Competition 2010", Korea Academic Society of Industrial Organization, Seoul, mimeo (in Korean).

Jung, Hee-Nam (2003), "Strategy for the Reform of Land-Use Regulations", Korea Research Institute for Human Settlements, Seoul (in Korean).

Jwa, Sung-Hee (2002), *The Evolution of Large Corporations in Korea*, Edward Elgar Publishing, Northhampton, Massachusetts.

Jwa, Sung-Hee and In Kwon Lee (eds.) (2000), *Korean Chaebol in Transition: Road Ahead and Agenda*, Korea Economic Research Institute, Seoul.

Kalirajan, K. (2000), "Restrictions on Trade in Distribution Services", *Staff Research Paper*, Productivity Commission, Ausinfo, Canberra.

Kim, Dong-Whan (2003), "Deregulation for Productivity in the Distribution Sector", Korea Chamber of Commerce & Industry, Seoul, mimeo (in Korean).

Kim, Jaehong (2002), "Entry Regulation: Theory and Practice", Korea Economic Research Institute, Seoul (in Korean).

Kim, Wan-Soon and Michael Jae Choo (2002), "Managing the Road to Globalisation: The Korean Experience", Korea Trade-Investment Promotion Agency (KOTRA), Seoul.

Kim, Yang Woo (2002), "Optimal Horizons for Inflation Targeting in Korea", *Economic Papers*, Bank of Korea, Vol. 5, No. 1.

Korea Development Institute (1997), "Moving toward a Competitive Market Structure", Seoul, mimeo (in Korean).

Kwon, O. Yul, Sung-Hee Jwa and Kyung-Tae Lee (eds.) (2003), *Korea's New Economic Strategy in the Globalization Era*, Edward Elgar Publishing, Northhampton, Massachusetts.

Lee, Changwon (2003), "Changing Labor Relations and Human Resources Management of Korean Businesses in China and Future Challenges", Korea Labor Institute Issue Paper No. 21, Seoul.

Lee, Jae-hyung (2002), "Analysis of Market Concentration in Korea: Mining and Manufacturing Sectors", Korea Development Institute Policy Study 2002-10, Seoul (in Korean).

Lee, Jang-Young (2003), "Market-based Approach to Credit Card Companies' Debt Problems", *Weekly Financial Market* 12-22, Korea Institute of Finance, Seoul (in Korean).

Lee, Wonduck and Byung-you Cheon (2004), "Flexibility in the Korean Labor Market", Korea Labor Institute Issue Paper No. 28, Seoul

Lim, Youngjae *et al.* (2003), "Developing and Measuring an Evaluation Index for Market Reform", Korea Development Institute, Seoul, mimeo.

McKinsey & Company (1998), "Productivity-led Growth for Korea: General Merchandise Retail Industry", Seoul and Washington.

Ministry of Planning and Budget (2002), *How Korea Reformed the Public Sector*, Seoul.

Ministry of Labour (2003), *Reform Proposal for Sound Industrial Relations*, Seoul.

Nam, Il-Chong *et al.* (2001), "Reforming tariff regulation in privatized network industries", Korea Development Institute, Seoul, mimeo (in Korean).

Nguyen-Hong, D. (2000), "Restrictions on Trade in Professional Services", *Staff Research Paper*, Productivity Commission, Ausinfo, Canberra.

OECD (1999), *Economic Survey of Korea*, Paris.

OECD (2000a), *Economic Survey of Korea*, Paris.

OECD (2000b), *Regulatory Reform in Korea*, Paris.

OECD (2000c), *Regulatory Reform in Road Freight and Retail Distribution*, Paris.

OECD (2001a), *Economic Survey of Korea*, Paris.

OECD (2001b), OECD *Economic Studies, Special Issue: Regulatory Reform*, No. 32, Paris.

OECD (2001c), *Territorial Reviews; Korea*, Paris.

OECD (2002), "Product Market Competition and Economic Performance", OECD *Economic Outlook,*, No. 72, December, Paris.

OECD (2003a), *After the Telecommunications Bubble*, Paris.

OECD (2003b), *Communications Outlook*, Paris.

OECD (2003c), *Economic Survey of Korea*, Paris.

OECD (2003d), *Science, Technology and Industry Scoreboard*, Paris.

OECD (2003e), *The Sources of Economic Growth in OECD Countries*, Paris.

OECD (2004), *Economic Survey of Japan*, Paris.

Office of Ministry for Trade (2003), *Review of EUCCK's Trade Issues & Recommendations* 2003, Seoul.

Park, Jong-Kyu (2004), "Macroeconomic impacts of bubble bust in the credit card industry", *Weekly Financial Market* 13-04, Korea Institute of Finance, Seoul (in Korean).

Rowthorn, Robert and Ken Coutts (2004), "De-industrialisation and the Balance of Payments in Advanced Countries", *Cambridge Journal of Economics*, forthcoming.

Shin, Inseok, Chinhee Han and Changkyun Park (2003), "Analysis of the delinquent borrower problem and future policy directions", Korea Development Institute, Seoul, mimeo (in Korean).

Sohn, Chan-Hyun (2002), *Korea's Corporate Restructuring since the Financial Crisis*, Korea Institute for International Economic Policy, Seoul.

Suh Yong-Ku *et al.* (2002), "Economic Effects of Structural Changes in the Distribution Industry", *Research Paper submitted to* MOCIE, Sookmyung Women's University, Seoul (in Korean).

Annex A

Overview of progress in structural reform

This annex follows up on recommendations from the 2003 OECD *Economic Survey of Korea*.

Recommendations in the 2003 *Survey*	Actions taken or proposed by the authorities
A. The corporate sector	
Further ease restrictions imposed on the chaebol in line with the development of market-based institutions for corporate restructuring.	The Korea Fair Trade Commission has proposed a "Three-Year Market Reform Roadmap" that would allow chaebol that improve their corporate governance practices and ownership structure to graduate from the regulations on equity investment.
Expand opportunities for shareholders to gain compensation for illegal management decisions, either through the introduction of class action suits or changes in derivative suits (2001 *Survey*).	Class action suits are to be introduced in 2005. However, they will be limited to large companies whose asset size is larger than 2 trillion won, and will cover only securities-related cases. Class action suits will be expanded to all listed companies in 2007.
Improve the workout programme (2001 *Survey*).	The workout programme, which continues for nine of the original 83 companies, is to be abolished in the near future.
Increase transparency by improving the quality of external audits (2001 *Survey*).	Three accounting-related laws were revised in 2003 to require the certification of financial reports by CEOs and CFOs, prohibit loans or collateral for major shareholders and executives, and strengthen protection for whistle-blowers.
B. The financial sector	
The Korea Asset Management Corporation (KAMCO) should continue to sell, according to its timetable, the non-performing loans (NPLs) that it has purchased.	Of the 110 trillion won of NPLs that KAMCO purchased between 1997 and 2002, 69 trillion has been sold. KAMCO is planning to sell an additional 3 trillion won in 2004.
The privatisation of commercial banks should be a top priority in order to enhance their role in corporate restructuring and establish a market-oriented financial system.	The remaining government stakes in two nationwide banks, Choheung and Kookmin, were sold in 2003. Privatisation of the holding company of Woori Bank is underway, while the authorities are mapping out plans to sell their remaining stakes in some of the other banks.

Recommendations in the 2003 *Survey*	Actions taken or proposed by the authorities
It is important for the FSC to monitor potential future risks to asset quality related to the surge in bank lending to households, the increased use of credit cards and asset price fluctuations.	Provisioning and other prudential regulations for the banks and credit card companies have been tightened, helping to bring the latent delinquency problems to the surface and thus limit the scope of the problem and improve the soundness of financial institutions.

C. The labour market

Ensure that employment protection for regular workers does not hinder restructuring of the corporate and financial sectors.	The reform proposal submitted to the Tripartite Commission by the government in 2003 includes a shortening of the consultation period for collective dismissals. The related laws are to be revised in 2004, after deliberation by the Commission.
An extension of the social safety net to non-regular workers should accompany an easing of employment protection for regular workers to limit the development of a dualistic labour market.	The worksite-related health insurance and the National Pension Scheme were extended to part-time employees. The coverage of the Employment Insurance System was further expanded to cover daily workers such as construction workers.
Use the Tripartite Commission to forge a consensus on bringing Korea's industrial relations practices into line with internationally accepted norms.	The government announced the "Roadmap for Industrial Relations Reform" in 2003 to make labour regulations more consistent with internationally accepted norms. The Tripartite Commission has been considering the reform proposal.
The Korea Confederation of Trade Unions (KCTU) should rejoin the Tripartite Commission in order for it to function effectively.	Efforts are continuing to persuade the KCTU to rejoin the Commission.
Employment subsidies with large deadweight costs should be phased out.	The amount spent on wage subsidies declined by 30 per cent between 2001 and 2003, and the target of the programmes has been focused more clearly.

D. The land market

Increase the holding tax on property and make the current system less regressive.	The effective tax rate on property has been raised by setting the tax base closer to the market price and abolishing size-related adjustment factors. In addition, the current taxation framework will be changed in 2005 by introducing a comprehensive property tax on buildings and land and imposing progressive tax rates.

E. Increasing competition

The Regulatory Reform Committee (RRC) should prevent civil servants from imposing regulations that are not backed by legislation.	Under the *ex ante* deliberation scheme for new or revised regulations, the RRC has blocked regulations that are not backed by legislation or whose burden exceeds the expected benefit. In 2002, the RRC considered 280 regulation proposals. Of these, it recommended that 26 per cent be changed and 9 per cent be rejected.

Recommendations in the 2003 *Survey*	Actions taken or proposed by the authorities
Continue the "Clean Market Project" to help consumers realise the benefits of increased competition.	The Project has resulted in significantly lower prices in some of the sectors chosen. The Korea Fair Trade Commission implemented the Project in six sectors in 2003, and it will continue its efforts in eight sectors in 2004.
Complete the 1998 privatisation programme and consider whether the privatisation of other state-owned enterprises (SOEs) would enhance efficiency.	Eight out of the eleven SOEs selected in the 1998 privatisation programme have been privatised, while 67 of the 77 SOE subsidiaries, which were selected for consolidation, have been restructured through privatisation, liquidation or merger.

F. Specific sectors

Telecommunications

Further reduce mandatory contributions from service providers and limit government intervention.	No action taken. The mandatory annual contribution for R&D remains at 0.5 per cent of revenue.
Establish an independent regulatory authority and streamline the licensing process to facilitate the entry of new firms.	No action taken. Although the Korea Communication Commission has developed into a semi-independent regulatory body, the Commission lacks autonomy in staffing, budgeting and crucial regulations, such as licensing and pricing.
Impose price caps in markets where Korea Telecom remains dominant while limiting intervention in all other markets.	No action taken.
Further ease the remaining restrictions on foreign ownership in the telecommunications sector.	No action taken. The ceiling on foreign ownership of Korea Telecom was raised from 33 to 49 per cent in 2002, the same limit as for other facility-based service providers.

Electricity

Accelerate the ten-year reform plan in order to bring the benefits of competition to households earlier.	No action taken.
Establish an independent regulatory authority.	No action taken. The Korea Electricity Commission lacks autonomy.

Agriculture

Accelerate the shift from market price supports to direct payments to farmers.	Direct payments increased from 6 per cent of total support to farmers in 2001 to 9 per cent in 2002. The government recently announced a long-term plan to raise direct payments from 9 per cent of total support in 2003 to 23 per cent by 2013.
Accelerate farm consolidation to boost the average farm size.	Numerous measures such as the Farm Size Optimisation Programme and the Farmers' Retirement Programme have been implemented. The average farm size rose from 1.36 hectares in 2000 to 1.44 hectares in 2002.
Increase market access for imported rice when the "minimum access commitment" ends in 2004.	No action taken.

Recommendations in the 2003 *Survey*	Actions taken or proposed by the authorities

G. Creating a knowledge-based economy

The education system

Liberalise centralised control to increase the autonomy of individual schools, while also ensuring their accountability.

The government has been delegating authority related to basic education to province-level education authorities or principals of individual schools. The related laws and regulations are in the process of further delegation.

Expand the pilot project of allowing independent private schools.

No action taken. Independent private schools, such as alternative schools, specialised schools and self-financing independent schools, are to be expanded within the framework of the Equalisation Policy.

Consider increasing spending on tertiary education by raising support for private institutions, which educate the majority of students.

No action taken. Meanwhile, the government formulated a plan in 2003 to promote the competitiveness of tertiary education by granting more autonomy, downsizing and fostering a better research environment.

Provide sufficient loans and grants to ensure access to tertiary education.

The amount of loans for tertiary education rose 19 per cent in 2003, providing 783 billion won to 303 thousand persons. Related government expenditure also increased from 56 to 75 billion won in 2003.

Research and development

Increase the role of universities in the R&D effort by boosting incentives for research by professors.

Government expenditures on basic research, which is primarily done in universities, increased from 19 per cent of the total R&D budget in 2002 to 21 per cent in 2004. It is to rise further to 25 per cent by 2007.

Encourage interaction between R&D in universities, the private sector and government research institutes (GRIs) by promoting labour mobility and enhancing opportunities for networking.

The government has introduced numerous co-operation programmes, such as *i*) participation of the private sector in the National Science and Technology Council and the boards of the research councils of the GRIs, *ii*) preferential treatment of the private sector in funding the national R&D programmes, and *iii*) reduction of block funding to the GRIs to encourage them to seek external funds from the private sector.

Increase international linkages in the R&D area.

To attract foreign R&D investment, a special committee was created in the Office of the President in 2004. The establishment of foreign R&D centers, such as Pasteur and Cavendish, in Korea is an example of strengthened international linkages. In addition, the government is to launch the International Science and Technology Co-operation Foundation to further international linkages.

Exercise caution in designating specific technologies as the focus of R&D programmes.

No action taken.

Recommendations in the 2003 *Survey*	Actions taken or proposed by the authorities
Venture business	
Reduce the government's role in providing equity and guarantees in this sector, while encouraging participation by other investors, such as business angels and institutional investors.	No action taken.
Consider whether the government should continue to designate certain firms as venture business, and if so, whether the criteria are sufficiently objective.	At the end of 2002, the designation criteria were changed to a two-step process by adding an innovation capability evaluation, which is assessed by independent entities. The current designation system is to be terminated in 2005.
Small and medium-sized enterprises	
Reduce the amount of support and the number of programmes to small and medium-sized enterprises (SMEs) to avoid waste and duplication.	In 2003, the number of programmes was reduced from 88 to 79, with related public expenditures diminishing by 2 per cent in 2003.
Continue to lower protection given to SMEs.	The number of business lines reserved for SMEs was reduced from 86 to 45 in 2002. The protection scheme is to end in 2004.

H. Sustainable development

Air pollution	
Extend the Seoul emission permit-trading scheme to other areas, based on accurate data on emissions.	In 2003, the Special Act on Air Quality Improvement in the Capital Region was enacted, effective in 2007, which adopted a regional cap and emission trading system.
Strengthen enforcement by increasing the role of independent inspections and separating the monitoring and ownership functions of local authorities as regards the local incineration plants.	The plants owned by lower-level local governments are inspected by upper-level local governments, while the plants owned by the latter are inspected by the central government's regional environment offices.
Reduce tax advantages for diesel, and raise emission standards and fuel quality for diesel vehicles. Tighten heavy-duty vehicle emission standards in line with other OECD countries.	Diesel fuel price has been raised according to the five-year (2002-2006) tax reform schedule. Beginning in 2006, the sulphur content standard for diesel fuel is to be lowered from 430 ppm to 30 ppm, and the emission standards on vehicles are to be tightened to the level of other OECD countries (California's LUEV for gasoline vehicles and Euro-IV for diesel vehicles).
Expand the use of road pricing and improve traffic management policies in order to reduce congestion.	Road pricing was applied to 24 highways and 16 tunnels and roads in 2002. In particular, the traffic volume in two toll tunnels in Seoul diminished by 3 and 9 per cent in 2002.
Waste management	
Gradually increase the price of garbage bags used for municipal waste.	The price of garbage bags rose 7 per cent on average in 2003.

Recommendations in the 2003 Survey	Actions taken or proposed by the authorities
Carefully monitor the system of extended producer responsibility (EPR) for recyclable products to ensure that recycling does not generate excessive costs in relation to alternative waste disposal methods.	Eleven associations were organised to monitor compliance and seek for a more effective recycling method. In addition, a comprehensive analysis of the ERP is under way in collaboration with the OECD to further improve the system.
Allay opposition by residents to the construction of new, modern waste disposal facilities by compensating them and introducing tougher monitoring of such facilities.	The law to provide support to nearby local communities was revised in 2003 to expand the scope of facilities included. The law requires up to 10 per cent of the total construction costs to be earmarked for support.

I. Sustainable income for retirement

Take advantage of the window of opportunity through 2008 to enact fundamental reforms to introduce a three-pillar system that relies more on private-sector saving.	The reform of the National Pension Scheme (NPS) was submitted to the National Assembly in 2003, but has not been approved yet. Meanwhile, the introduction of a corporate pension scheme is being studied.
Reform public occupational pensions and integrate them with the National Pension Scheme.	The government established a Task Force in the Prime Minister's office in 2003 to consider how to introduce portability between the public occupational pensions and the NPS.
Ensure that the social assistance system is providing the minimum subsistence income to all elderly in need, as well as other eligible individuals.	The Basic Livelihood Security Programme, introduced in 2000, is intended to provide minimum subsistence income to all eligible persons. The definition of subsistence, including minimum living costs, has been updated annually.

J. The tax system

The personal tax base should be broadened by reducing allowances and credits, as well as improving taxation on the self-employed.	The income assessment method for the self-employed was changed by requiring evidence for tax deductions. To further improve taxation on the self-employed, a new system for issuing receipts for cash payments is to be introduced by 2005.
Increased taxation of fringe benefits is needed to broaden the tax base.	Taxation on income gained from the exercise of stock options and purchase of stocks at below market prices through employee stock ownership plans (ESOP) was introduced in 2002.
Broaden the corporate income tax base by eliminating or streamlining various incentives provided for SMEs, investment and R&D.	Tax preference for SMEs was reduced by abolishing the tax deductibility of investment reserves and by lowering the tax credit ratio from 30 to 15 per cent of the tax base in 2004.
The tax base of the VAT should be broadened by reducing the number of exemptions.	The special treatment (or simplified tax regime) for small businesses has been reduced significantly. The threshold was tightened from 150 to 48 million won in 2002, and the portion of taxpayers receiving the special treatment declined from 90 per cent in 2001 to 46 per cent in 2003.

Recommendations in the 2003 *Survey*	Actions taken or proposed by the authorities
Reform taxation of capital income, which is low and uneven across sources.	The comprehensive financial income tax system, which had been temporarily suspended after the financial crisis, was re-implemented in 2001. The tax exemption on long-term deposits to the insurance companies was tightened in 2004.
Continue to raise taxes on holding property and lower transaction taxes.	The effective tax rate on property has been raised by setting the tax base closer to the market price and abolishing size-related adjustment factors. In addition, the current taxation framework will be changed in 2005 by introducing a comprehensive property tax on buildings and land.
Reduce the use of quasi-taxes (charges that are not imposed by tax laws).	The number of quasi-taxes increased from 95 in 1999 to 102 in 2002, while the total revenue increased by 82 per cent.

Annex B

Chronology of main economic events

2003

January

The Bank of Korea sets its 2003 inflation target at 3 per cent, plus or minus one percentage point, the same as in 2002.

The Ministry of Finance and Economy extends the coverage of the National Fiscal Information System to all national agencies.

February

The Ministry of Construction and Transportation introduces measures to prevent land speculation prompted by the plan to create a new administrative capital by designating eleven areas where prior approval of land transactions is required.

Moody's lowers its outlook for Korea's credit rating from positive to negative, while maintaining a grade of A3.

March

The government introduces measures to cope with shocks resulting from the war in Iraq, including policies to ensure energy supplies for Korea and the adoption of expansionary monetary and foreign exchange rate policies.

The authorities announce policies to restore the financial stability of the credit card companies by requiring self-rescue efforts by the companies.

April

The government requests financial institutions to co-operate in rolling over credits to the credit card companies and investment trust companies in order to stabilise the financial market.

The strike by workers at the national railroad is settled, in part by ruling out the possibility of privatisation.

The government presents a plan to reform the corporate governance and accounting systems, including a compulsory change of outside auditing companies at least once every six years.

May

The Bank of Korea cuts the overnight call rate by 25 basis points to 4 per cent.

The Korea Cargo Workers Federation goes on strike.

The Ministry of Finance and Economy presents a plan to merge the Korea Stock Exchange, KOSDAQ, and the futures market under a single operating company.

June

Legislation to reform the railroad industry is enacted. The Korea National Railroad, a government agency, is to be separated into two state-owned enterprises, which will be responsible for facilities and operations.

The National Assembly passes a first supplementary budget for 2003, which totals 4.5 trillion won.

July

The Bank of Korea cuts the overnight call rate by 25 basis points to 3.75 per cent, the lowest level on record.

The special consumption taxes on cars, televisions and air conditioners are reduced to boost domestic consumption.

August

Choheung Bank is privatised by selling the government's 80 per cent ownership stake to the Shinhan Financial Group.

Six-party talks, including South and North Korea, the United States, China, Russia and Japan, begin in Beijing to discuss the North Korean nuclear issue.

The "Foreign Workers Employment Scheme" is introduced to grant foreign workers the same rights (basic labour rights, industrial accident compensation insurance and minimum wage) as domestic workers. Their maximum work period is set at three years.

The Incheon area is designated as a "free economic zone" to attract foreign investment.

The five-day workweek is implemented through a revision of the Labour Standards Act.

September

The Financial Supervisory Commission approves the takeover of the Korea Exchange Bank by Lone Star.

October

The National Assembly passes a second supplementary budget for 2003, which totals 3 trillion won.

Busan/Jinhae and Kwangyang Bay are designated as "Free Economic Zones".

The government announces a comprehensive policy package to stabilise the overheated real estate market by expanding the supply of housing, strengthening the tax system and reinforcing regulatory measures.

November

Eight credit banks provide 2 trillion won to LG Card, the largest credit card company, which is suffering from liquidity problems.

December

The National Assembly approves the 2004 budget of 118.3 trillion won.

The government sells its remaining 9.1 per cent ownership stake in Kookmin Bank in the market.

The National Assembly passes three laws for the balanced development of the nation; the Special Act on Construction of the New Administrative Capital, the Special Act on Balanced Development of the Nation, and the Special Act on Decentralisation.

The National Assembly lowers the corporate tax rate by 2 percentage points to 25 per cent, effective in 2005.

2004

January

The revised Bank of Korea Act takes effect. The Act introduces a medium-term inflation target in place of the annual one and strengthens the independence of the central bank by replacing one of the outside members on the Monetary Policy Committee by the vice governor of the Bank of Korea.

The Monetary Policy Committee set a medium-term inflation target of 2.5 to 3.5 per cent for the period 2004 to 2006.

The creditor financial institutions agree to rescue LG Card by providing more liquidity.

The National Assembly approves class action lawsuits for such practices as stock price manipulation and disclosure and auditing violations, effective in 2005.

The Ministry of Information and Communication implements number portability for mobile phone service.

February

Mr. Hun-Jai Lee is appointed as a Deputy Prime Minister and Minister of Finance and Economy.

The Monetary Policy Committee fully liberalises interest rates by abolishing remaining restrictions on demand deposits.

The free trade agreement (FTA) with Chile is ratified by the National Assembly, 18 months after the completion of negotiations between the two countries.

KorAm Bank, the sixth-largest in Korea, is acquired by Citibank, and Hyundai Investment Trust Company is taken over by Prudential Financial.

The second round of six-party nuclear talks is held in Beijing.

March

The newly established Korea Housing Finance Corporation begins operations to replace banks' short-term housing loans with long-term mortgage loans.

The government announces a comprehensive policy package to deal with delinquent borrower problems, in part by establishing a bad bank.

The National Assembly passes an impeachment motion against President Roh Moo-hyun.

April

In the general election, the Uri Party wins more than half of the seats in the National Assembly, and the Democratic Labour Party gains seats for the first time.

May

The Constitutional Court overturns President Roh Moo-hyun's impeachment.

BASIC STATISTICS

BASIC STATISTICS:

INTERNATIONAL COMPARISONS

	Units	Reference period[1]	Australia	Austria	Belgi...
Population					
Total	Thousands	2000	19 157	8 110	1022.
Inhabitants per sq. km.	Number	2000	2	97	33.
Net average annual increase over previous 10 years	%	2000	1.2	0.5	0.
Employment					
Total civilian employment (TCE)[2]	Thousands	2000	9 048	3730 (99)	385.
of which:					
Agriculture	% of TCE	2000	4.9	6.2 (99)	2.
Industry	% of TCE	2000	22.0	30.6 (99)	24.
Services	% of TCE	2000	73.1	63.2 (99)	68.
Gross domestic product (GDP)					
At current prices and current exchange rates	Bill. USD	2000	388.5	188.7	228
Per capita	USD	2000	20 158	23 270	22 33
At current prices using current PPPs[3]	Bill. USD	2000	507.6	219.0	268
Per capita	USD	2000	26 338	27 001	26 19
Average annual volume growth over previous 5 years	%	2000	3.9	2.6	2.
Gross fixed capital formation (GFCF)	% of GDP	2000	22.7	23.6	20.
of which:					
Machinery and equipment	% of GDP	2000	...	8.0	9.
Residential construction	% of GDP	2000	4.5	5.4	4
Average annual volume growth over previous 5 years	%	2000	0.5	0.2	0
Gross saving ratio[4]	% of GDP	2000	18.3	21.8	26.
General government					
Current expenditure on goods and services	% of GDP	2000	18.2	19.0	20
Current disbursements[5]	% of GDP	2000	32.1 (98)	46.9	46
Current receipts[6]	% of GDP	2000	33.7 (98)	47.1	47
Net official development assistance	% of GNI	2000	0.27	0.23	0.3
Indicators of living standards					
Private consumption per capita using current PPPs[3]	USD	2000	15 829	14 910	13 85
Passenger cars, per 1000 inhabitants	Number	1999	510 (98)	496	44
Internet subscribers, per 100 inhabitants	Number	2000	12.7	6.00	10
Television sets, per 1000 inhabitants	Number	1998	548 (97)	331	3.
Doctors, per 1000 inhabitants	Number	1999	2.5 (98)	3.0	3
Infant mortality per 1000 live births	Number	1999	5.7	4.4	5
Wages and prices (average annual increase rate over previous 5 years)					
Wages (earnings or rates according to availability)	%	2001	2.8	2.5	2
Consumer prices	%	2001	2.3	1.6	
International trade[7]					
Exports of goods, fob	Mill. USD	2000	63 920	64 226	187 9
As % of GDP	%	2000	16.5	34.0	82
Average annual increase rate over previous 5 years	%	2000	3.8	2.2	
Imports of goods, cif	Mill. USD	2000	67 742	69 058	177 1
As % of GDP	%	2000	17.4	36.6	77
Average annual increase rate over previous 5 years	%	2000	3.4	0.8	2
Total official reserves[8]	Mill. SDR's	2000	15 455	11 017	7 9
As ratio of average monthly imports of goods	Ratio	2000	2.7	2.1	(

1. Unless otherwise stated.
2. According to the definitions used in OECD *Labour Force Statistics*.
3. PPPs = Purchasing Power Parities.
4. Gross Saving = Gross national disposable income minus private and government consumption.
5. Current disbursements = General government final consumption expenditure plus subsidies plus property income plus current taxes on income, wealth, etc. plus social benefits other than transfers in kind plus other current transfers.
6. Current receipts = Operating surplus plus taxes on production and imports plus property income plus current taxes on income, wealth, etc. plus social contributions plus other current transfers.

Questionnaire on the quality of OECD publications

We would like to ensure that our publications meet your requirements in terms of presentation and editorial content. We would welcome your feedback and any comments you may have for improvement. Please take a few minutes to complete the following questionnaire. Answers should be given on a scale of 1 to 5 (1 = poor, 5 = excellent).

Fax or post your answer before 31 December 2004, and you will automatically be entered into the prize draw to **win a year's subscription to *OECD's Observer magazine*.***

A. Presentation and layout

1. What do you think about the presentation and layout in terms of the following:

	Poor	Adequate		Excellent	
Readability (font, typeface)	1	2	3	4	5
Organisation of the book	1	2	3	4	5
Statistical tables	1	2	3	4	5
Graphs	1	2	3	4	5

B. Printing and binding

2. What do you think about the quality of the printed edition in terms of the following:

Quality of the printing	1	2	3	4	5
Quality of the paper	1	2	3	4	5
Type of binding	1	2	3	4	5

Not relevant, I am using the e-book ❏

3. Which delivery format do you prefer for publications in general?

Print ❏   CD ❏   E-book (PDF) via Internet ❏   Combination of formats ❏

C. Content

4. How accurate and up to date do you consider the content of this publication to be?

1   2   3   4   5

5. Are the chapter titles, headings and subheadings…

Clear   Yes ❏   No ❏
Meaningful   Yes ❏   No ❏

6. How do you rate the written style of the publication (*e.g.* language, syntax, grammar)?

1   2   3   4   5

D. General

7. Do you have any additional comments you would like to add about the publication?

....

....

....

Tell us who you are:

Name: ....   **E-mail:** ....

Fax: ....

Which of the following describes you?

IGO ❏   NGO ❏   Self-employed ❏   Student ❏
Academic ❏   Government official ❏   Politician ❏   Private sector ❏

Thank you for completing the questionnaire. Please fax your answers to:
(33-1) 49 10 42 81 or mail it to the following address:
Questionnaire qualité PAC/PROD, Division des publications de l'OCDE
23, rue du Dôme – 92100 Boulogne Billancourt – France.

Title: OECD Economic Surveys 2004, Korea

ISBN: 92-64-01663-5 **OECD Code (printed version):** 10 2004 10 1 P

---

* Please note: This offer is not open to OECD staff.